The 7 Stages of Marriage

Laughter, Intimacy and Passion

Today, Tomorrow and **Forever**

Sarí Harrar *and* Rita DeMaria, Ph.D.

Reader's Digest

The Reader's Digest Association, Inc.
Pleasantville, NY/Montreal

Project Editors: *Suzanne Beason, Kimberly Casey*
Copy Editors: *Jeanette Gingold, Jane Sherman*
Proofreader: *Barbara Booth*
Indexer: *Andrea Chesman*
Illustrator: *Tracy Walker*
Project Designer: *Nick Anderson*
Associate Art Director: *George McKeon*
Editor in Chief, Reader's Digest Books: *Neil Wertheimer*
Associate Director, North America Prepress: *Doug Croll*
Manufacturing Manager: *John L. Cassidy*
Director of Production: *Michael Braunschweiger*
Associate Publisher: *Rosanne McManus*
President and Publisher, Trade Publishing: *Harold Clarke*
Chief Executive Officer: *Eric Schrier*

Library of Congress Cataloging-in-Publication Data

The 7 stages of marriage : Laughter, intimacy, and passion: today, tomorrow, and forever.
   p. cm.
  Includes index.
  ISBN-10: 0-7621-0725-1
  ISBN-13: 978-0-7621-0725-4
  1. Marriage. I. Reader's Digest Association.
  HQ734.S485 2006
  306.81—dc22
               2006022852

Address any comments about *The 7 Stages of Marriage* to:
  The Reader's Digest Association, Inc.
  Editor in Chief
  Reader's Digest Books
  Reader's Digest Road
  Pleasantville, NY 10570-7000

For more Reader's Digest products and information, visit our website.
www.rd.com (in the United States)
www.readersdigest.ca (in Canada)

Printed in the United States of America

1 3 5 7 9 10 8 6 4 2

Note to Our Readers
The information in this book has been carefully researched, and all efforts have been made to ensure its
accuracy and effectiveness. However, each marriage is unique; for significant marital issues or discord,
seek expert help. The Reader's Digest Association, Inc., the authors, and the individual experts interviewed or cited in this book do not assume any responsibility for any injuries suffered or damages or losses incurred as a result of following the instructions in this book.

Acknowledgments

I would like to thank the many relationship counselors, researchers, and observers who generously shared their ideas and experiences, as well as the couples—including many from the Association for Couples in Marriage Enrichment—who spoke so frankly and eloquently about their marriages. I am also indebted to my coauthor in this book, Rita DeMaria, Ph.D., for her invaluable partnership and wisdom. Thank you to all the people at Reader's Digest who worked so hard to make this book such a wonderful reality. In particular, my gratitude goes to Genevieve Bonadonna and Kristina Swindell, who oversaw the *Marriage in America Survey* and answered my many questions both calmly and smartly; to George McKeon for his design work; and to Jeanette Gingold and Jane Sherman for their precise copyediting. Most of all, love and thanks to my husband, Dan.

—**Sarí Harrar**

My sincerest thanks go out to:

My husband, Richard, for his love and confidence in me, and to my children, Amanda and Jeff, for their support and interest in my work;

Reader's Digest, for identifying the need for this book and including me in this exciting and rewarding project;

Diane Sollee and my colleagues within the Coalition for Marriage, Couple and Family Education, who share their knowledge and skills so graciously year after year to help couples and families;

Steve Treat and my colleagues at the Council for Relationships, who create such a dynamic and positive working environment;

Lori Gordon, for the creation of the PAIRS program, and to the PAIRS network for their dedication and support;

And finally, to all the couples who have allowed me to guide and support them in their quest for love, laughter, and passion.

—**Rita DeMaria**

Contents

Introduction   v

viii   **Part One:** A Well-Lit Path to Lasting Love

3   **Marriage and Happiness** *A Practical, Lifelong Map*

15   **Marriage Today** *What 1,001 Peoples Report*

31   **Measuring Your Marriage** *The 7 Stages Quizzes*

53   **How to Fix a Marriage** *Universal Tips and Rules*

64   **Part Two:** The 7 Stages

67   **Stage 1** Passion

97   **Stage 2** Realization

133   **Stage 3** Rebellion

165   **Stage 4** Cooperation

195   **Stage 5** Reunion

223   **Stage 6** Explosion

261   **Stage 7** Completion

288   **Part Three:** Extra Wisdom

291   **Premarriage** *Smart Relationship Steps to Take Before You Say "I Do"*

301   **Remarriage** *How the 7 Stages Apply the Second Time Around*

311   **Getting Help** *Finding the Best Counselors and Enrichment Programs*

319   **The Best Ever** *Surprising Words of Hope from Everyday Marriages*

Marriage Resource Guide   326

Index   334

About the Authors   352

Introduction

Go to a party and observe the couples in a room, and chances are you'll have a difficult time telling which ones have struggling marriages. Knowing which couples are *happy,* though, is easy. The evidence is right there—in the smiles, the glances, the body language. It's there in the way they listen to each other, or stay close to each other, or tend to each other's needs. It's there in the way that other people are drawn to them, as if the couple's good fortune and joy were a contagious condition that others would gladly catch.

When we observe a truly happy couple, walking hand in hand, talking, laughing, flirting, we are naturally touched. Seeing successful marriages gives us all hope; it reminds us that even more than work, or a pretty house, or impressive vacations, the best thing in life is still a deeply shared, lasting love.

The 7 Stages of Marriage is not simply a book about the ups and downs, the pushes and pulls of marriage over a couple's lifetime together. It is a book about hope. The hope, mostly, that each of us can achieve the joys and benefits that a good marriage can provide—but also the hope that, as a social institution, marriage is not decaying, despite what so many pundits will tell you.

We acknowledge that their evidence is compelling: The divorce rate in America, at roughly 50 percent, is depressingly high. That statistic suggests that the majority of the people who are married are generally *unhappy,* secretly wishing for an alternate, more fulfilling, freer lifestyle. Since this must be true, some experts note, then surely marriage is an institution that has passed relevance.

We don't buy it. And neither do tens of millions of happily married American couples. When Reader's Digest surveyed 1,001 people about all aspects of their marriages, the results were a welcome respite from all the negativism. These people—a statistically valid cross section of married adults of all ages, from diverse backgrounds and locations—gushed far more than they griped. They reported that their marriages were very important in their lives and that the pleasures of matrimony far outweighed the hassles. While certain stereotypes still hold true—Husbands, can't you clean a little more? Wives, can't you communicate a little more directly?—many truisms about marriage are actually fallacies. Marriage can be fun, adventurous, liberating, and stimulating, our survey respondents told us, at all ages and stages.

Of course, we need to be realistic. Since marriage today is less obligatory than it once was, and divorce so readily attainable, one could argue that those who stay married are naturally happier with their decision and lifestyle. And the research makes it clear that all marriages have some challenges and points of tension. In writing this book, however—a process that involved incalculable amounts of reading, interviewing, studying, and observing—the emotion that kept coming forth was hope. At every stage of marriage, the difference between war and peace, misery and joy, tears and laughter, is often not that great. Listening better, enjoying each other a little more, showing greater compassion—these are not brutally hard changes to make, but their benefits are greater than you can imagine.

We made sure that there are many aspects of *The 7 Stages of Marriage* that distinguish it from other books on marriage. The first is obvious: the 7 stages themselves. We believe these stages capture the evolutionary path of a relationship more succinctly and accurately than any previous attempt. More important, we believe our core message—that the joys and issues of marriage are distinct at each stage and need to be handled in ways appropriate to the stage—represents a new paradigm for how we counsel couples and improve marriages. Intuitively, that makes sense—yet surprisingly many of us treat marriage as a static state, without growth or change or evolution. Living day to day causes this shortsightedness: It's hard to see change when life plays out in such a slow and steady flow. This book will open your eyes to how much your relationship has evolved and will evolve, and why being conscious of change is crucial to attaining the contentment you seek.

There are many other new ideas here, as well as many "Aha!" moments. One example is the incredibly important role of laughter in a marriage and the decreasing importance of sex. (Yes, sex is still important, but it is far less of an issue for most couples than some experts would have you believe.) We also worked very hard to come up with quizzes, exercises, and advice that will both surprise and delight you—first, because they are fresh and new, and second, because they are so easy to do!

Finally, you will meet a wonderful cast of characters as you read. More than 1,000 married people shared with us their insights, frustrations, and stories during the making of this book. Their comments and anecdotes are bound to touch your heart and stimulate your mind.

The 7 Stages of Marriage is not a relationship-repair book—though you can use it that way and it will do the job wonderfully. Rather, it is a road map to greater happiness, no matter what stage you are in, and no matter how blissful or melancholy your relationship is today. You will learn why your marriage has progressed as it has, as well as where it may be headed in the future. Most of all, we believe this book will give you hope that the joy, passion, and love that brought you to marriage in the first place is not only sustainable but ready to grow anew with just a little tending. Be open, give our advice a try, and enjoy the journey!

—*Sari Harrar*

—*Rita DeMaria, Ph.D.*

PART ONE

a well-lit path

marriage and happiness

a practical, lifelong map

Fantasies can fill our hearts with joy and our souls with hope. But one should never mix them up with reality—and the reality is that life is not perpetual bliss, and marriage is not a perpetual honeymoon.

After the pink and white roses have faded and the rental tux has been returned, the romantic bubble of wild, newlywed passion eventually drifts back down to Earth. The descent may be as slow as the fall of an autumn leaf or as swift as the plunge of a meteor. But inevitably, all couples land with a thud in an unfamiliar country: real marriage.

At first, it may not seem so wonderful. This is it? you wonder as newlywed bliss collides with nitty-gritty reality. Your partner isn't Romeo or Juliet, you realize one day. He or she is imperfect, unvarnished ... even irritating. His endearing athletic socks on the bathroom floor? They belong in the hamper. Her little habit of forgetting to pay the bills? Irresponsible—not proof of a mind on a higher plane. That long, long pause before he answers a question? Perhaps he's tuned you out—it's not that he's thinking lofty thoughts, as you once imagined. Her readiness to organize absolutely everything? It's frenetic, not refreshingly energetic. And pillow talk? Now it's tense negotiations about absolutely everything: Will I always be the one who has to mop up spaghetti sauce splattered on the kitchen floor? What kind of house should we buy? Why are you always in charge of the TV remote? Isn't it about time we had kids?

For all its challenges, marriage remains among the sweetest, happiest, and most fulfilling things a person can experience.

Building a real relationship based on love, honor, and respect has never been easy in this world—not even in the days when men's and women's roles as husband and wife were much more strictly defined and divided. "Keep your eyes wide open before marriage, half shut afterwards," Declaration of Independence signer Benjamin Franklin once quipped. (Meanwhile, his own marriage—he called it "the state in which you will find solid happiness"—lasted 44 years.)

In the 19th century, England's world-weary Marguerite Gardiner, Countess of Blessington, sighed, "Love-matches are made by people who are content, for a month of honey, to condemn themselves to a life of vinegar." Humorist James Thurber, whose first marriage ended in divorce and second lasted the rest of his life, adds this 20th-century barb: "The most dangerous food is wedding cake." Like all veterans of matrimony, they knew that nurturing intimacy and joy can mean facing down boredom, betrayal, disappointment, irritation, bewilderment, fiery power struggles, sub-zero silences, loneliness, and infidelity—stuff that romance alone can't ease.

And it's tougher today than ever before. Historians say the venerable institution of marriage has changed more in the past 30 years than in the previous 3,000. The reasons: social upheavals that put women and men on an equal plane; 21st-century economics that leave both spouses overworked and stressed out; sky-high expectations for mutuality and closeness (we want a soul mate, sexual athlete, and stimulating conversationalist across the kitchen table, not just a homemaker or good provider!); and the easy availability of divorce.

Ahhh, but the rewards! For all the challenges we've just noted, a good marriage remains among the sweetest, happiest, and most fulfilling things a person can experience in all of life. A healthy marriage offers everything you need for long-term happiness: love, hope, laughter, security, purpose, friendship, intimacy, care. Research shows there are many other benefits as well. As we discuss later on, married people have more—and better—sex. They're healthier and wealthier, and some studies show they live longer than their single counterparts do.

And while modern times have made marriage more complicated, having greater equality between husband and wife makes the rewards sweeter as well. "When a marriage works well today, it works better than anyone in the past ever dared to dream," notes historian Stephanie Coontz, Ph.D., author of *Marriage, a History*.

"Saying 'I love you' on a day-by-day basis, telling my wonderful wife how much I prize her, finding the ways she likes to hear that she's loved, that means the world to me," says Hollie Atkinson, 70, of Georgetown, Texas, who will soon celebrate his 50th wedding anniversary with his wife, Janell. "Our marriage, while not a perfect one, is a good one, and it is not as good as it will be next year.

"There's nothing better for delivering a big wallop of love than locking eyes and asking her about her day," Hollie adds. "Nothing better."

The question is, why don't more of us have this kind of marital success? An estimated 40 to 50 percent of first-time couples break up (as do 50 to 60 percent of remarriages). Half of those breakups are within the first seven years of matrimony. Many who stick it out are privately gritting their teeth: Just two years after saying "I do," an estimated 20 percent of couples make love fewer than 10 times in a year, researchers say. And polls have found that as many as 40 percent of still-married husbands and wives have considered leaving.

So what is the secret of marital success? What is it that Hollie Atkinson knows that the rest of us don't? The answer, experts agree, is as simple as two words. To have a great marriage, *embrace change*.

The Timeline of Marriage

All marriages evolve over time. So say the nation's top relationship researchers, who've been busy analyzing the inner secrets of successful marriages for nearly two decades. They've scanned couples' brains, measured their pulse rates and the hormones in their bloodstreams, videotaped their most ordinary, ho-hum conversations, and tracked their physiological reactions during easygoing chats and stormy arguments alike, all to reach a simple yet profoundly useful consensus: *The true story of married love is change.*

Every marriage is unique, of course, yet most follow a strikingly similar story line shaped by biology, changing needs, major life events, and the demands of 21st-century life. The journey can be pleasurable and unexpected, revealing and challenging, as it carries you and your spouse through what research shows are seven distinct, dramatically different relationships within your marriage. These stages range from the starry-eyed intensity of the honeymoon phase to the sudden collision with everyday life in the rebellious "seven-year-itch" stage to the shattering adjustments required by a major illness or financial crises in the "explosion" stage.

Change never, ever stops: Couples interviewed for this book who've celebrated their 30th, 40th, and 50th anniversaries said they're still grappling with serious issues, finding new pleasures, and constantly being surprised by their mature marriages. Quiet contentment in the golden years, we're happy to report, is a myth.

So where are you right now? Don't try to guess based merely on the number of years you've been married. Some stages arrive with a bang. Parenthood, for example, rocks your world the moment your first child arrives. Some stages arrive like a whisper, such as the "honeymoon's over" phase, when you may notice yourself growing more critical of your spouse as your initial passion wanes and your deeper wants, needs, and worries slowly resurface. This cooling period may last for just a few months or persist for 20 years. Likewise, you may revisit an earlier stage if new stresses catapult you backward into old ways of getting along. You may even be in two stages at once!

The notion that a marriage unfolds in stages isn't new—everyone's heard about the honeymoon stage, the seven-year-itch, and the empty nest, for example. What's revolutionary is this: Marriage experts now say that understanding the mission, the strengths, and the work of each stage can give you a clear road map for navigating in rough times—something couples need today more than ever before. In each stage, the things you and your spouse require in order to feel happy, secure, and satisfied can shift without warning. If you know your stage, you'll know what to do and what not to do, what your spouse needs and doesn't need, and why the subtle, unspoken "rules" of marriage seem to have been rewritten overnight.

But that's not all. We believe the power of *The 7 Stages of Marriage* goes beyond its utilitarian purpose as a great set of marital power tools. Appreciating your marriage as an incredible, inevitable journey will help you see the good in your partner, your relationship, and yourself during the most difficult moments. This *Aha!* lifts guilt, buoys your hopes, and gives you the freedom to set aside your struggles more often in order to enjoy the real core of your partnership: the two of you.

The marriage-saving benefits of living your stage also include:

A reenergized sex life. One in three American marriages are "low sex" or "no sex." We'll show you how to rediscover your passion, with tips tailored for exhausted new parents, distant empty-nesters, and independent-minded rebellious types.

Better communication. More than 30 percent of women and 25 percent of men give their marriages low marks for communication. But the way to improve communication changes with each stage. Respect never goes out of style, of course, but chances are that the sexy love talk of the honeymoon stage won't win your partner's heart in the early years of parenthood.

More quality time together. Husbands and wives say the best way to improve their relationship would be to spend more time together. But thanks to jobs, kids, TV, the Internet, hobbies, and home and family responsibilities, the average couple spend just *four minutes a day* together. We'll show you how to get together more often—in stage-specific ways that bolster, not torpedo, togetherness.

An "affair-proofed" relationship. An astounding 60 percent of married adults have had at least one affair. A smart combination of drawing each other close and giving each other space can cut your odds dramatically.

Lowered odds for divorce during the most vulnerable stages. Breakup risk is highest in the Rebellion stage of marriage, when personal needs and interests sometimes surpass the interests and needs of a marriage. We'll show you how to use commitment as a tool for strengthening your marriage and erasing reluctance—and give you insider tips for avoiding "contagious" divorce.

Protection from advice that could doom your marriage. The number of marriage therapists in the United States increased 50-fold between 1970 and 1990, yet the divorce rates haven't budged much. The danger: Many (but not all!) therapists employ techniques that work well in individual

Marriage by the Numbers

Should you stay—or should you go? Let these statistics from various national surveys help you decide.

- Cost of the average wedding: $20,000
- Cost of the average divorce: $20,000
- First marriages that end in divorce: nearly 50%
- Second marriages that end in divorce: 67%
- Third marriages that end in divorce 74%
- Percent of miserable couples who stayed together and felt happier 5 years later: 86%
- Number who were very happy 10 years later: 80%
- Spouses who say their sex lives are better married: 73%
- Relative increase in wealth for married couples versus single or divorced people: 85%
- Longevity bonus for married men over unmarried men: 1.7 years

therapy but can seriously damage a married couple, experts say. If you decide you need professional help, we'll show you how to find a counselor who's firmly pro-marriage.

The flexibility to thrive despite so-called irreconcilable differences. Experts say most couples—even those in happy marriages—have 6 to 10 areas of disagreement that may never be resolved. Solving what you can, working on issues where you must take a stand, and learning to tolerate the rest is a hallmark of strong, happy marriages. And living with the exciting friction of difference keeps your marriage fresh, alive, energized. You'll learn how to handle—and value—your differences here.

Seven Stages at a Glance

In Part 2 of this book, you'll delve deeply into each of the seven major stages of marriage. You'll discover how a cast of hidden forces moves you from stage to stage in ways that usually cannot be seen or felt.

But to get you started, here is a synopsis of the seven stages of marriage.

Stage 1: Passion This is the honeymoon stage, when romance and intense attraction bond a couple together and lead to commitment. In retrospect, it often seems as short-lived as springtime—by two years, most couples have usually lost that initial magic, though one couple interviewed for this book said their Passion phase lasted for seven. But when it is happening, the Passion stage is a fortissimo wave of feel-good brain chemicals orchestrated by Mother Nature to make the two of you forsake all others and take action to ensure the survival of the species.

Even if you're marrying later in life, or for the second time, nature supplies these delicious bursts of neurotransmitters to make you bond. Couples not only frolic and fall madly in love in the Passion stage—they begin to establish the trust, respect, and emotional intimacy that will support their relationship forever.

Stage 2: Realization In this stage, the honeymoon ends, and a more real vision of the rest of your life together begins. In this stage, you discover your spouse is not only human, he also doesn't load the dishwasher or lower the toilet seat. Disappointment and early conflicts are the hallmarks of this difficult, unavoidable period, as the two of you make the first steps toward accepting each other for who you really are.

The mission and challenge? No less than laying the groundwork for a long future together based on acceptance, respect, and openness to change. You'll need to assertively discuss and empathetically listen as you both introduce your deepest personal needs and wants. This creates a foundation for being truly known, understood, and supported in the years ahead.

Stage 3: Rebellion She misses her friends; he misses his cool toys. She wants to travel; he wants to play weekly softball. She wants to build her career; he wants to build his career. Even for couples who successfully navigate the Realization stage of marriage and lay the foundation for a happy, respectful coexistence together, a time inevitably emerges when self-interest often overtakes the interests of the marriage. And when this happens, be ready for the battles.

Love amid the power struggles of the Rebellion stage is tricky business. You both believe you're right, so of course your partner's wrong. That means you're simultaneously offended at being called wrong and claiming the moral high ground. Is this any way to run a marriage?

Experts say the dramas of the Rebellion stage are unavoidable. Learning the art of the good fight is the mission now—often it is the nature of the battles, rather than the substance of the discussion, that leads to trouble. Why? Rebellious thoughts, when met with anger and frustration, often lead to rebellious actions, such as infidelity, outlandish spending, or saying yes to the sudden offer from work to transfer to a new city. Any of these can spell disaster for a marriage.

Stage 4: Cooperation As marriages progress over time, they inevitably become more complicated. Careers grow, houses get bigger, personal commitments grow deeper, and children arrive. In the Cooperation stage, marriage takes on a businesslike personality. Set aside all that love and emotion and personal-realization stuff: There are mortgages to be paid, investments to be handled, careers to be directed, health to be managed, and—first and foremost—children to be raised.

Making the transition from lover to household partner to parent can threaten your relationship. Many researchers have found that marital satisfaction takes a sharp nosedive when a baby arrives. University of Buffalo sociologists say the "rules" for good marriages seem to change drastically in the Cooperation stage. Meanwhile, you are too time starved and sleep deprived to try and figure out what the heck's going on. Your marriage is the bedrock of your family—we'll show you how to keep it strong.

Stage 5: Reunion If you have children, the Cooperation stage often lasts 10 to 20 years—then suddenly, it is gone. Your parenting commitments are lessened, your finances established, your career set, your mortgage paid. What then? For happy couples, it is a time to appreciate each other again, not as parents and providers but as lovers and friends, thinkers and seekers. Achieve this, and there's peace, happiness, and reconciliation.

That all sounds wonderful, but this ideal is often hard to achieve. The embers of passion need stoking; the disillusionment and distance of middle age need to be managed; the roles and expectations of the marriage need recalibrating.

Stage 6: Explosion Job loss, major health problems, a move to a new city, financial troubles, the illness or death of a parent—as you pass through midlife and into the golden years, major life developments seem to come one upon the other. In the Explosion phase, either you, your spouse, or both of you are dealing with major, life-shaking events that could affect your relationship for a day, a year, or the rest of your lives. While the other six stages tend to occur in order, the Explosion stage can happen at any time in a marriage, though it happens most as we pass through our 40s and 50s.

Confronted by a personal crisis, your marriage can be a source of solace or be sorely tried by the unexpected pressure of new roles, new limitations, and new fears. The mission of the Explosion stage: Deal the best you can with life's challenges and changes, but at the same time, keep yourself happy and healthy. Letting your marriage see you through can be as simple as sharing daily joys, provided you sometimes practice the Zen-like art of putting aside fear and stress.

Stage 7: Completion It's no coincidence: Lots of surveys find that marital happiness soars after several decades of a shared life. Experts say simply that it's because the kids are grown, and couples know each other very, very well. But there's more to it than that. "Knowing" each other isn't merely about tolerating each other's habits, quirks, and needs. In the Completion stage, "knowing" each other has a far deeper meaning—and a bigger payoff as well.

Part of being a happy man is to never lose the boy within; the same goes for women—there is the spirit of a young girl inside, no matter how many wrinkles edge the eyes. Maintaining a childlike love of life, laughter, nature, and each other is the real secret to a perpetually blessed relationship. It is also living in the present, not the past. In the Completion stage of marriage, there is never a belief that the best times are over—they should always be today and tomorrow.

A Journey Worth Taking

Something else happens in the decades after the wedding cake, the roses, the gown, and the tux become just memories tucked into an album: Married people thrive. More than divorced or never-married people, those who say "I do" enjoy a staggering wealth of benefits that no one bothers to mention when you tie the knot. We believe wholeheartedly in marriage—and in its benefits for a couple and their children—and we want you to stay together for the joys, the deep closeness, and the richness of long-lasting love. But don't forget this treasure chest of surprising, significant bonuses:

More happiness: Marriage does more to promote life satisfaction than money, sex, or even children, say Wake Forest University psychologists who analyzed a nationwide survey of women and men ages 25 to 75. How big a factor is it? English economists who computed the magnitude of change in happiness levels among people experiencing big life events (such as getting married or getting a raise at work) say marriage's happiness boost is equal to that of pulling down a six-figure salary.

Better sex: It's a myth that married sex has to be tepid and infrequent. In one large national study, married women and men said they have more sex—and better sex—than unmarried people did. They also enjoy it more on physical and emotional levels.

When Divorce Is the Right Choice

About 30 percent of American divorces happen in "high-conflict" marriages. These are relationships in which violence; physical, sexual, or mental abuse; or a threat to the life of a spouse or children is most likely. In these cases—or when there's chronic addiction or substance abuse, psychosis or extreme mental illness, or a pattern of chronic infidelity—getting out is the right choice.

The litmus test: If you feel frightened for yourself or your children, your first priority is to ensure your safety. Call a friend, relative, the police, or a local women's shelter to find a safe place to live. Your well-being matters most.

More wealth: Compared to confirmed bachelors and bachelorettes, married people accumulate about four times more savings and assets, say Ohio State University sociologists who analyzed the marital status and tracked the net worth of 9,055 women and men over 15 years. Those who divorced had assets 77 percent lower than the ever-single group.

A longer, healthier life: When University of Chicago researchers checked mortality records for 6,000 women and men over an 18-year peri-od, they discovered that many more married women and men were still alive at age 65 than were divorced, widowed, or never-married people. And in a University of Pittsburgh study that tracked 7,524 women ages 65 and older for six years, simply being married cut the risk of dying by 17 percent. Why? A recent study from the federal Agency for Health Care Policy and Research offers this clue: Married elderly people were more likely to take simple, health-promoting steps on a daily basis, such as eating breakfast, wearing seat belts, getting physical activity, having regular blood pressure checks, and not smoking.

Marriage also reduces stress and gives a couple more time, money, brainpower, and motivation to ward off health problems, say researchers from the Center on Aging at the University of Chicago. In a study of 12,000 middle-aged women and men, they found that married people were significantly healthier than singles.

What's in Store

Throughout this book, you'll discover how to harness your marital "stage" to boost harmony, get closer, and enjoy your marriage more—every day. We'll show you the best conversation-starters, stress-coolers, great dates, exercises (for one or both of you), and conflict-resolution strategies, tailored for every stage.

The benefits of taking action to improve your marriage should be pretty clear. But to help, here are some extra specifics on what this book promises.

You'll understand the core mission of your marriage, which changes with each stage. Knowing your relationship's real priorities—such as sexy bonding, assertively getting to know one another, developing independ-ence, or simply raising children well—will help you build a rock-solid, deeply intimate, joyful marriage.

You'll develop new strengths for the journey ahead. Too many couples bemoan a loss of passion. But endless physical passion and romance (at the expense of other things) is not only next to impossible—it's bad for a marriage. A good spouse not only evolves but also changes his or her contribution to and role in a marriage as time progresses. Men in particular tend to get stuck in a single role, thinking that they should not change from the "man she married."

You'll sidestep advice that could threaten your marriage. Friends, marriage counselors, and TV shrinks may be steering you wrong if you—and they—don't get what your relationship needs right now.

You'll avoid time- and effort-wasting wrong moves. Trying the wrong tactics at the wrong time (for example, fixating on your mellowing sex life in the Realization stage, rather than exploring each other's *nonsexual* being) won't help bring you lasting closeness. This book identifies the key things couples *need* to do in each stage and explains why they work.

You'll enjoy an immediate payoff in pleasure and fun. Simply knowing where you are on the marriage journey is very reassuring. A rough patch doesn't necessarily mean your relationship is broken or that you're hitched to Mr. or Mrs. Wrong. Instead, difficulties often simply signal the arrival of a crucial new stage.

You'll rediscover pleasure and play—now. Sure, we'll help you through the big, tough challenges of marriage—how to argue, living with stuff you will never resolve, how to adjust to each other's changing priorities and needs. But underlying it all is a simple message: Marriage is about fun. At every stage, we'll encourage you to laugh, get away, pamper yourselves, indulge, play, have sex, relax, and even tease each other. For what is a good marriage if not joy?

marriage today

what 1,001 people report

Inside the American marriage, love, honor, and laughter are still alive.

That's welcome news in an era of broken promises, a divorce rate hovering just below 50 percent, and dire predictions about the "death of marriage" as more and more couples live together and postpone the walk down the aisle—or never take it at all.

When Reader's Digest asked married women and men across the nation in-depth questions about their attitudes and beliefs about marriage, the results were heartwarming and surprising. In this comprehensive survey, a total of 1,001 respondents said that deep down, they value trust, forgiveness, and good communication much more than whether the housework is fairly divided. Partners told us that fun, laughter, and spending time together are four to five times more important than sex. That they'd marry their spouse all over again. And that divorce isn't the answer.

The survey—a candid look at the American marriage, from the inside out—was conducted via the Internet with U.S. adults of all ages, geographic locations, and economic levels. Answers were anonymous; however, participants were asked to elaborate on our questions with written comments, and many were quite forthcoming (you'll find their comments throughout this book, and they comprise the entire last chapter).

What's most important to a marriage? Trust and fun, say survey respondents.

The survey results reveal that in private, we're so proud and pleased with our mates that we've grown a bit smug: A majority of participants said their marriages are better than their parents', their friends', and the typical American marriage. And we feel both lucky and grateful: Most said their relationships are better than their own vision of the way marriage should be. "There are so many [cherished moments]," one husband said. "I cannot say that any one is more outstanding than any other."

But we're not without contradictions. Americans ranked sex very low on a list of must-have ingredients for a happy marriage. And we admitted that we make love less often now than we did in the passionate, early days of our relationships. Happily, we also think the quality of our lovemaking is better—a testament to emotional closeness as much as improved technique. But the reality's not so simple. While some husbands and wives are perfectly happy with less sex, others are longing for more kisses, hugs, and physical intimacy. And while we gave sharing the housework a low rating on that same list, women are still shouldering more domestic responsibilities than men despite the fact that most are also working outside the home.

Over and over again, husbands and wives say their marriages are forever—and they're ready to roll up their sleeves and work on their relationship:

- 85 percent say, "Marriage is a partnership."
- 79 percent say, "I intend to stay married for the rest of my life."
- 75 percent say, "I believe that to have a good marriage you have to constantly work at it."
- 56 percent say, "Divorce is not the answer."

About the Survey

The Reader's Digest *Marriage in America Survey*, conducted online February 10–24, 2006, asked a random sample of married American women and men about their marriages. In total, 1,001 people responded. Who were they? The details:

Women   53%

Men   47%

Married just once   66%

Married twice   25%

Married three or more times   9%

Ever considered divorce   24%

Average length of marriage   17 years

Married less than 2 years   10%

Married 2–10 years   32%

Married 11–20 years   22%

Married 21–40 years   26%

Married more than 40 years   10%

Average age when married   29 years old

Percentage with children   83%

With kids living at home   42%

This high level of dedication gives American couples the drive to make their relationships happier, more harmonious, and better able to last through the tough times, says psychologist and marriage expert Howard J. Markman, Ph.D., director of the Center for Marital and Family Studies at the University of Denver. "People who are dedicated are less likely to feel trapped and more likely to be optimistic about their future together," he says. They're also less likely to think the grass is greener on the other side of the fence and to fantasize about dating or marrying someone else.

In one of the most encouraging findings from the survey, partners said that they intend to work hard to stay married—despite the odds. "Marriage is what you make it—you *always* have to keep working at your relationship; otherwise, it will slide," one husband said. "Marriage is a business, and both people need to work at it to make it run," said another. Self-sacrifice and an open mind help too, said this man: "We both willingly give up our wants for our needs and for the other's benefit. We have always bolstered each other and tried to keep our criticisms in kindness, never bringing each other down intentionally and always willing to forgive and forget quickly and go forward with new enlightenment."

We hope the findings of this important survey will enlighten you and encourage you as you work toward a more satisfying, durable marriage.

Finding No. 1: Marriage Isn't Broken!

Is matrimony on the rocks? TV, newspapers, and magazines would have you believe it is. Experts weigh in daily on its grim decline. Some warn that the U.S. is going the way of Scandinavia, where fewer and fewer couples get married at all. Marriage counselors and divorce lawyers are doing a booming business. Talk shows are packed with tearful couples on the brink of messy breakups.

But real couples in committed relationships clued us in to a far happier reality. Over and over, husbands and wives said they'd marry their mates all over again. And a few did—either by renewing their vows or remarrying the same spouse after a divorce. "Loving" and "secure" were their top descriptions of their relationships, while "cold" and "distant" were rarely chosen. "My husband is my best friend, my soul mate," one woman told Reader's Digest. "We both believe that we were lucky to have found the perfect mate and will be married for eternity."

The Statistics

Percentage of survey respondents who agreed with the following statements:

I would marry my spouse all over again	71%
I love my spouse even more than when we were first married	62%

Percentage of respondents who say their marriages are better than:

The typical American marriage	58%
How they envisioned marriage should be	54%
Their parents' marriage	53%

Respondents were given a list of 18 adjectives and told to pick three that best describe their marriages.

These four were chosen most often:

Loving	41%	Trusting	30%
Secure	33%	Blessed	29%

These four were chosen least often:

Disconnected	6%	In crisis	4%
Cold	4%	Volatile	2%

Whether they'd just celebrated their first wedding anniversary or had been married more than 40 years, husbands and wives alike said they were more in love with their mates today than when they walked down the aisle. "I was one of the few people that ever got to find their real 'bone of my bone and flesh of my flesh' soul mate," one husband proudly reported. "We have never had a raised-voice argument in all our years together. I have never cheated and never will." Added another happy husband: "In this wonderful marriage, there are *no* regrets. I'm sure she agrees with my statement." A third was succinct: "It is all good. Every day is great."

How great? Couples surprised us by rating their own marriages higher than the marriages of their parents and their friends and higher than the typical American marriage. They even said their relationships are better than they envisioned they would be. "Just better than I ever expected," is the way one wife described her marriage. "My husband is my very best friend in the whole world, and I would be lost without him," said another woman. "I am very lucky to be married to my husband. He takes good care of me, financially and otherwise. He does have some faults, as do I, but we get along well—and he cooks for me almost every night."

And here's the icing on the cake: They also said that in most important areas, their marriages had improved with time. More than 50 percent said trust, forgiveness, and problem-solving were better than ever; over 40 percent said compatibility, verbal affection (those little "I love yous"), time together having fun, and the sharing of household duties had improved.

Couples told us about an enduring, private happiness at the heart of everyday marriage. "Every woman should meet and marry someone like my husband," a wife said. "He is my lifetime companion," said another. Added a besotted husband, "I can't believe how lucky I am to have the woman of my dreams. I cherish every moment of every day that I'm with her."

More than chemistry or sex or romance, partners said dedication and daily good deeds made the difference in their marriages. "My husband is very supportive of me," one wife said. "Since I have gone back to college, he calls me his 'hardworking student' and will take over my household responsibilities when I have a lot of homework to do. It is so precious to me that he respects whatever I attempt to do." Added another, "My spouse stuck by me and supported me through a very trying time with my mother. It made me realize that love can carry us through some bad moments."

The little things matter. One husband's most cherished moment happens quietly, near daybreak. "Waking up each day and seeing this beautiful person lying next to me," he said. One wife's moment comes after work. "Anytime I've had a stressful day or just feel depressed, my husband will listen to me while sitting on the couch rubbing my feet. He thinks that it's funny that it makes me fall asleep within less than 15 minutes," she said.

Could this avalanche of bliss be for real? "The truth is, we're optimists," says marriage researcher Blaine J. Fowers, Ph.D., head of the department of educational and psychological studies at the University of Miami and author of *Beyond the Myth of Marital Happiness: How Embracing the Virtues of Loyalty, Generosity, Justice, and Courage Can Strengthen Your Relationship.* "In a sense, the numbers don't make sense, given what we know about how people complain and put up with mediocrity in their lives and often get divorced. But there's more to the picture. Most people put a positive spin on reality—including their marriage. This makes good things happen.

When you see your spouse in a positive light, she or he is more likely to respond positively to you. It sets up a good cycle."

Digging deeper, Dr. Fowers says survey participants are talking about loyalty, gratitude, and friendship—marriage-sustaining qualities that experts are only beginning to appreciate. "When you look for your partner's virtues, you begin seeing and feeling them everywhere, every day, in your relationship. This adds depth and resonance and meaning to your marriage," he says. "And it's a skill anyone can learn." While relationship researchers have been looking at communication skills, pleasure, and sexual intimacy as keys to a good relationship, Dr. Fowers says they've overlooked this bedrock sense of regard. "Part of loyalty is simply marching through life, arm in arm. It's having worthwhile things in your life that you value together. And it's going through hardships together. When you have that, you have a deep understanding. And when you cherish your partner for these reasons, it doesn't matter whether you say exactly the right words to each other. You have a deep connection."

Better yet, you can practice these qualities and improve your marriage. "Spouses who characteristically act generously, loyally, fairly, courageously, and with goodwill create good marriages," he says. "These acts of character happen every day in small as well as large ways. You can choose to do this, and love can flourish."

Finding No. 2: It's Really about Trust

"We always have people that are envious of our marriage," a blissfully wed woman told Reader's Digest. "They don't understand that most of it is trust and respect. We are like one."

More than friendship or laughter, forgiveness or compatibility, spouses name trust as the element crucial for a happy marriage. Survey-takers ranked this old-fashioned virtue as five times more important than good-quality sex—and most said the level of trust had improved in the years since they first became husband and wife.

In today's stressed-out marriages, where we need more from each other than ever before yet have less time in which to give it, trust is no longer a given. "Trust may be even more important than love itself," says Terry Hargrave, Ph.D., a professor of counseling at West Texas A&M University

The Statistics

Survey respondents were given a list of traits and asked to pick which were most important to their marriages. These five were rated highest.

Trust	63%
Time spent talking, laughing, having fun	52%
Compatibility	30%
Ability to resolve differences effectively	30%
Forgiveness	27%

Respondents were also asked to rate from 1–10 how happy they were with important elements of marriage. Given are the percentages of people who rated the element either 9 or 10.

Trust	66%
Freedom of personal/career growth	60%
Compatibility	58%
Ability to forgive	58%
Verbal affection	51%

and author of *The Essential Humility of Marriage*. "We write songs and poetry about love, but too often we ignore this other important pillar of marriage. I'm glad to see it was named and counted as important."

Trust is all about fairness and balance—it's both partners doing their share of the work in a relationship. It's something that each partner is always aware of, on some level. And like money in the bank, trust is an important relationship resource that can be used well or squandered. "Done right, it takes on a magical quality: If you trust your spouse, you can give freely and happily. But when there's a lack of trust, spouses withdraw or manipulate or threaten," Dr. Hargrave says. "A lack of trust can destroy love. But a lack of love can't destroy trust—in old-fashioned arranged marriages, those with a high level of trust could actually generate love even if a husband and wife barely knew each other at the start."

Dr. Hargrave points to a crisis of trust underlying the nation's high divorce rate. Sometimes the breach of trust is huge: infidelity, alcoholism, drug abuse. But more often, we fail each other in smaller, everyday ways that erode trust slowly but surely. "A working marital relationship is built on trust," he says. "Its success is based on how you answer the underlying questions: Can we give equally to each other? Can we accomplish the work of marriage—nurturing children, becoming financially secure? Can I treat you in a respectful way? Can we do what we need to do in our community? In families where both spouses work, the acts that build trust are different than they are in traditional families. A wife is going out to work, so a husband needs to take up more domestic responsibilities. If this doesn't happen, you have trust problems—and ultimately, frustrated and overworked wives who may decide that they're better off divorced."

Sometimes the act of getting married switches on a spouse's "responsibility gene," as one survey participant found: "The day we married, he changed from someone who I could never trust to someone I trust completely." For others, trust was part of the marriage pact itself, as one woman told us. "We promised to talk, to trust each other, not go to bed angry, to listen to our children, not to be judgmental, and if we disagree with each other, never to express that in front of our children, family, or friends," she said.

The good news: While you cannot conjure love from thin air, you can bolster the sense of trust in your marriage today. "Doing your share, not letting your spouse down can go far toward repairing relationships and building love," Dr. Hargrave says. "The fact that people are naming trust as a vital element in marriage is an encouraging sign. It cannot be taken for granted."

Finding No. 3: Laughter Is More Important Than Sex!

Want to be happy? Set aside the *official* list of things every marriage needs—such as sex as incandescent as Fourth of July fireworks, a diplomat's savvy for resolving conflicts, and endless reserves of saintly patience. Instead, go out for ice cream together. *Now.*

Don't stop to change your clothes, wash the dishes, or figure out who forgot to pay the cable bill. *Just go.* Laugh. Chat. *Be.* And don't come home for at least an hour.

You just made an investment in your relationship. "The most important thing in a marriage," one woman confided, "is being able to laugh together and just plain have fun." A contented husband agreed, describing

The Statistics

When wives and husbands chose the factors *most* important for a good marriage, the items that rose to the top—and sank to the bottom—of the list surprised us.

Time spent talking, laughing, having fun	52%
Compatibility	30%
Quality of sex	13%
Frequency of sex	9%

Next is the percentage of respondents who agreed with the following statements regarding how they spend their time.

My partner and I share many interests and hobbies	47%
My spouse and I do *not* spend a lot of time together	22%
I spend a lot of time with my *own* friends	9%

his most cherished moment with his spouse as "the two hours we spent relaxing and talking while eating an early morning breakfast (3 A.M.) in a small town miles from home."

Partners in our survey surprised us when they ranked "time spent talking, laughing, having fun" as one of the most important elements in their marriages—ahead of forgiveness, problem-solving, and housework and far ahead of frequent or high-quality sex. Only trust earned a higher rating. Frivolous? Not at all, says psychologist Howard J. Markman, Ph.D., director of the Center for Marital and Family Studies at the University of Denver and co-author of *Fighting for Your Marriage: Positive Steps for Preventing Divorce and Preserving a Lasting Love*. "Spending time together connecting as friends is at the heart of a marriage," he says. "Our research clearly indicates that having a sense of safety and connection with the person you want to spend the rest of your life with is vital—and spending time together, building a friendship, accomplishes that. And it doesn't have to be sky-diving or a two-week vacation. Any time when you can be focused on each other, talking as friends and having fun—and not dealing with conflict or the kids or the routine issues of everyday life—will do that."

Indeed, survey respondents regaled us with stories of marriage moments that were special simply because they happened outside of the worries and cares of everyday life. Some happened in all-night diners, others at luxurious and exotic resorts. "Traveling with my wife to Jamaica and enjoying the time alone with her," is how one husband described a special time with his spouse. "I feel it is important to get away with your spouse and enjoy the things together which make life worth it all. Vacationing in Jamaica was like taking a time-out. It allowed us to grow closer. It was wonderful."

For others, a special time happened in the quiet after tragedy, as this husband related: "We once drove across America together just after 9/11, and the days in the car together were wonderful as we just drove all day for three days." He also said that anything out of the ordinary was a tonic for

Sexual Satisfaction: Husbands vs. Wives

We asked survey-takers about the level of satisfaction in their marriages with four aspects of romantic love. "High" means they rated it 9–10 out of 10; "medium" means 6–8; and "low" means 1–5. Here is how the men compared with the women:

Physical Displays of Affection (e.g., Hugs, Kisses, Hand-holding)

	Women (%)	Men (%)
High	51	42
Medium	26	38
Low	23	19

Verbal Statements of Affection

	Women (%)	Men (%)
High	55	46
Medium	28	36
Low	18	18

Frequency of Sex

	Women (%)	Men (%)
High	39	24
Medium	34	34
Low	28	42

Quality of Sex

	Women (%)	Men (%)
High	53	37
Medium	30	34
Low	18	29

his marriage, including "time outside of work and home when we travel and play together, golfing, hiking and attending sporting events."

One bride learned the lesson of these special time-outs in a kitchen the night before her wedding. "The day before my husband and I were married, we spent the night cooking and preparing for our reception the next day," she recalled. "We laughed and played around the whole time, and my mother-in-law was there helping. It meant a lot to see that we were in this marriage together. I play that day over a lot because it makes me smile all the time."

These couples created the ideal environment for growing a strong friendship: special time together, with a focus on fun and a ban on heavy-duty talks about relationship issues and everyday concerns. The trick? Making time for each other right now, regardless of what else is going on in your lives. That's especially challenging for couples busy raising kids, holding down jobs, and fulfilling commitments to community and religious organizations during the hectic Cooperation stage. In our survey, those couples were most likely to be unhappy with the amount of time they were spending together.

And yet, that's probably when it's most crucial to find bits of downtime to spend together. "In our seminars and retreats, we stress that you're always going to have problems and disagreements—but you shouldn't put off fun, friendship, and romance until all your other problems are resolved, because they'll never all be settled," Dr. Markman says. "Happy couples make time to relax and focus on each other, regardless of what else is happening in their lives."

And sex? If your friendship is strong, you'll have the strong, easy emotional connection that leads comfortably to sexual intimacy. It's not that American husbands and wives don't value sex. They've just got their priorities in order. "We don't push ourselves to make fun times happen, but sometimes you have to. Fun comes easily early in marriage, but later on, you have to create it," says Dr. Markman, whose research-based retreats help couples brainstorm ways to have fun together, then "teach" them about fun by scheduling wine tastings, bicycle repair clinics, reflexology, and more. "People have a blast and help their marriage at the same time," he says.

Finding No. 4: Guys Get Gushy about Marriage, Too

Forget media-fueled images of monosyllabic grunters and strong, silent types. Husbands are effusive, heartfelt, and articulate in their appreciation of both their partners and their marriages. In our survey, the guys were nearly as gushy as the women—and in some areas, gushed even more. Most said they loved their wives more now than on their wedding day—and would do it all over again. They also had no fears about being openly tender and romantic.

Here's what a few men shared when asked to describe their most cherished marriage moments.

- "Kissing in the snow."
- "My wife's face when our two daughters were born and recently our first grandchild."
- "Snuggled up in bed on a cold winter day, warm under the covers."
- "The look of joy and happiness on her face as she came toward me at the altar."
- "The first and every time we make love."
- "I can't believe how lucky I am to have the woman of my dreams. I cherish every moment of every day that I'm with her."
- "When we first danced together. We both love to dance and enjoy the art of dance, and we connected as soon as we danced. It was as if we had expressed our affection and attraction with body language word for word."
- "The moment I realized she was the person I wanted to be with forever."

Guys told us that their wives went above and beyond expectations in some surprising areas—including a sense of humor, open-mindedness, kindness, and having good emotional skills. Paying attention to these key touch points can give wives a road map for reaching an even happier union. Tops on the list: more respect for being funny.

"The women in the survey weren't saying 'my guy is funnier now than when I married him,' but many men said their wives were funnier—and they liked that," notes Brown University psychiatrist Scott Haltzman, M.D., author of *The Secrets of Happily Married Men: Eight Ways to Win Your Wife's Heart Forever*. "That tells you that humor is very important to married men. Studies suggest that a wife's sense of humor can help a husband feel more content when there's been discontent in a marriage. But the opposite isn't always true: A husband's sense of humor doesn't soothe his wife when they've had problems. Men want their wives to laugh with them and to realize that you can solve serious problems while you're laughing. Too often, women marry a man who makes them laugh, but afterward humor is seen as a sign that he's not taking things seriously."

Men also value open-mindedness in their wives—two in five praised their wives for being better than expected in this area that embraces flexibility, tolerance, and acceptance. Dr. Haltzman links open-mindedness to a woman's ability to show respect for her mate's ideas, plans, and abilities. "What's clear to me from my own work and research is that men genuinely want to feel appreciated. What men have to offer, more than their emotional connection to their wives, is their capacity, their knowledge, their skills, their desire to fix things and improve things. When that is ignored, it's kind of like 'What am I here for?'"

They also deeply appreciated their wives' emotional skills. "Men realize that they rely on women to take the lead when it comes to emotions," Dr. Haltzman notes. "Many men have told me they really respect that their wives have a better sense of emotional intelligence. Women process emotions more quickly, have a more sophisticated level of emotional awareness, and can interpret facial expressions with greater ease. Any husband worth his salt will try to learn from his wife's emotional skills."

Finding No. 5: Challenges Make Us Stronger

From illness to job loss, from the death of a parent to the need to care for aging parents, all but a few survey participants said they had coped with at least one big crisis in their marriages. And for many, the worst of times had a silver lining that ultimately deepened their relationships.

"My husband is my hero," one wife told us. "He has had many physical challenges, ranging from broken bones, loss of one eye, severe burns, etc., but he has never complained or felt sorry for himself. He just goes on and deals with the injuries. He is always cheerful and would do anything to help another person."

"My spouse stuck by me and supported me through a very trying time with my mother," another said. "It made me realize that love can carry us through some bad moments."

Facing a challenge together unlocks hidden reserves of love. "My husband tries to act macho and gruff. But just before I was about to have surgery, I looked at him and saw tears running down his face," one wife said. It can also reveal a spouse's full ability to be generous, compassionate, and courageous. "When I became disabled," one husband said, "my wife took care of us and the family without any 'poor me's' and with great stamina and closeness to God." Spouses also sacrificed for each other. "The way he took care of me when my mother died is something that I will always cherish," one grateful wife said. "It was so hard for him, as he loved her as much as I did, and yet he was my rock, waiting a full three months to finally break down and cry his heart out too."

"When a crisis shocks your marriage, it gives you a second chance," says Wayne M. Sotile, Ph.D., director of psychological services for the

The Statistics

Ninety-four percent of husbands and wives said they had experienced challenges in their marriages. The outcome was sometimes negative, but surprisingly there were instances when it was positive. Here's how a variety of challenges affected their marriages.

Crisis	Percentage Who Experienced It	Positive Effect	Negative Effect
Death of a parent	50%	37%	34%
Job loss	47%	31%	54%
Depression	42%	25%	63%
Parent's illness	28%	36%	38%
Major illness	27%	58%	29%
Becoming obese	25%	20%	50%
Caregiving for parent	25%	42%	32%
Addiction	20%	26%	65%
Major weight loss	15%	61%	13%
Personal bankruptcy	15%	46%	34%
Infidelity	13%	20%	67%

Wake Forest University Healthy Exercise and Lifestyles Program. "It's not that we discover something new to love in one another, it's that we're reminded of what we already love. A psychological, spiritual, and existential reawakening happens. At our clinic, 65 to 68 percent of our patients say three to four years after their diagnosis with heart disease that this was the best thing that ever happened to their marriage."

In our survey, significant numbers of couples said that even the most difficult and emotionally draining challenges—such as depression, job loss, and caring for an ill parent—had a positive effect on their relationships.

Couples, Dr. Sotile says, grow closer in crisis because they appreciate each other's strengths. They also feel especially loved and comforted just when feeling most vulnerable. "Your partner's love touches you in a way you'll always remember," he says. "And the experience makes us grow up and get beyond childish illusions that we'll live forever and have a perfectly stress-free journey. You realize that you don't have everything, but you do have each other."

measuring your marriage

the 7 stages quizzes

Even with just one reading of the list, you probably have a good sense of which of the seven stages of marriage you can call your own. And chances are good that you are correct.

The truth is, most stages are distinct. They have clear differences from what's gone before or will come afterward. Got school-age children? You're in the Cooperation stage, running fast to keep up with the daily demands of family, job, home, and community. Just kissed your youngest child good-bye at the door to his or her college dorm room or first apartment? You're most likely a Reunion-stage empty-nester, ready to resume your love affair with your spouse—or revisit unresolved conflicts that (surprise!) have been waiting in the wings for two decades. Dealing with a sudden upheaval—such as a major illness, job loss, or move? Your marriage is surely rocked by the challenges of the Explosion stage.

So far, so simple. But love and marriage are never *un*complicated—and sometimes pinpointing your stage *isn't* simple.

Here's why: Each marriage is like a well-written novel, a journey that inevitably takes sudden, unpredictable turns. It is a two-steps-forward, three-steps-back, one-step-to-the-side adventure, not a straight-line narrative in which everything flows logically and predictably.

That's why we won't assign you to a stage, "diagnose" your individual marriage, or force you into a mold. Determining the current stage of your marriage is *your* task.

And it's a fun one. The rest of this chapter offers seven quizzes that can help you get a handle on the stage (or stages) your relationship may presently occupy. But relax—this is hardly a college entrance exam, in which the scores are crucial to your future. Rather, these questions are tools to help point you in the right direction. So compare your answers to your own instinct. Ask your spouse to take a crack at the quizzes on his or her own, then see how your answers line up. Or just meander through to get a sense of what lies ahead in this book. No one knows your marriage better than you do. Ultimately, only you can assess your stage.

Are We in the Passion Stage?

Are you still in the glorious honeymoon phase of your relationship—and are you making the *most* of every passionate, romantic, spontaneous moment? Take this quiz to find out.

1 If our relationship were an object, it would be a:
- **a.** chili pepper—hot, passionate, intense, spontaneous
- **b.** quilt—warm, comforting, cozy
- **c.** railroad—fast-moving trains by day; side by side, deep in sleep at night
- **d.** video game—push the button, a new battle starts

2 When I think about my spouse, I feel:
- **a.** hot and tingly
- **b.** loved and secure
- **c.** safe, perhaps a little bored
- **d.** irritated and untrusting

3 We don't share household chores and duties equally, but:
- **a.** I don't care—just being together is pure bliss
- **b.** we're working it out
- **c.** I'm resigned to it
- **d.** I'm fed up

4 Our love is:
- **a.** overpowering, like a tidal wave
- **b.** blissful, like a quiet, warm bath
- **c.** comfortable, like a pair of old slippers
- **d.** flickering, like the embers of a once-large fire

5 When we're apart for the day, I:
- **a.** crave my partner's embrace
- **b.** have occasional loving thoughts about him or her
- **c.** think little about him or her, secure that all is fine
- **d.** feel relieved to be alone

6 My spouse and I could be happily stranded on a desert island for:
   a. years—all we need is each other
   b. weeks—we love each other's company, but in a short time we'd crave the other parts of our lives
   c. days—just long enough to have some laughs and catch up on our sleep
   d. hours—any longer and we'd be at each other's throat

7 We do romantic things for each other:
   a. every day, every way
   b. once a week, when our schedules allow it
   c. a few times a year, such as on birthdays and Valentine's Day
   d. almost never

8 We have a repertoire of special touches, kisses, and phrases, and we "practice" our private language of love:
   a. every day, sometimes even in public
   b. occasionally, and always in private
   c. rarely—we were young and foolish when we did that stuff
   d. never—and never will

9 If we were offered airline tickets to Paris tomorrow—or to anywhere else we find romantic and special—we would:
   a. immediately say yes
   b. ask for a few hours to see if we could make arrangements to go
   c. decline—our kids, jobs, and household duties come first
   d. argue—one of us would want to, the other would insist on being "responsible"

10 When we both get home from work, we:
   a. kiss passionately and sometimes head straight to the bedroom
   b. give each other a warm kiss and hug, then sit down and share our days
   c. give each other a peck on the cheek and then get busy with chores and cooking
   d. head straight to the TV or refrigerator, barely acknowledging each other

Your Score

If your answer to question No. 1 was *a* and your answer to even one other quiz question was an *a*, then congratulations! You are most likely to be in the Passion stage. The more *a* answers you have, the more deeply you're into the glorious, passionate, honeymoon phase of your relationship. Fun and frolic now aren't frivolous—passion and spontaneity are the key elements of your relationship. Learn how—and why—you should revel in this most luxurious of stages by turning to page 67, Stage 1, Passion.

If your answers included a few *a*'s and mostly *b*'s, your marriage may be shifting from the Passion stage to the Realization stage, when the real world—and your real needs, desires, and expectations—intrude upon your love nest. To see if you're really in the Realization stage, take the quiz on page 36.

If your answers included mostly *c*'s and *d*'s, your marriage has probably moved even farther along—into the power struggles of the Rebellion stage or the busy years of the Cooperation stage, in which raising kids, securing your future, and managing your home takes precedence over physical or emotional passion.

Some lucky—or hardworking—couples hold on to the honeymoon feeling long after the Passion stage has ended. If your answers included lots of *a*'s but you've been married more than two years, have children, or are juggling lots of real-world responsibilities with your spouse, you're among the lucky. If that's you, or you'd like to recapture the passionate love that drew you together, our chapter on the Passion stage can show you how.

You may be in the Passion stage if:

- you see yourselves as newlyweds
- you feel madly in love
- you crave your partner when you're apart, and when you're together, you live in your own private romantic world
- your relationship is all about passion, excitement, sex, and intimacy
- you have a hard time focusing on things other than your relationship
- you've been married for two years or less (though some couples report the honeymoon phase lasting five years or longer!)

Are We in the Realization Stage?

The Realization stage can rock any marriage. Hormonal shifts turn down the volume on wild passion, and in its place, you feel the need to share likes and dislikes with your partner that you may have edited or muted during the Passion stage. At the same time, the two of you discover that each of you isn't perfect and doesn't intuitively know everything about the other's wants, needs, and desires. Are you here yet? Take this true-or-false quiz to find out.

1. I *thought* I knew my spouse well, but over the past year I've come to observe imperfections that surprise and disappoint me.

2. Lately I've found myself thinking that our marriage isn't automatically unfolding as I expected.

3. Recently I've begun to notice attractive people of the opposite sex again.

4. I'm starting to notice that there are more lengthy silent moments when we are together than there used to be.

5. I miss the excitement and passion of our first months together.

6. When I want my spouse to understand my wants and needs, I'm not quite sure what to do or say.

7. Recently my spouse and I have found ourselves arguing over things we never previously talked much about, like religion, politics, or career strategies.

8. I've recently discovered that my spouse has had major life experiences that he or she never revealed to me.

9. Lately we've had spats due to our different tastes regarding entertainment, decorating, cooking, or how to spend free time.

10. I've begun to form a mental checklist of how I want my spouse to improve.

11. I've recently made the surprising discovery that sometimes I'd rather do things *without* my partner.

12. I find that when we have disagreements, it's becoming harder to reach a compromise or conclusion.

Your Score

If you answered "True" to 4 of our 12 questions, it is likely that you are in the Realization stage, and the more "True" answers, the more certain it is. Looking back at the questions, you'll see that most are about recent changes—and that is the key point. A couple might spend their lives arguing about politics, for example, and that probably is very healthy and normal. In question 7, however, it is the newness of the argument, the sudden discovery that you have different opinions, that suggests you are in the Realization stage.

The keys to success in the Realization stage are to enjoy the process of discovery about each other, to learn how to communicate your needs and desires, and to discover ways to function as a team, as opposed to just lovers. If you were able to answer "False" to most of the questions, it means that you have accepted and embraced your spouse's quirks and differences—a key element in long-term marital success.

You may be in the Realization stage if:

- the initial romance and passion of your marriage are waning
- you find yourselves negotiating things you never worried about before
- you are frequently explaining things about yourself to your partner
- you spend lots of time establishing rules for how you'll function as partners
- your partner suddenly seems less than perfect—you discover he or she has flaws and imperfections just like everybody else
- for the first time, you find your spouse irritating, annoying, even boring
- you have asked yourself recently if you made the right choice in a mate
- you've been married for at least six months (couples may start experiencing the challenges of the Realization stage even sooner, or as long as two years after marrying)

Are We in the Rebellion Stage?

If you or your spouse feels a powerful pull to break out of your marriage—by pursuing new interests, spending more time apart, or even having an affair—your relationship may have entered the stormy Rebellion stage. This stage is frequently marked by power struggles, intense conflict, secrets, and angry rebellion. However, it can be a very positive stage as well, if you and your spouse allow each other the freedom, security, and time to allow your true selves to take flight. To make that happen, you'll need to negotiate schedules, learn to accept differences, work through conflicts, and build a present and a future that you *both* love. Are you in rebellion, and is it healthy or harmful to your marriage? Take this two-part quiz and find out.

A. Am I in Rebellion?

The following is a list of acts that are often hallmarks of being in marital rebellion. Please place a check for each instance in which you have thought about taking action, said something to your spouse, and/or actually acted on it.

	Thought about it	Told my spouse about it	Actually acted on it
Pursue a new job or career			
Pursue a work promotion			
Consider moving			
Consider going back to school			
Restart an old friendship			
Start a new hobby			
Start a new sport			
Join a religious group			
Have regular social outings without my spouse			
Take a vacation without my spouse			
Buy an expensive "toy" for myself			
Stop eating dinner together			
Flirt with a co-worker			
Contact a former flame			
Pursue a romantic interest			

B. Does My Marriage Satisfy Me?

The following multiple-choice questions will help establish the level of hostility or satisfaction in your marriage today. Choose the answers that most accurately describe your situation as it exists now.

1 My interactions with my spouse right now are:
   a. mostly power struggles
   b. guarded and distant
   c. warm and positive
   d. fun-filled, loving, and open

2 My emotions for my spouse right now are:
   a. more hostile than positive
   b. mixed up, with moments of anger sometimes overshadowing moments of love
   c. caring and appreciative
   d. deeply loving and committed

3 Our disagreements turn into arguments:
   a. almost all the time
   b. more than half the time
   c. sometimes
   d. never

4 When we argue, we both think we're right and the other person is wrong:
   a. almost all the time
   b. more than half the time
   c. sometimes
   d. never

5 What I need most from my marriage right now is:
   a. more freedom
   b. less arguing
   c. understanding and affection, the usual stuff
   d. exactly what I've been getting!

6 I have been growing and changing. My spouse:
   a. is too self-absorbed to have noticed
   b. makes occasional comments, often more teasing or challenging than positive
   c. is appreciative, interested, and supportive
   d. is so pleased and impressed that he or she wants to join me on my path

7 When I talk about my spouse to my friends, I am:
   a. surprisingly critical and uncomplimentary
   b. cool, rational, and dispassionately descriptive
   c. kind, generous, and occasionally teasing
   d. effusive, loving, and deeply supportive

8 If my spouse were to go on a weeklong business trip, I'd be:
   a. almost certain he or she was doing inappropriate things behind my back
   b. wondering, always wondering, but never knowing
   c. fine—unless a call didn't come every 24 hours
   d. trusting and supportive, confident that it's all about work

9 If I found myself attracted to another person, I probably would:
   a. secretly pursue the relationship, wherever it goes
   b. flirt—it's harmless
   c. not take action, but fantasize about the things that could have been
   d. shut it right down—my spouse is my one and only!

10 Our sexual relationship is:
   a. barely there
   b. a once-a-week experience
   c. I gotta say, still pretty good!
   d. hot, frequent, and loving

Your Score

A. Am I in Rebellion?

There is nothing inherently wrong with any of the first 12 "rebellious" acts. All of us want to grow and experience new things. The question is, are you doing things in a way that hurts your marriage? To score yourself, give yourself a point for each of the top 12 actions that you have thought about or done and told your spouse about. Give yourself a negative point for every one that you've seriously thought about but not expressed to your spouse. Then give yourself negative two points for each one you've acted on without telling your spouse. Are you in the plus or minus category? If you are in the minus category, chances are you are in the Rebellion stage.

Then there are the last three, all having to do with the opposite sex. Taking action on any of these three is indicative of a rebellion against your spouse that you need to deal with immediately if your marriage is to last.

B. Does My Marriage Satisfy Me?

If you answered *a* three or more times, you are likely not only to be in the Rebellion stage but also in need of marital help. If your *c* and *d* answers outnumber your *a* and *b* answers, congratulations! Even if you or your spouse wants greater freedom or change, your marriage can probably support it, thanks to your positive, accepting attitudes.

The Rebellion stage is a turning point in your marriage and is often the toughest period to move past. In this chapter, you'll discover ways to turn power struggles into productive conversations that support your emotional needs, resolve "solvable" differences, and reach toward acceptance of differences that aren't solvable—at least for now.

You may be in the Rebellion stage if:

- you and your spouse are having regular power struggles
- you or your spouse has had an affair—or is close to having one
- one or both of you feel a consistent desire for freedom and independence to pursue individual interests
- you find yourself backing away from your spouse and your marriage
- you've been married for at least two years—although the Rebellion stage can start early in a marriage (especially if you lived together first or dated for a long time before your marriage) and last for years or even decades

Are We in the Cooperation Stage?

After the passion and the rebellion comes the partnership—intensely busy years when you're raising your family, investing in your career, making your home exactly the way you want it to be, creating savings for retirement, and contributing time and effort to community or religious organizations. The joys of this building phase are enormous—but they can take a toll on your marriage. How good is the cooperation in your marriage? Take our two quizzes.

A. The Marriage Intensity Test

Put a check next to each item that is true about your marriage.

○ We have one or more children living at home (8 points)

○ We both have full-time jobs (4)

○ We own a home or condominium (4)

○ We are undertaking major redesign or renovation to our home (2)

○ We have a yard and/or garden to take care of (2)

○ We have retirement savings accounts (2)

○ We have credit card debt over $5,000 (2)

○ At least one of us has a professional career that is on the rise (2)

○ At least one of us regularly travels for business (2)

○ One of us owns a business (2)

○ At least one of us works more than 50 hours a week (2)

○ At least one of us volunteers, coaches a team, or is involved in community or political activities on a weekly basis or more frequently (2)

○ We have dinner guests, parties, or formal social engagements more than four times a month (2)

○ We host holiday or birthday gatherings three or more times a year (2)

B. The Partnership Assessment Test

How functional is your marriage in terms of day-to-day life management? Answer these true-or-false questions about you and your spouse to find out.

1. We have a set routine for keeping our home clean.

2. We work well as a team to get dinner on the table and then clean up afterward.

3. We speak by phone frequently to make everyday arrangements and solve everyday problems.

4. We have a face-to-face "check-in" with each other at least once a day to make sure all is well with each other.

5. If one of us were sick in bed for a week, the other would keep the household running just fine.

6. Both of us have an honest and equal understanding of our financial situation.

7. Both of us are comfortable with the way our home and family duties are split.

8. We share similar expectations for neatness, organization, and punctuality.

9. We frequently "cover" each other's responsibilities so the other can have a break.

10. We frequently say thank you to each other for helping each other out.

11. We both do our part in getting errands run (e.g., shopping, shuttling kids).

12. If I ask my spouse to do something, he or she will get it done in a reasonable time, without constant reminders.

13. We can point out to each other errors, things forgotten, and better ways to do something without getting hostility or resentment in return.

14. No matter how intense work, children, or daily life gets, our marriage is always my top priority.

15. No matter how intense work, children, or daily life gets, my spouse and I always manage to get in a few hugs, kisses, and laughs.

Your Score

A. The Marriage Intensity Test

Add up the points for the statements that you checked. Then see where you fall.

16 and over: You have a thoroughly hectic, modern marriage, the type in which everyday living can get in the way of emotions and love. You are almost certainly in the Cooperation stage.

12–15: Your marriage is busy, and you may be in the Cooperation stage (or on the edges), but be relieved that your marriage is saner than that of the typical middle-aged married couple.

8–12: Aspects of your life are very busy, but chances are you have the time and resources to handle it.

Under 8: Congratulations on the mellow life! Chances are you are either young or of retirement age, and most likely not in the Cooperation stage.

B. The Partnership Assessment Test

This one is simple: The more "True" answers, the more functional your marriage is. Be very happy if you answered "True" to 12 or more, and be reasonably satisfied if you answered "True" to 8 to 11 of the questions. But if fewer than half the questions got a "True," you and your spouse have work to do to become an effective team.

These two quizzes do a great job of pointing out the level of craziness in your everyday life. But they don't reveal one thing that's crucial to marital success in the Cooperation stage: your ability to make time for yourselves and each other. We'll show you how to balance the daily craze with your personal needs in the Cooperation stage chapter.

You may be in the Cooperation stage if:

- you have children living at home
- you have bought a house or condominium in the past five years
- both you and your spouse have dynamic professional careers
- money management is a big issue due to lots of money either coming into or going out of your accounts
- your to-do list on any given day is so long it could never be completed in 24 hours
- you've been happily married for more than five years

Are We in the Reunion Stage?

Your nest is empty, your career's cruising along nicely, your future looks secure. It's time to enjoy a well-deserved breather and savor the fruits of your labor. Reunion-stage couples turn back to each other—and you may find open arms, be surprised by the reemergence of old disagreements, or struggle to reconnect if you've grown far apart over the years. Find out if you're truly in the Reunion stage—and what type of marriage you have—with this quiz.

A. Are We Ready to Reunite?

Place a check next to each statement that is true for you or your marriage right now:

○ Our children are old enough to take care of themselves most or all of the time.

○ Our careers are stable.

○ Our routines for running our home are established and work well.

○ I'm wiser and calmer than I used to be.

○ We have a nice home filled with objects we cherish.

○ Money is less an issue today for us than it was 10 or 20 years ago.

○ I'm finding I have more time in the evenings than I used to.

○ I've been running so fast for so long, I'm ready to slow down a little.

○ I have little interest anymore in the hobbies of my early adulthood.

○ I spend three hours or more each evening watching TV or working on the computer.

○ A large part of my social life happens without my spouse.

○ We no longer consult with each other when shopping for clothes or food.

○ My spouse and I have become comfortable sitting in a room together and not speaking.

○ We eat dinner separately the majority of weekday evenings.

B. How Well Do I Know My Spouse?

Answer yes or no to the following questions.

Do I know...

_____ where my spouse would like to go on vacation?

_____ what my spouse thinks about his or her boss?

_____ the issues my spouse is dealing with these days at work?

_____ exactly how my spouse spends his or her day?

_____ what book my spouse is currently reading?

_____ my spouse's dreams for retirement?

_____ my spouse's favorite restaurant?

_____ what my spouse would like for his or her birthday?

_____ what is the easiest way to get my spouse sexually aroused?

_____ if there are any celebrities my spouse has a crush on?

_____ the last time my spouse changed his or her hairstyle or hair color?

_____ what my spouse's favorite Internet sites are?

Your Score

A. Are We Ready to Reunite?

This quiz contains both life-status and relationship issues that are common to couples in the Reunion stage of marriage. Here's how to score.

9–14 checks: You are very likely to be in the Reunion stage.

5–8 checks: There is a good chance you are about to enter the Reunion stage.

0–4 checks: You are probably not in the Reunion stage.

B. How Well Do I Know My Spouse?

After years of worrying about kids, career, and home improvements, it is often shocking for established couples to discover that they really don't know each other as well as they did early on in their marriage. Here's how to score.

9–12 "Yes" answers: Congratulations! You have weathered the craziness of life well, and are poised to have a fun, love-filled Reunion stage.

5–8 "Yes" answers: Not bad. You have work to do to become truly intimate again, but there is still a good level of closeness between you and your spouse.

0–4 "Yes" answers: Your lack of knowledge about your spouse reveals that you've put your marriage on the back burner. If you don't take quick steps to improve it, you face real troubles.

Settling into the Reunion stage is a lot like getting off a roller-coaster ride: You've been through a lot together, your head is spinning, and at last—calm and quiet again. At the same time, the ride through the previous stages of marriage has changed both of you. Your answers to our pair of quizzes can help you see whether you're there yet—and measure the distance or closeness that's grown up between you. Time for togetherness is the theme of the Reunion stage, but the transition can be both scary and awkward.

This is the perfect time to look at the strengths of your marriage and to draw on them in order to make some new dreams come true now that other areas of your life have settled down. Investing in your relationship right now is at least as important as investing in your retirement savings account. Ignore this, and you may find yourself living in the cold waters of an "emotional divorce" or even see your marriage end. Make a new commitment, and you'll find yourselves enjoying a second—and even better—honeymoon phase.

You may be in the Reunion stage if:

- your children have left home or can take care of themselves
- your careers are running smoothly
- you have more time for yourselves
- your finances are at least somewhat secure
- the two of you can start and finish a conversation without frequent interruptions
- you perceive your spouse more as a business partner than as a soul mate
- you've been married 15 to 25 years

quiz 6

Are We in the Explosion Stage?

A crisis never knocks first. Job loss, illness, injury, financial trouble—even retirement or relocation—can swiftly overturn comfortable routines, change the way your future looks, even reweave the fabric of your marriage. Are you in the midst of the upheaval of the Explosion stage—and how well are you coping? Take our quiz to find out.

A. The Explosion Test

The following are significant life events that can strongly affect a marriage—sometimes for the better, sometimes for the worse. Place a check next to any event that has happened in the past year within your immediate family (that is, you, your spouse, or a child living at home) or is very likely to happen in the coming six months.

◯ Layoff from work

◯ Launch of a new business

◯ Personal bankruptcy filing

◯ Move to a new house

◯ Move to a new city

◯ Death of a parent

◯ Death of a child

◯ Life-threatening illness

◯ Life-altering injury

◯ Conviction for a crime

◯ Home disaster (e.g., flood or fire)

◯ Major crisis with child (e.g., drug addiction, dropping out of school, pregnancy)

◯ Prolonged depression

◯ Sudden, significant religious or spiritual change

◯ Major trouble with obesity

B. The Coping Test

The following is a list of 20 positive attributes we typically want in our spouses during a time of crisis. For each one, write down your level of agreement as follows.

1. strongly disagree
2. somewhat disagree
3. neither agree nor disagree
4. somewhat agree
5. strongly agree

My spouse...

_____ is a great listener

_____ is optimistic about life

_____ is resilient

_____ is open with his or her feelings

_____ is accepting of my weaknesses

_____ is a problem-solver

_____ is fair and honest in his or her dealings with others

_____ has unconditional love for his or her family

_____ is prudent with our money

_____ is focused on the present and future

_____ is reliable and resourceful

_____ is a loving, fair parent

_____ is a good public speaker

_____ is unselfish with his or her time

_____ knows how to calm me down

_____ knows when to give me space

_____ knows what to say to me at tough times

_____ has a good work ethic

_____ puts family first over work and personal interests

_____ makes me feel secure about the future

Your Score

A. The Explosion Test

This isn't really a test, and there really isn't a score. All it takes is one checkmark to hurl your marriage into the Explosion stage. If you checked more than one, then the marital issues of the Explosion stage will be far more pronounced. Your goals: successfully deal with the crises at hand and do so in a way that causes no harm—and hopefully brings some good—to your marriage.

B. The Coping Test

Add up the total number of points. The total should land somewhere between 20 and 100. Here's how to read your number.

80–100: Congratulations! Not only can you rely on your spouse in times of crisis, but you clearly have a strong, loving marriage.

60–80: Very good! The plusses outweigh the perceived minuses, meaning you are mostly favorable to your marriage. However, there is work to be done to grow your teamwork and reliance.

40–60: Not so good. The minuses outweigh the plusses, meaning you probably don't trust your spouse to be there for you in times of trouble. You two need to make a serious commitment to being a more positive, supportive, and assertive team.

20–40: Crisis! Scores this low mean that your spouse has few if any of the attributes important for weathering the storms that will inevitably hit. Be prepared for some hard conversations and a strong commitment to change!

No life challenge is easy, and no two are the same. What is common through all, however, is your need to have a spouse you can rely on, and not just emotionally. You want a spouse who is practical too, who will commit to doing the right thing to solve the problem or rebound from the challenge. No matter how you're coping, the chapter on Stage 6, Explosion (page 223) will give you a deeper understanding of this life-altering stage and offer insights and tips for keeping your marriage strong and supportive during tough times.

You may be in the Explosion stage if:

- you or your spouse has just experienced a major career, health, or parenting crisis
- catastrophe has struck your home or family
- a major positive experience has just happened, like winning a lottery or getting a promotion that dramatically changes your role at work and at home

Are We in the Completion Stage?

Partners in the Completion stage share a long, rich history—glorious joys savored together, difficult challenges met as a team, and plenty to look back on with pride and satisfaction. You've weathered the storms, but are you still enjoying each new day together and looking to the future with happy anticipation? This quiz will help determine whether you've reached the Completion stage—and have mastered the art of honoring your past while you enjoy the sweetness of the present, work on marital issues that never go away, and confront new challenges.

A. Are We Complete?

Please rate your marriage on a 1–10 scale on the following criteria, with 1 being the lowest and 10 being the highest score.

_____ Level of trust between you and your spouse

_____ Compatibility

_____ Ability to resolve differences effectively

_____ Ability to forgive each other

_____ Freedom to pursue personal and/or career growth

_____ Time spent talking, laughing, or having fun together

_____ Verbal statements of affection

_____ Physical displays of affection

_____ Sharing of everyday household duties

_____ Level of respect you have for your spouse

_____ Richness of memories of past times together

_____ Ability to improve each other's moods

B. The Words-of-Love Game

Here's a simple one: Just choose three words from the following list that you think best describe your marriage today.

Trusting	Reliable	Frustrating
In crisis	Cold	Secure
Blessed	Growing	Joyful
Hectic	Challenging	Disconnected
Complete	Warm	Passionate
Distant	Loving	On autopilot

Your Score

A. Are We Complete?

Add up your 12 scores. A perfect score is 120; if you have 100 or higher, chances are great that you are in the Completion stage of a happy, successful marriage. An 80–99 score is very solid but suggests that your marriage hasn't fully culminated. Below 80, and you have work to do before you can call your marriage "complete."

B. The Words-of-Love Game

When we asked more than 1,000 married people the same question in the Reader's Digest *Marriage in America Survey*, we were pleased at the positive nature of the responses. The top five words were Loving (41%), Secure (33%), Trusting (30%), Blessed (29%), and Complete (19%). There's no formal scoring here, but if you are in the Completion stage of marriage, at least four of the five adjectives should be positive in nature. If you chose words like Distant or Disconnected, then there's work to be done to reconnect with the person you have shared so many years of life with.

You might be in the Completion Stage if...
- the "building" stages of your marriage—kids, career, saving for the future—are over
- health and happiness are more important issues today than career and child-raising
- fighting between you and your spouse has declined substantially in recent years
- you've been married more than 25 years

how to fix
a marriage

universal tips and rules

Marriages can break down at any time, for any number of reasons. This is true if you are newlyweds, young and free career people, harried parents, or marriage veterans who've already weathered many storms together.

There is nothing wrong with an occasional breakdown—virtually all marriages have them in some shape or form. What matters is that you quickly take steps to fix things as they emerge. And that's why we're here.

In the chapters that follow, you will discover marriage remedies that are customized to the unique stages of marriage. But don't turn the page just yet, because there is important news! Regardless of your marital stage, several fundamental rules apply when it comes to making your relationship stronger, deeper, and more loving. These rules apply at every stage of your marriage, no matter the size of the problem or the number of anniversaries you've celebrated.

The rules? Some are so simple, a kindergartener could ace them: Share your lunch. Listen. Hold hands when you cross the street. Don't be nasty. Laugh. Sing. But if it were only that easy, there would be no marriage crisis in America—no 48 percent divorce rate or shadow epidemic of still-marrieds longing for something better. Truth is, it's not always simple. But fixing your marriage is possible—if you know what really works. And these rules do work.

So start applying them today—and keep on using them every day—to build a healthier, happier relationship. Based on research from the nation's top relationship experts, these "new fundamentals" are modern enough to withstand the unique pressures and stresses of real-world, 21st-century relationships, yet old-fashioned enough to uphold the enduring pillars of marriage: love, honor, and respect.

Here are our three golden ground rules.

Ground Rule 1

Keep Your Eye on the *Real* Prize: Play, Pleasure, and Joy

At many marriage-enrichment weekends, the first assignment that hurting, distant, and improvement-minded pairs receive is surprisingly counterintuitive: Put aside all the "he said, she said" confrontations and go have fun tonight. The next morning, the breakfast room is packed with sparkly-eyed, hand-holding, shyly exuberant couples. The rationale: You've already spent hundreds of painful hours obsessing about what's gone wrong, parsing the blame, and shouting about how to fix it. It's time to recapture the playfulness and pleasures that really make a good marriage sing.

A little too Pollyanna, you say? Shouldn't you hash out all the tough issues before you taste—or even deserve—dessert? Top marriage researchers say doing precisely the opposite is crucial.

In a Florida study of 20 couples married for at least 25 years, 40 percent of satisfied husbands and wives reported that they have fun together—and treasure the experience. Humor and affection weren't even on the radar screens of less-satisfied married folk. And University of Michigan, Ann Arbor, researchers who followed 373 just-hitched couples for four years found that expressing a loving, positive attitude was the most powerful predictor of marital quality.

We know. Boredom, frustration, and everyday irritations can erode the spark between you—but more of the same won't feed that flame. Making the good stuff your top priority will. Here's how.

Keep your love account in the black. It takes 5 to 20 *positive* statements (the number varies with the marriage expert) to outweigh the damage wrought by a single negative remark—or even by a steely squint or an impatient "hmph!" Do more of the former, less of the latter. Opportunities to build up your "love bank" abound—compliment your spouse on her new shoes or his new blue button-down shirt; thank him for his contributions to keeping your household running smoothly; dial her office number for a quick afternoon "I was thinking of you" check-in (do *not* discuss household chores or the dinner menu, unless you're buying it, cooking it, or taking her out for it). Make sure your compliments and thank-yous are heartfelt and specific: "I can always count on you to make sure my car is safe and ready to use." "You're always thinking of ways to make our home pleasant—this new tablecloth is nice." If the two of you haven't been exactly showering each other with appreciation lately, it may take a little clever attention-getting to help your spouse notice and absorb all the new warm fuzzies you're sending his or her way. Aim for eye contact when you smile or offer a compliment; make a little joyful noise (a small, happy sigh, for instance) when delivering an affectionate, unexpected touch.

Eight Marriage-Busters to Give Up Today

We'll say it straight up: There's no good reason in the world to continue practicing these.

1 Nagging, nagging, nagging. We know about the squeaky wheel, but complaining loud and long gets you only short-term gains and builds up powerful discontent on your spouse's side.

2 Blaming, criticizing, and name-calling. These tactics belittle the person you promised to love, honor, and cherish; let you play angel to his or her devil; and don't address the responsibility you both share for your marital happiness.

3 Bullying, rudeness, and selfishness. These ugly power plays tell your partner that he or she doesn't count at all in your eyes.

4 Peacekeeping and passive placating. A "whatever you say, Dear" attitude may keep your home quieter but leaves you in the martyr's role. You get to be angry, defensive, and a drudge. What fun is that?

5 Deploying logic all the time. Life isn't the starship *Enterprise*; playing the dispassionate Mr. Spock not only cuts you off from your feelings but also subtly tells your spouse that his or her feelings don't count either.

6 Throwing up distractions. Being hyperactive, fooling around all the time, and refusing to focus—in conversation or in life—is a frustrating attempt to avoid intimacy or difficult issues.

7 Stonewalling. Another stall maneuver, stonewalling stops arguments and constructive discussions cold. Not much can happen when one spouse just won't talk about it.

8 Making unilateral decisions about the big things. Sometimes you have to pick the bathroom paint color on your own. But if you're making major decisions about your money, your time, your kids, and your family life, you're acting without accountability and cutting off the possibility of joint decision-making.

Study the art of small acts of love. You know how to push Mr. or Mrs. Right's hot buttons, and if you think about it, you know how to push his or her joy buttons too. We don't just mean sex, but it's not a bad place to start. Greet him with a "glad to see you" hug and kiss when you get home. Surprise her by delivering coffee, bedside, some rainy Thursday morning (and stay to talk). Notice and appreciate her sterling qualities; let the faults slide. (She's probably doing the same thing for you.) Give his waist a quick squeeze when you two pass in the hallway; flash your "I'm so happy we're here together" smile as you schlep the recycling bin out to the curb. Unload, reload, and run the dishwasher, and don't even mention it. Resolve to enjoy a 10-second kiss before you turn in each night. Laugh at his jokes, even if you think Dave Chappelle's version on Comedy Central was far funnier. You'd do this for your kids, why not your spouse?

Touch. Human touch triggers the release of feel-good endorphins—for giver and receiver alike. Nonsexual touch is the unsung arrow of love. Link arms as you walk into the grocery store; brush her cheek with your fingertips when you smooch good morning; while he catches up on some extra work at night, kiss that cute spot on his head where his hair circles outward in a little whorl. Revive little ways you touched or kissed during your most passionate days—maybe it was the little smooch on the back of his earlobe, or running your hand through the back of her hair while you drove cross-country.

Touch is a rich, complex language—it pays to improve your vocabulary. Use it to show affection and support, create a mood-lifting sense of play, and strengthen your rituals (for example, a special hello or good-bye hug and kiss).

Jealously guard the "we" of your marriage. You love the kids, the dog, the cat, the goldfish, and the hamster. But you need a couples-only weekend away once in a while—a week would be even better—to rekindle the glorious sizzle that brought you together. But don't wait until vacation rolls around to restring the ties that bind. A woman and a man who form a tight unit—a haven, a cozy castle with strong walls and a figurative moat to keep out the world—are safe from any storm. Support your soul mate— take his or her side in difficulties if she feels alone. (An "Oh, you poor dear" works so much better than "Gee, Honey, I think your boss was right" when emotional support is needed.) Keep your spouse's secrets to yourself, even when everyone in your office or social circle is spilling their best husband or wife woes. Short of an actual emergency, accept no interruptions of couple time. That's what voice mail and bedroom door locks are for. Create and protect your private world. Added benefit: Guarding your little kingdom can help affair-proof your marriage.

Find two kinds of time for each other. You clear your schedule for hair appointments, grade-school band concerts, favorite TV shows, and your book group—how about your spouse? Spend 20 to 30 minutes a day chatting together about your daily lives, your dreams, and your plans. And make time for intimacy—even if it means scheduling it in your day-planner.

The only ground rule for chat time: Keep household management issues and "what's happening to our relationship" talk off the agenda. It's reconnect time. You're building your friendship. A St. Louis, Missouri, study of happy couples found that being friends was a more potent "glue" than even sex or the kids. And expect some dividends: Building your friendship, say University of Washington researchers, guarantees a closer, even sexier, marriage over the years.

Why schedule sex? Sure, spontaneity makes you feel like you're still in the Garden of Eden. But if you or your partner isn't getting enough affection and physical loving, show him or her that it matters by setting aside time just for the two of you.

Celebrate victories. Super Bowl champs, Stanley Cup winners, and Olympic gold-medal bobsledders have one thing in common: After a victory, they party like crazy. If your marriage is humming along nicely, that's a triumph worth celebrating. Dine at the place where you proposed; take a picnic to a secluded woodland meadow; try one of those midwinter, midweek travel deals to Paris or London or Prague. You've earned it.

Ground Rule 2

Change Yourself, Not Your Spouse

Your partner ain't broke, so don't try to fix him (or her).

It's tempting to blame your significant other when you're feeling angry, disappointed, bored, betrayed, or stressed out about your marriage. And it's just a short hop to seeing your mate as the bad guy or bad girl who's gotta change so that your marriage can improve.

But that's a cop-out. Trying to improve your spouse—and expecting him or her to change *first*—puts your partner on the defensive and casts

Forget starter marriage, no-fault divorce, and the on-again, off-again "wedded bliss as swinging door" examples set by the likes of Brad Pitt, J Lo, and Great-Aunt Tillie, who divorced three guys four times. Instead, think commitment.

Shutting the exit doors—by truly believing that you and your spouse are together, no matter what, for the duration—can give you the security you need to focus on the important stuff. It also simply buys you time: In University of Chicago studies of 700 miserable, ready-to-split spouses, researchers found that two-thirds of those who stayed married were happy five years later.

They survived some of the toughest problems couples face: alcoholism, infidelity, financial straits, and serious illness among them. Their strengths? A mix of stubborn commitment, a willingness to work together on issues, and a healthy lowering of unrealistic expectations. The added benefit: They avoided the financial and emotional stresses of divorce. The obvious exception: Physically violent couples were better off divorced.

you in the dreary role of Joan of Arc. Stalemate! Nobody changes; nobody takes responsibility; everybody's unhappy. Casting your spouse as the evil Snidely Whiplash or the treacherous Catwoman inevitably causes you to ignore the 80 to 90 percent of him or her that is good. Is that fair?

The real fix: Change yourself. Very few problems are one person's "fault." When you fix up your side and seek the best in your spouse, magic happens. You feel more optimistic. Your spouse is happier because he or she is being appreciated, not chastised. And you'll both feel motivated to change in ways that make each other even happier.

Some ways to start:

Embrace your *wabe-sabe* marriage. The Japanese philosophy of imperfection, *wabe sabe* (pronounced "wah-bee sah-bee") applies well to real-life love. Next time your guy or girl does something that makes you bristle, take a breath, mutter, "Wabe sabe," and remind yourself that her intentions are sterling, even if the execution wasn't. Accept him for who he is. You want your spouse to love and honor your true self in the same way, so lead the way—humbly and without expecting anything in return.

Bite your tongue; open your ears. We've hidden this nugget throughout this book because it may be the single most powerful step you can take to keep your marriage from going south. Blaming, insulting, criticizing, bullying, and being domineering predict a bad end, or at least a living hell. (So do being defensive, denying responsibility, and withdrawing.) Resolve instead to listen well and speak with love.

Take a crash course in spouse appreciation. Every day this month, choose an aspect of your spouse that you like—it could be fleeting or enduring, large or small. ("He always holds the door for me." "She always smiles at me over dinner.") Name the trait—for example, "My wife is thoughtful" or "My husband puts our marriage first." Then think up a specific act that supports it: "She brushed the snow off my windshield after the blizzard last week." "He always checks with me before scheduling a night out with the guys."

Honor your own imperfect nature. We don't simply blame our partners; sometimes we blame ourselves for all that's off-balance in our relationships. Accepting too much guilt is paralyzing. You're human. Your heart is good. To convince yourself, use the same approach suggested above, but turn your love light on yourself. Think of qualities that are important to you, tell yourself you have them, and back it up with a real-world example, such as, "I am honest—I tell her what I'm really thinking."

Make yourself happy, healthy, and energetic. The most classic piece of advice experts give to singles looking for the perfect match? Be "the One" so that you'll attract "the One." Same goes in marriage. The happier you are, the happier your marriage will be—and the easier it will be to manage disagreements without falling into nasty fights. (Doesn't more stuff roll off your back when you're happy? Sure it does!) Yes, you depend on your spouse. But if 15 minutes of morning yoga, a walk, a switch to decaf, a new hobby, or a new hairstyle give you a new, relaxed zing, the good feelings can't help but spill over into happier, richer moments together.

Never underestimate the power of good grooming. Once, you combed your hair and obsessed about the sexiest item to wear to bed. Now it's either the circa-1998 sweats or the size XXXL T-shirt with Goofy on the back. Clearly, its time to ramp up the visuals—but don't go overboard. No need to wear lipstick or aftershave for Saturday morning Cheerios, but do comb your hair, brush your teeth, and wear the robe that doesn't have holes.

Feeling good about yourself makes your eyes sparkle—you'll be more likely to make eye contact, which sends the spark to your spouse, and you know what to do next!

Ground Rule 3

Fight Fair

Conflict doesn't mean your marriage is in trouble—it means you're still alive. Happy couples disagree about as many things, and the same kinds of things, as unhappy pairs do. (How could any two people sharing a house, a mortgage, jobs, kids, in-laws, pets, and a future not spar on occasion?) Everyone, and we mean everyone, disagrees. When Ruth Graham, wife of famed evangelist Billy Graham, was once asked if there were fights in her own household, she quipped, "I hope so. Otherwise we would have no differences, and life would be pretty boring."

There's a world of difference, however, between dirty fighting and constructive engagement. In a Florida study of longtime couples, joint problem-solving ability was cited as a key factor for 70 percent of satisfied pairs, while just 33 percent of unsatisfied couples seemed to have mastered this skill. Why it matters: With the right tools and mind-set, conflict becomes the gateway to deeper intimacy—the chance to be seen for who you truly are; to accept your mate's adorable, vulnerable, quirky real self; and to build a strong union without caving in or silently seething.

"All married couples should learn the art of battle as they should learn the art of making love," notes one close observer of human nature. "Good battle is objective and honest—never vicious or cruel. Good battle is healthy and constructive and brings to a marriage the principle of equal partnership." The philosopher? Advice columnist Ann Landers. We agree. Our ground rules for the good battle:

Ban blame—and outlaw the words *never* and *always*. Criticism, contempt, confrontation, and hostility are like gas on a fire—and can burn up a marriage. When University of California researchers followed 79 couples for more than a decade, they found that early divorcers fought loud and long and were constantly on the attack—or defensive. Happy couples avoid verbalizing every critical thought and work to keep discussions from escalating.

Sometimes a good idea is really a bad idea in disguise. This trio of well-intentioned fix-up moves is a case in point.

Fix-Up Flub 1: The Big Confrontation

This is your marriage, not reality TV. Slamming your partner, cold, with a tidal wave of anger, frustration, and demands for major changes right now is a scorched-earth policy—not the path to a deeper, more intimate, more loving and playful relationship. Trust us.

Sure, you've got a laundry list of serious complaints, ancient hurts, and old scores to settle. We've all got gripes. But starting your journey to a better marriage with the Big Talk is too hot, too explosive, too negative, and too likely to leave you both feeling even more defensive, hurt, distant, and frustrated. Even worse: You'll continue operating under the false assumption that the two of you must resolve all your problems before you can be happy.

The real fix: Build trust and happiness first and use our "fight fair" techniques to settle differences gently.

Fix-Up Flub 2: The Big Announcement

Declaring that things are going to change for the better from this moment onward might seem the perfect way to start a better future. But even the sunniest "Honey, we're going to make this better, and here's how" conversation can backfire, marriage experts say. Here's why: It comes across as a big to-do list, loaded with code words. Does "make it better" really mean he's bored with you? Does "get closer" mean she'll leave if we don't?

The real fix: Skip the big pronouncement. Be subtle. Lovingly stealthy. Show, don't tell. Hire a baby-sitter, get out of the house for the evening, and make sure both of you have a great time. Then do it again. Take a small thing the two of you do naturally, such as sharing coffee and conversation before the kids wake up, and make sure it happens every day.

Fix-Up Flub 3: Constant Compatibility

Like sinking the perfect putt, perfect harmony is blissful—and all too rare. Having the goal of always agreeing, or believing that all your time together should be pure pleasure, sets you up for repeated disappointments and frustration. At worst, the myth of constant compatibility could lead you to conclude—falsely—that your mate isn't the One.

The real fix: Don't expect your marriage will feel like an *Ozzie and Harriet* rerun or like a Katharine Hepburn/Cary Grant movie. Revel in the differences that make good sparks fly when you're working together.

Keep a verbal fire extinguisher within reach. If an argument is heating up despite your best efforts, try one of these fire prevention techniques: Change the subject, inject gentle humor, empathize, or show your spouse some extra appreciation. Too late? Bail out now. Agree to walk away, and resume when you've both cooled off.

Getting in deep? Make sure it's the right time and place. If you're not well rested and well fed, postpone serious, potentially difficult relationship talks until you are. Hunger and fatigue can unleash the demons behind regrettable remarks. Ban alcohol for the same reason—break out the merlot, microbrew, or bubbly after you've achieved détente.

Focus, focus, focus. Turn off the TV, the radio, and the laptop. Put down the catalog. If you're preoccupied or on your way out the door, arrange a time to pick the discussion up again. Resolving differences with your main squeeze is too important to do on the fly. Giving your spouse your undivided attention builds empathy and opens lines of communication—you *both* feel closer and more interested in talking together.

Does this discussion have a G rating—and a happy ending? If not, cultivate the strength to stop—and reschedule—loud, long arguments until the kids aren't around. And when they are, keep disagreements respectful and productive. Research shows that children thrive (and absorb good relationship skills) when parents resolve issues, but they develop insecurities and even behavior problems when Mom and Dad engage in hopeless shouting matches. (Sparring behind closed doors doesn't spare little ears.)

Listen, listen, listen. Yes, you can accurately predict precisely what your mate's going to say within the first three seconds, but this isn't a data download. It's about feelings—and his or hers need to be heard. Don't interrupt, offer a solution, or defend yourself too soon; nod, rephrase, or provide a soft "um-hum" to show you're honoring the emotions behind the words. Sometimes all we need is someone to really listen.

Rehearse this useful phrase: "I'm sorry." We all make mistakes. Apologies—humorous, heartfelt, or clumsy—are crucial for the continuing happiness of your marriage. Experts say that these "repair attempts" can predict the success of your relationship.

Solve the easy stuff—pronto—and back off on the rest. There are two types of marital conflicts: eternal and solvable. Nearly 70 percent may be perpetual or take decades to sort out. Sigh, shake your head, and try to laugh at those. Then solve the rest. You'll feel better.

PART TWO

the
7 stages

stage 1

passion

For every couple in love, there was a moment when you melted and caught on fire at the same time. You can't predict when such a moment is coming, and you can't force it to arrive. But magically, you realize you are passionately in love—laughing, glowing, falling over the furniture. Suddenly you feel as if you're levitating. You lose your appetite and think of nothing but your beloved. Time stands still for hours, months, and occasionally even years as you float in a delicious, magical universe built just for two.

This extraordinary passion ignites during courtship, inspires your decision to marry, and carries you through the early months or even years of your marriage in bliss. Now you understand the subtle, soaring, piercing qualities of love described so vividly by the Arab writer Ahdaf Soueif. In the novel *The Map of Love*, she writes of eight types of love, all of which you seem to experience in the Passion stage:

> "*Ishq* is love that entwines two people together, *shaghaf* is love that nests in the chambers of the heart, *hayam* is love that wanders the earth, *teeh* is love in which you lose yourself, *walah* is love that carries sorrow within it, *sababah* is love that exudes from your pores, *hawa* is love that shares its name with 'air' and with 'falling,' *gharm* is love that is willing to pay the price."

Have you experienced passion this full? Such a love changes you forever—and you never forget the moment it all begins, as couples we interviewed for this book showed us time and time again.

"Our first date symbolizes our whole marriage," says Margaret Martin, 56, married to husband, Rich, for 30 years. "I was smitten with Rich, and I bought a stunning red silk pajama pantsuit to wear on our date … and Rich showed up at the door in the ragged jeans he'd worn backpacking through Europe the summer before! As we drove down the interstate, he handed me a bag of balloons and asked if I wouldn't mind blowing some up and wearing them on my head! That way, we would get a discount at the Great Southeast Music Hall in Atlanta. At that point, I'm thinking, This guy's not only weird, he's cheap! But he was so cute, and there was such a physical attraction between us. He made me laugh. We talked and talked, and our strong, common bond grew quickly. We met in August and were married the following June. And we've never stopped talking."

"Greg came all the way from Idaho to sweep me off my feet—and I couldn't resist," recalls Karen McGreer, a marriage and sex therapist from Medford, New York, now married for 11 years. "I had already been married twice before—and was divorced once and then widowed. I knew Greg, but I didn't know he was keeping tabs on me all these years through mutual friends. He came to New Jersey just to be with me. He was the kindest man I'd ever met—very remarkable, very wise, a real Renaissance man. He's intellectually brilliant. He can fix anything. He was, and is, so attentive to me. I can honestly say the honeymoon lasted for almost 8 years."

And sometimes adversity can kindle this early passion.

"Larry and I came back from our honeymoon in Key West to a snowstorm in Baltimore," says Susan Saunders, a clinical social worker at the University of Maryland. "Our car wouldn't start in the airport parking lot. When we finally got to Larry's apartment, where we were going to live, a window had been left open and a cat had gotten in. There was cat pee on everything—the furniture, the linens, the towels. The trash cans were all overturned. It was cold and it stank. Larry said, 'Why don't you have a nice shower, and I'll find us something to eat.' Well, the hot water gave out just when I was all soaped up. I was thinking seriously about trying to get my old apartment back when Larry came into the bathroom with a clean, fluffy yellow towel and a watering can full of warm water he'd heated on the stove. He rinsed me off and wrapped me up in the towel … as he played our vows from our wedding day on a tape recorder. Okay, I said to myself, I think we can make this work!"

The Love Cocktail

Welcome to the first stage of marriage: Passion. "The euphoria of early, intense love really is an altered state of consciousness—a change in brain chemistry," notes marriage and sex therapist Pat Love, Ed.D., author of *Hot*

Monogamy and *The Truth About Love*. The force behind the Passion stage? A special "love cocktail" of neurotransmitters that contains three primary ingredients. The first is the amphetamine-like compound phenylethylamine. This is the same "love molecule" that peaks in the brain during orgasm and is also found in chocolate candy. When you're deeply in love, your brain also produces extra dopamine, a feel-good neurotransmitter, and norepinephrine, which revs you up for sex.

Italian researchers have also found higher-than-normal levels of hormones called neutrophins, which they dubbed "lust molecules," in blood samples taken from people in passionate relationships. They also note that women's levels of libido-enhancing testosterone were higher during intense love. Put it all together, and you've got a natural high—and a mix so potent, so exhilarating, and so alluring that supplement manufacturers have tried to reproduce and market it as pills and even nasal sprays with names like Passion Rx.

A "love cocktail" of brain chemicals is what makes passion so real.

But there's nothing like the real thing. This blend of naturally produced chemicals alters your personality, boosts your energy, and suppresses your need for sleep and food. You feel euphoric, giddy, fearless, and more alive than ever before. Defenses are down; optimism is up. You're convinced that your lover is perfect—no matter what your friends may tell you or what those socks on the bathroom floor reveal about her laundry habits.

Alas, this glorious idyll in paradise will come to an end. Honeymoon passion usually sustains itself for six months to two years, researchers say. Yours may last longer—or vanish before you've unpacked all the wedding gifts. Some married lovers brag that their passion persisted for years and years, while others grouse that theirs evaporated quickly. This much is true: Bliss this delicious can't last forever. Those love chemicals eventually settle down. The "ga-ga phase" ends. Real life knocks on your front door.

We'll get to that in the Realization stage. Meanwhile, enjoy your passion to its fullest. But even in this period of hazy, passionate love, you've got work to do. The truth is that unbridled passion won't do much to help the two of you navigate the decidedly unromantic and difficult challenges of making a real life together. For a long-lasting marriage, don't write off the Passion stage as just a wild romp before you crazy kids get down to the serious business of marriage. Now's the time to take your special bond very, very seriously. Smart Passion stage couples try to fully experience the romance and passion that connect them. They work hard to develop a strong sense of "we." And they use the unique closeness and openness of this 24/7 Valentine's Day to forge deeper trust, respect, emotional intimacy, and sexual closeness.

Your five-part Passion stage mission is all about love.

Savor—and remember—the glories of the Passion stage. Don't miss your own party! We've got dates and at-home activities to help you make the most of this special time—and ways to preserve it so that you can rekindle the chemistry later on.

Forge a rock-solid sense of "we." You can—and should—spend Saturday morning and afternoon rolling around between the sheets, ordering out for Chinese food, and jumping back into bed for a heart-to-heart chat and more lovemaking. Why not use this exclusivity as the springboard for strengthening your sense of "we"—the solidarity that will help you feel secure in your marriage for decades to come?

Practice your partner's native love language. Does your partner respond to soft words or properly inflated car tires, a candy heart or a heart-to-heart talk? The answer matters. At stake: whether your romance style makes your spouse feel deeply loved or misses the mark.

Build trust, respect, and emotional closeness. The special closeness of the Passion stage offers a great opportunity to work on emotional intimacy. You'll learn how to be more supportive and less judgmental, how to be trusted with your partner's most private secrets (and to dare to reveal your own), and to take the first step in accepting (yes, and respecting) your mate's weaknesses as well as his or her most sterling qualities.

Expand your sexual vocabulary through touch, pleasure, and a new sense of the erotic. Don't wait to feel turned on: Schedule a "touch date" with your partner and explore. It's fun—and you'll build skills and habits that deepen physical intimacy and will keep lovemaking on the agenda when stress, work, kids, and fatigue (and any libido differences) get in the way of spontaneous sex in the future.

Experts say the first two years of marriage are crucial for building skills to carry you past the inevitable disappointments ahead when the sizzle of passion cools. We're happy to report that this work is fun, loving, romantic, and sexy.

Mission 1

Savor the Passion

Anthropologists say the short-lived infatuation of the Passion stage is merely Mother Nature's way of ensuring the survival of the species. Luckily, it also provides a template for lifelong marriage. "Find a way to put all that passion in a bottle," suggests Dr. Love. "Keep a journal and write it all down. Take pictures. Save receipts and silly trinkets. Really record it so that you can remember it and bring it back later on."

Too many couples switch into old-married-couple roles once they've unpacked their honeymoon luggage. They want to get down to tasks like getting the bathroom painted and choosing a color scheme for the kitchen. "They've got checklists and lots of unromantic plans, but I think a lot of that can wait," Dr. Love notes. "This is a stage where you should really enjoy romance. It's free right now. Later on, you'll have to really work at it."

So buy or decorate a pretty box and keep mementos—in later years, they'll have the power to drop you back through time to the feelings that ran high on the day you ate that custard at the lake, had dinner at the little Italian place on a side street, or walked through the park during a twilight snowstorm. One woman interviewed for this book experienced this delicious time warp while cleaning out the basement with her husband. "We were moving boxes, throwing old trash away, when suddenly, my husband opened a file folder and pulled out the receipt from the first time we'd rented a cottage together by the Chesapeake Bay in Chincoteague, Virginia. It was the trip where we told each other we loved each other for the first time. I stood in my dirty old basement and cried in his arms—happy to remember it and happy he'd quietly saved the memory!"

Romantic remembrances aren't just a girl thing. Guys can—and should—be collectors too. "When I interviewed couples for one of my books, there wasn't one man who said he didn't love romance," Dr. Love says. "All the women liked it, but the men said they didn't get very much of it. They wanted more!"

Six Great Ways to Remember Your Wedding Forever

Frame your wedding vows. Whether you wrote your own; agreed to love, honor, and respect using the traditional vows of your faith; or were married by a justice of the peace, your wedding vows are your promise to each other—they recall the moment you made your "forever and ever" pledge. Hire a calligrapher or use one of the fancy typefaces on your computer to create a beautiful, frame-worthy version of your vows. Hang it proudly in your bedroom, the foyer of your home, or another place of honor.

Show off your bouquet. Hang your flowers upside down in a dry, dark place for two weeks after the wedding. Display in a china closet or under a glass dome: Dried flowers are lovely but fragile. Or ask your florist in advance to freeze-dry your bouquet so that it looks nearly as colorful as it did on your wedding day.

Finish your wedding album! If you haven't finalized your album yet, or didn't use a photographer who assembles an album for you, now's the time to get organized. Dedicate a weekend—or the evenings of a week—to sorting and choosing wedding photos for a simple album. Pick your favorite shot of the two of you and order a large copy (we like 8 x 10s). Hang it in your living room or bedroom.

Create a honeymoon shadow box. Assemble all the odds and ends you probably collected on your honeymoon—the napkin from that romantic spot where you had a glass of wine together, the ticket stubs from the boat ride, postcards, maps, brochures, stones, the flower you plucked on a walk at the botanical garden, the prized recipe a chef never gives away (except to a new bride like you!). Purchase a shadow box and double-sided tape at a craft store. Create a pretty collage you'll always love.

Turn minutiae into a montage. You've got your embossed wedding napkin, your invitation, the receipt for the cake, the wedding program, the cake-topper, the groom's bow tie (which he'll never wear again), the pearl-and-crystal clip you wore in your hair, and a copy of the sheet music for the song the harpist played as you marched down the aisle. Arrange these memories inside a large shadow box for a pretty way to relive your wedding day whenever you like.

Go candid. Find the most beautiful, artistic, spontaneous snapshot from your honeymoon. Have it enlarged (8 x 10 is perfect) and framed.

Why it's worth bottling up as many Passion stage memories as possible: This phase is packed with relationship-enhancing behaviors that happen naturally right now. Later, you may have to remember to treat your partner this well. Reminders from this period of your love can reignite romance, passion, and closeness. They can also inspire you to perform more of these relationship-building acts, Dr. Love says, such as affectionate touching, flirting, laughing, playing, supporting and appreciating each other, feeling positive about your future together, and giving each other the benefit of the doubt.

Mission 2

Forge a Sense of "We"

After Greg and Priscilla Hunt said "I do" in 1976, Greg worked hard to master the grammar of an unfamiliar new language: marriage. "I remember consciously shifting the way I talked, going from *I* and *me* to *us* and *we*," says Hunt, now senior pastor at the First Baptist Church in Shreveport, Louisiana. "I was constantly rephrasing as I moved from thinking in individualistic terms to thinking of us as a couple."

Getting to "we" seems like a given for newlyweds: You've planned the wedding together, tied the knot in front of friends and family, earned the marriage license that proves the two of you are an official legal entity. Yet experts say it's important to make a concerted effort to heighten and reinforce this new sense of oneness—and then to guard and protect it. "It's so important that couples form their own new, separate union together," says Claudia Arp, who with her husband, David, founded Marriage Alive International and co-authored marriage books including, *10 Great Dates to Energize Your Marriage*. "But we see a lot of husbands and wives who never, ever reprioritize their relationship after marriage. They're still entwined with their family of origin, putting their parents and siblings first. Or they've been on their own for years and don't realize that their friends or job or other interests no longer take precedence. You need to be able to say 'My spouse comes first.' Yes, you love and respect your parents. And you still get together with your friends. But this is your anchor relationship. If you establish this now, it will be easier to hold on to when life becomes more complicated later in your marriage."

The mental shift from *me* to *we* can be startling: You can't go home to your old apartment (or your childhood bedroom) anymore if you're bored or angry or need quiet time. You can't arrange a girls' night out or a poker afternoon without factoring in your partner. You're a team—and responsible to someone else in a new and profound way.

When University of Minnesota researcher David Olson, Ph.D., and his daughter Amy Olson-Sigg surveyed over 10,000 married couples, they found that togetherness was a top priority for 97 percent of happy couples but for only 28 percent of unhappy pairs. Enjoying free time together was important to 97 percent of the happy group but only 43 percent of unhappy husbands and wives. Nearly twice as many happy couples as unhappy twosomes made most decisions in their marriages jointly. And perhaps most telling of all: 81 percent of happy couples said their partners' friends and family rarely interfered with the relationship, compared to just 38 percent of unhappy couples.

Establishing a healthy boundary around your union isn't always easy: When University of California, Los Angeles, researchers interviewed 172 newlywed couples, problems with in-laws and other relatives ranked with communication, money management, and moodiness as top challenges.

"You really are forming a new system when you get married, and it needs care and feeding," says Dr. Love. "In our culture, we don't do 'we' very well. We're better at autonomy: I can take care of myself, I can give to you. But being a real unit means taking another step: making the relationship itself a priority. Other cultures do this much better—the Japanese have a concept called *amae*, which loosely translated means the delicious experience of interdependence. It's a goal worth striving for."

The first step for newlyweds? Revel in your exclusivity. You want to be together, just the two of you, so give yourselves permission to cocoon. Then try these couple-building tips.

Create couples rituals. Do something regularly that bonds you, such as 10 minutes to chat before bed, always having morning coffee together, or saving Saturday for date night.

Institute a daily check-in. Marriage experts recommend couples do something that big business has employed for decades to keep workers happy, productive, and in the loop: hold regular team meetings. Luckily, yours will be more fun than listening to Bob from accounting go over the last month's sales numbers. One version of the daily check-in helps couples keep communication flowing freely with an agenda.

- Start by appreciating something about each other.
- Offer up some new information from your day.
- Ask your spouse about something that has bothered or puzzled you (or something about yourself).
- Make a nonjudgmental, complaint-free request ("Please fold the towels when you do the laundry. I couldn't find any this morning after my shower.")
- And end with a hope that could be small ("I hope we can go see that new movie Friday night") or lavish ("I'd love to retire at age 50 and sail the Mediterranean with you.")

Ask: Is it good for our relationship? When you bump up against any important decision in your marriage, don't just talk about whether it's good for you and for your spouse. Make it a point to talk about and think about whether it's good for your marriage. "You'll know the answer almost intuitively if you stop and ponder it," Dr. Love notes. This may come down to how much time something will take away from your time together, whether it will make things stressful between you, or if it involves people who in

FOUR PERFECT DATES
for the Passion stage

Get out your calendar and write these dates in with pen—you don't want to miss these eye-opening, passionate, relationship-stretching experiences!

The over-the-top romantic night(s) out. Fantasize about the most romantic evening you can imagine, then think of ways to make it happen on your timetable and budget. Making love by a stream in the moonlight? A candlelit picnic in the park? A dressed-up night at the opera, then a midnight supper at an artsy café? Plan at least two super-romantic nights out: one that matches your wildest dream, one that matches your spouse's.

The $10-or-less cheap date. Think of ways to have a great time without spending more than $10. The goal: Stretch your creativity and keep the focus on ways the two of you can make your own fun—not the thrill (and anxiety) of spending a bundle.

The sensual date. A soak in a hot tub or hot spring, an hour-long massage date (massage each other or find a team of masseurs who will knead you both), an afternoon at a spa. Wear your most luxurious fabrics—silks, velvets, that baby-soft fleece top. And top off the occasion with a sensual meal that includes foods such as oysters, chocolates, or champagne.

The dream date. Find a place with a great Empire State Building–caliber view. It could be a rooftop restaurant or observation deck, a mountaintop, a spot in a local park with a scenic wide-angle view. Take along blank paper, pens, and some snacks. As you take in the long view around you, consider the long view that's your future. Now's the time to dream big—and get ready for the goal-setting in the next stages of marriage that will get you there.

some way threaten your relationship (lunch with your ex, for example). If you don't even want to ask the question, that's a red flag that whatever it is—from working late to "surprising" your spouse with an expensive new living room sofa to making individual plans on your usual date night—isn't going to be good for your marriage.

Build healthy boundaries. Marriages need what experts call a semi-permeable boundary that allows friends and family to connect with you but that doesn't interfere with your own desires and plans. This can be especially complicated when it comes to your families of origin.

The biggest challenge is often deciding how you'll handle the holidays. Will it be his family's house for Thanksgiving, yours for Christmas? Yours for Rosh Hashanah, his for the Passover Seder? Or will you start a new tradition in your own home? How often will you talk on the phone—and how much will you share about the details of your marriage? If in-laws are nearby, decide how often you'll visit—and when you'll be at home to receive family visitors. Some parents and siblings respect a new couple's needs; others may need gentle reminders. "Parents can work with or against a new couple," Claudia Arp says. "They need to be getting on with their own marriage, going from being child-focused to partner-focused. Your marriage can be a transition time for them as well. Don't cut them off—you really need that love and support. Do communicate your decisions about your needs in a kind, calm way."

Cheer each other on. "One of the most important things to me is that my wife, Rebecca, is for me and I'm for her," says Lee Potts, a retired computer programmer from St. Louis, Missouri. "It sounds simplistic, but it's really important. I've been married twice before, and I don't think we had each other's best interests at heart like this. We had our own agendas." Arp suggests that encouraging your partner is one of the most important things you can do for your relationship. "If we don't, who will? Our bosses and co-workers? Don't count on it! Our children and teenagers? Ridiculous!" she says. "Our mates need our encouragement." Three strategies she and her husband recommend in their workshops: Look for the positive in your new spouse; develop a sense of humor; and give honest, specific praise—describe what you appreciate about your spouse.

Schedule time for your marriage *first*. Don't relegate your relationship to scraps of leftover time. "In mapping out your schedule for the next several weeks, why not start with writing in date times for you and your mate?" suggest Claudia and David Arp. "Then add discretionary things like golf, shopping, and community volunteer activities."

No time? Wonder why? Do a calendar review. You're overcommitted if friends, visits with your parents and extended family, hobbies, clocking overtime hours on the job, or volunteer and community commitments have crowded out the three kinds of time you need with your beloved: casual catching-up, scheduled dates, and intimate encounters. Same goes if your evenings are TV marathons or Internet extravaganzas. "Unless you're willing to make your relationship a higher priority than other relationships and activities, you won't have a growing marriage," notes Claudia Arp.

Disconnect from the 24/7 office. Push the "off" button! Heavy use of cell phones and pagers, BlackBerry devices, and high-tech walkie-talkies—the little gizmos that keep us connected with family, friends, and the office 24/7—can mute your happiness and dial up stress in your home, University of Wisconsin-Milwaukee researchers found recently. The study tracked the technology use and moods of 1,367 women and men for two years. Those who sent and received the most calls and messages were also most likely to say that this "work spillover" left them tired and distracted at home. "Technology is really blurring the lines between home and work," says lead researcher Noelle Chesley, an assistant professor of sociology at the university. "That's not necessarily a bad thing. It may give you more flexibility. But your boss doesn't tend to call you with the good news—you don't hear that you've done a great job on the project; you do hear that suddenly there's a deadline crisis."

Setting limits could lift on-call stress: Talk with your boss or your company's human resources department if work calls are burning you out. Check e-mail once in the evening. If a call's not urgent, muster the courage to say, "I'll look into it first thing in the morning." And simply turn off your cell phone at a certain time in the evening (same goes for the laptop). Ahhh … quiet.

Create a code word for love. Remember the elementary school joke about "olive juice"—say this silly phrase, and your mouth automatically makes the same movements as when you say "I love you." Find a secret way to express your love that only the two of you understand. It comes in handy if your spouse calls when the boss is standing beside your desk, and creates that "just us" feeling anytime you use it.

MARRIAGE MAGIC
Praise, and Praise Some More

Track the number of positive and negative things you say to your spouse for the next 24 hours. It takes a minimum of 5 positive remarks to offset damage done by a single negative comment. A ratio of 7, 10, 15, or even 20 supportive remarks for each downer is even better!

Over the next few weeks, set aside time to discuss these topics and come to an agreeable plan.

1. Your families of origin. How will the two of you handle:

   a. Holidays. Visit one side of the family, both sides, invite them to your place, rotate each year, or spend some (or all) of the time alone?

   b. Visits. How often will the two of you visit? How often would you like to be visited by your families? How often will one of you go home alone to see parents and other relatives?

   c. Phone calls. How often do you talk on the phone with your mother, father, siblings, or other close family members? Will frequent calls disrupt your couple time or blend with your plans? Do you need to change this in any way?

   d. Intrusions. How will you handle family members who ask for too many personal details about your life together, offer too much advice, or try to take over aspects of your home (such as buying unwanted home furnishings), your finances (by offering too many opinions about how the two of you handle your money), or your future (such as your plans to have children, move to a new place, buy a home, or change careers)?

2. Individual and mutual friends. How will you:

   a. Maintain friendships with people just one of you knows or enjoys?

   b. Build a network of mutual friends, especially other married couples?

   c. Balance individual friendships with your need to socialize as a couple?

3. Your marriage. Do you:

   a. Have hobbies, interests, or recreational activities that you both enjoy? Will you pursue these together?

   b. Have interests that just one of you likes? If yes, how much personal time is reasonable for each of you to devote to them?

   c. Have interests you would like to pursue together? If yes, how do you get started?

exercise

The Love List

One way to build team spirit in a new marriage—and pave the way for appreciating differences rather than feeling irritated or even betrayed by them later on—is to take an inventory of your strengths. Often, couples complement each other. Maybe you're good at organizing new projects but don't have the stamina to stick with it till the end, while your mate's better at the follow-through. Perhaps one of you is great with finances and all things mathematical, the other a whiz at planning social occasions and dates.

Spend 5 to 10 minutes sharing what you think your strengths are and what you think your partner's are; then it's your partner's turn. As you fill in the spaces below, remember that any positive quality you admire counts as a strength—from a beguiling laugh to warm feet in bed, from loyalty to courage to making a mean pot of chili. Then look for ways your strengths complement each other.

Her Strengths   **His Strengths**

_____   _____

_____   _____

_____   _____

_____   _____

_____   _____

_____   _____

_____   _____

_____   _____

_____   _____

_____   _____

Mission 3

Learn Your Love Languages

Every February 14, Bea and Jim Strickland of San Jose, California, display a pair of 20-year-old Valentine cards. They serve as reminders of an important love lesson: Romance is in the eye—and heart—of the beholder. "Twenty years ago, I gave Bea this beautiful Valentine's Day card. It was black, with a picture of a red Corvette on the front," recalls Jim. "Inside was a really simple message, just 'I love you' or something like that. I thought it was really great! But Bea was really disappointed, and I couldn't understand why."

Meanwhile, Bea gave Jim a frilly card decorated with lace and hearts and flowers. Jim wasn't thrilled. The pair talked and came to a surprising realization: "I was giving her the card *I* liked, and she was giving me the card *she* liked," Jim says, laughing. "I realized that you don't give someone the gift you want, you give the gift *they* want. Every year, I now make an effort to find the really right words—hopefully the right lace and flowers. She likes warm, fuzzy messages inside. And she gives me back that same old Corvette card!"

This was more than a lesson in the art of choosing the perfect greeting card. Showing love in the way your partner needs to experience it deeply connects you both. The right "I love you" speaks directly to the heart—and fills your partner's need for love in just the right way. Using the *wrong* love language would be like using Icelandic to communicate with someone from Tokyo: The message might be heartfelt, but it would be incomprehensible. And like filling an electric car with diesel fuel or topping off a freshwater fish tank with seawater, using the wrong language won't get the results you want: a happy partner who feels well loved by you. Not knowing your partner's love language could mean years of frustration, misunderstanding, and feeling rejected and *un*loved despite your best efforts.

Some lovers know this instinctively—and offer love poems or trinkets, a foot rub or a kiss, a kind word or a home-cooked meal, depending on what really rings their partner's chimes. One marriage therapist who has thought deeply about the power of speaking the right love language is Gary Chapman, director of Marriage and Family Life Consultants, Inc., and author of *The Five Love Languages*. He maintains that when you get the message right, it fills your partner's inner "love tank."

Chapman's work as a marriage counselor led him to identify five different love languages that can fill deep emotional needs inside us.

1. Words of affirmation: compliments, appreciation, encouragement, kind words.

2. Quality time: togetherness, shared activities and interests, good conversation about feelings, thoughts, and ideas.

3. Receiving gifts: tangible symbols of love, large and small.

4. Acts of service: taking care of the house, the car, the laundry, the meals, the yard, the finances, the computer.

5. Physical touch: affection, cuddling, making love.

The trick? As the Stricklands learned with their valentines, you and your spouse probably speak different love languages—and tend to give love in the language you understand best even if it's not the one your partner can best receive. Genetics and childhood experiences shape your own instinctive language. Learning your spouse's native language requires careful observation and a little detective work. The rewards? A happier spouse—and new confidence in your own abilities to please, support, and nurture your mate. "I had to learn to say 'I love you' in the way my wife, Janell, could really hear it," says Hollie Atkinson of Georgetown, Texas. "I like to take care of her by fixing things around the house and by making sure her car is always tuned up and the tank is full of gasoline—she just has to turn the key and go. She likes that, and feels loved by that, but I realized that it wasn't making her feel deeply loved. What Janell really needed was for me to sit down with her, lock eyes, and say, 'Tell me about your day. How are you feeling about it?' Now *that's* mega-communication. *That's* when her eyes really light up."

Why start now, so early in your marriage? "The newlywed stage is an 'imprinting' time—when two partners' minds and psyches are open to learning new habits in a way that they'll never be again," Dr. Love says. "This is the time to learn how best to relate to each other. To find out what each of you really needs. The patterns you establish now will last for the rest of your marriage."

Here's how to discover, and learn to speak, your partner's love language.

Expect to feel a little awkward at first. Your own preferred love language is a deep groove, shaped early on by nature and nurture, then reinforced through decades of experience. Speaking your partner's language is going to feel a bit like the first day in junior high school French class. Don't worry about perfection—just give it your all. "At one point in our relationship, Bea asked me if I liked being touched," Jim Strickland recalls. "I said, 'Well, it's okay. It really doesn't matter.' But we tried to be more physically affectionate. It felt different to me. I had to accommodate it. But it's worked out really well. Now a very nice moment is to take a 10-minute break from whatever we're doing and lie down on the bed and just hold each other."

Discover your mate's unique "dialect"—and find your own. A Texas twang, the flat lilt of a lifelong New Englander, and the soft cadences of a central Florida native—all speak English, yet the language sounds different coming from each speaker. Love languages have their fine distinctions too, Chapman notes. Perhaps you crave quality time, specifically time spent in heartfelt conversation with lots of sharing and careful listening. Perhaps you need affection, and feel best-loved when you're kissed often. Pay attention to the little nuances that really make your partner's eyes shine—and that fill your own heart.

Strike a balance—keep using your own language too. "Hollie likes it when I do things for him," Janell Atkinson notes. "That's a joy for me. But I think I do some things for Hollie that he doesn't necessarily need. I enjoy picking out cards and sending them. Sometimes I do things for him that I enjoy very much, even if it's not a big deal for him. And he loves being the handyman around the house. If anything gets out of kilter, it gets fixed, sometimes better than before it was broken. He does that out of love for me, even though it's not my top love language."

MARRIAGE MAGIC
Do You Speak Love?

For the next five days, experiment with various "love languages" to see which one your partner responds to most strongly. Try words of love, little gifts, time together, physical affection, and doing special things for your spouse.

exercise

The Language of Our Love

How does each of you prefer to be shown affection? Use this very simple approach to find out.

1 Start by writing down eight acts of love that would really make you feel great.

_____   _____

_____   _____

_____   _____

_____   _____

2 Next, write down eight acts of love you believe would make your spouse feel great.

_____   _____

_____   _____

_____   _____

_____   _____

3 Next to each of these, write down a one-word "love language" category the act falls into:

Words	*Gifts*	*Touch*
Time	*Service*	

4 If your spouse is amenable, have him or her do the same exercise.

5 If both of you have done the exercise, hold a 30-minute summit and share results. If not, study the results on your own. First, analyze the categories. Are there surprises? Did you not realize that gifts or nonsexual touch were so important to your spouse? Then look at the specific entries. Are they romantic? Creative? Do they involve humor or drama? Use these observations as guidelines for the future as you work harder to successfully speak your spouse's unique love language.

Mission 4

Build Emotional Intimacy

In her late 40s, Susan Saunders developed a disorienting crush on a male friend. "Every time he was nearby, I felt tongue-tied. I blushed. It was a real mess," says Saunders. "I told my husband about it and how much I didn't like what was happening." His response amazed her: "My husband made an effort to get to know this man so that we'd have opportunities to all talk together. He was helping me get over it." It's a prime example of why she says, "I trust my husband more than any other person on Earth."

For Priscilla Hunt, trust in the early days of her marriage meant knowing that her husband, Greg, understood the vulnerabilities she developed as the child of alcoholic parents. "We had a lot of serious conversations about that stuff," says Priscilla, a Shreveport, Louisiana, training coordinator for the Association for Couples in Marriage Enrichment, a program that trains "marriage mentors" across the nation. "There were some places in our lives where it took years before we could really trust each other, or even had enough self-awareness to know what was going on. But we always worked on trust." Says Greg, "I had to pay attention to how Priscilla's childhood affected her. There were things that would really set her off and go way down into the visceral fears of the wounded little child."

Trust—the intangible asset that Barry McCarthy, Ph.D., a psychology professor at American University in Washington, D.C., calls "the emotional bedrock of a good marriage"—takes decades, if not a lifetime, to build and nurture. Along with respect, it forms the core of emotional intimacy—the comforting sense that your marriage is a safe place where you will be valued for who you really are and where you can safely reveal yourself. "Trust, respect, and emotional intimacy create a tough, resilient bond between two partners that can withstand a crisis without crumbling," says Dr. McCarthy, a marriage and sex therapist and author of *Getting It Right the First Time—Creating a Healthy Marriage*. "You may not feel you need this in the early months of your marriage, but that's the time to build this bond."

Why? For one thing, most people aren't aware of the things that best build—or break—trust. The biggest trust-breaker? "People think it's an extramarital affair or jealousy. Those are big," Dr. McCarthy notes. "But the biggest, most common break in a couple's trust bond is when one spouse publicly puts the other spouse down in front of friends, colleagues, or family. When that happens, you need to repair the breach with a genuine apology, by taking responsibility for breaking trust, and talking about trust in your relationship."

What information must be kept safe and secure in a trustworthy relationship? "It's different for every couple," Dr. McCarthy says. "If you come from a family that had money problems or even bankruptcy, financial issues could be a vulnerability. You may have trouble getting close if you had a former dating partner who humiliated you in public. In other families, hypocrisy about religious beliefs creates vulnerable feelings. In my own life, it's the fact that I cannot use machines. I cannot type, and even running fax machines is hard for me. So I'm very sensitive about people making fun of me about that stuff. My wife and I don't like my difficulty with machines—it's very inconvenient—but she never puts me down about it."

Knowing and accepting your spouse's stellar qualities as well as his or her idiosyncrasies, irritating habits, and truly weak points "flies in the face of romantic love," Dr. McCarthy says. But it's the strong foundation of your marriage. "Romantic love is about an ideal, perfect illusion of your spouse," he says. "Respect means seeing your spouse for who he or she truly is—warts and all—and still being loyal and loving. You don't have to agree with everything your partner believes or does. You can acknowledge problems without demeaning or losing respect."

Respect validates your partner on a deep level. To give it, listen and acknowledge feelings when your partner shares his or her daily experiences with you. Don't demean your spouse—either in your own thoughts, in conversation with him or her, or to friends and family. "Be a supporter, not a critic," Dr. McCarthy says. "Listen with empathy."

Emotional Intimacy 101

The two of you are close ... but could you be closer? Sharing feelings, concerns, hopes and dreams is the core of emotional intimacy, notes American University psychologist and marriage expert Barry McCarthy, Ph.D.

Creating trust in your marriage is a matter of daring to tell the truth—about your past, your feelings and actions in the present, and your desires and hopes for the future. But self-revelation is only half of the equation. Deep trust also requires listening to your spouse without judgment—and keeping the information to yourself. No retelling a top-secret truth to your best friend, bringing it up casually in the company of friends, or hurling it back at your spouse in anger.

To strengthen the trust between new partners, Dr. McCarthy suggests the following exercise.

- Find a quiet time, anywhere from 30 to 60 minutes, when the two of you can sit down and talk.

- Take a deep breath and share something from your past that you haven't yet revealed. It could be a time when you failed yourself or your family—flunking out of college or getting yourself into debt—or that reveals a part of you that has long been set aside—the "rock and roll" days or the years of rebellion against your parents.

- Rules for speakers: Don't talk about something to hurt your partner or simply trigger sympathy. The idea is to clear the air, get closer, and get one flawed, hidden part of yourself accepted. If the secret involves troubling behavior, assure your spouse that you're committed to not doing it again. "It's a sad chapter of your life, not the essence of you," Dr. McCarthy says.

- Rules for listeners: See yourself as a partner in healing. You don't have to fix the problem or minimize its importance to make your spouse feel better. The simple yet powerful act of listening, accepting, and telling your partner you love him or her as much as ever is profoundly healing.

Scared? The value of summoning all your courage and telling the truth is that you let your partner in on who you really are, deep down. You head off a potentially devastating, or at least disappointing, moment of truth later on if your partner should discover your secret on his or her own. You strengthen your marriage bond when you feel that your spouse knows you deeply—and when you offer respectful understanding and acceptance in return.

Mission 5

Expand Your Sexual Vocabulary

When writer Miriam Arond and her husband, psychiatrist Samuel L. Pauker, M.D., surveyed hundreds of newlywed couples across the nation, they discovered that 85 percent had made love before tying the knot, yet the frequency and quality of unmarried sex had little to do with the reality of married lovemaking. Nearly half said that after marriage, they didn't have sex as often as they'd like; 20 percent of new wives reported low sexual desire. For a fourth of the wives, sex meant painful intercourse or elusive orgasms, while 1 in 10 husbands experienced premature ejaculation, and 1 in 20 had erection problems.

Whatever happened to athletic, swinging-from-the-chandeliers, "did-the-Earth-move-for-you-too" prenuptial lovemaking? The deep, mystical, Tantric communing of two spirits? Hours of Hollywood sex complete with mood music, flickering candlelight, and satin sheets?

"The excitement of getting married gives couples a hit of dopamine— a feel-good brain chemical that increases sex drive. For a few months after marriage, things may stay hot," says Dr. Love. "And while you still love each other and feel passionate about each other, the dopamine does settle down. You're back to real life. Your normal sex-drive set point kicks back in. Your expectations about married sex take over. It's the perfect time to do the delicious work of deepening your sexual bond."

"The challenge for couples is balancing a sense of intimacy and safety and security with a sense of unpredictability and creativity and eroticism," says Dr. McCarthy. "When sexual intimacy is strong, making love plays a healthy 15 to 20 percent role in energizing your marriage. The paradox is that when sex is problematic, it plays an inordinately powerful, negative role in new marriages."

Understanding the real sexual issues that newlyweds face can help you keep sex fun and fulfilling—now and for the rest of your lives. Experts say these hidden concerns can cool the hottest love life in the early days of marriage.

Mismatched sex drives. "When your sex drive returns to its normal level in the months after you get married, couples start to notice a frustrating desire discrepancy," Dr. Love says. "It's perfectly normal. You've just got to work it out."

Testosterone, the hormone of desire, fuels sex drive in men and women. But, Dr. Love says, relatively low levels of natural testosterone mean that two-thirds of all women *don't* walk around thinking about sex all the time. "For these women—and I'm one of them—you don't feel like having sex until you're already having it," she says. "That's perfectly normal. It just means you have to approach sex a little differently. You have to make time for touching, time for sex. You can't rely on being aroused to get things started. You have to start with relaxed touching and kissing to raise your arousal level."

Clashing sex-pectations. On the last night of a romantic two-week honeymoon, Priscilla and Greg Hunt bumped up against a radical difference in expectations and desire. "We had been making love three times a day on our honeymoon," Priscilla recalls. "It was wonderful, but we were about to go back to real life. To work and school and doing the dishes and responsibilities. I had to say, it's time to talk about moderation." Says Greg, "Sexuality was a real issue. We were both learning about it in our college courses, but experiencing it firsthand was strikingly different. My testosterone levels were extremely high. We were not evenly matched for libido. We had to work hard to communicate. Sexuality is a very sensitive issue—you have all sorts of feelings and insecurities wrapped up in it."

Their solution? A fluid, flexible compromise: "There were times he wanted sex when we didn't have it and times I didn't want sex but we did. Thankfully, there were more times when we both wanted to make love. There's been a natural ebb and flow. It's something we still have to talk about," Priscilla says. "This is the reality for every couple: You're wired differently. If you have enough sexual experiences together that are positive for both of you, you'll be able to work out the differences."

This is an issue for many couples who've enjoyed a lusty sexual intimacy before marriage and/or during the honeymoon but who settle into different rhythms during day-to-day married life. The solution? Talk it out so that you don't feel rejected, frustrated, or bored.

First Base, Revisited

Don't wait for all that sexy dopamine to wear off. Using the heat, passion, and "let's jump back into bed now" sexual urgency of your first months

Scenes from the Reader's Digest *Marriage in America Survey*

When we asked respondents in the Reader's Digest marriage poll about the most cherished moments in their relationships, here's how four responded.

"A cherished moment was when we first danced together. We both love to dance and enjoy the art of dance, and we connected as soon as we danced. It was as if we had expressed our affection and attraction with body language word for word."

"Three seconds after I first saw her, I knew she was the one for me. It was like my heart left my body and wrapped around her, and she also told me the same thing. There she was, standing about 10 feet away with her hair down below her knees, a cig in one hand and a cup of coffee in the other, with a button-down pocket shirt and jeans and her black boots. We were married 21 days after we met, and we both cherish every minute of our life together, 24 years now."

"It was the first night that I met him at a bar, and after the bar closed, I always went to this all-night diner, and I asked him if he wanted to go for breakfast. Actually, I asked everyone that was at our table, so much to my surprise, he said yes. We both drove our own cars and met there. He just sat there and listened to what I had to say and was so sweet. He even picked up the bill. Then, as we were leaving to go to our cars, it was raining, and we just couldn't say good-bye. It took about 10 minutes standing in the rain, but it was great, and then he asked me if he could call on me. I was thrilled!"

"The day I told him I was a victim of incest, physical and emotional abuse, the week before we married (I wanted to give him the opportunity to back out if he so desired). He just opened his arms to me and said, "Forever and always." I had his wedding ring engraved with those words, and we have signed every note, card, or written correspondence with those same words ever since."

together to explore and expand your repertoire of touch. "The first two years of marriage are critical for building a sexual style that includes shared pleasure and deeper intimacy. Aim for that. Otherwise, sex problems can become the focus of your relationship," Dr. McCarthy notes.

The sexual prescription? First, go back to first, second, and third base—touching for physical pleasure, not necessarily orgasm or intercourse. And get past old-fashioned man/woman sex roles that stand in the way of an emotionally close and erotic sex life. "Men are often socialized to value performance more than intimacy or pleasuring," Dr. McCarthy says. "Women are taught to value relating and to see eroticism as the realm of wild, crazy women—not wives.

"Not all pleasurable touching can or should lead to intercourse," he notes. "When a couple becomes comfortable touching inside and outside the bedroom, they're building a closer, more solid sensual and sexual bond that will make them feel happier, closer, and even sexier now—and help protect against sexual problems in the future."

Couples should experience the full range of the joy of touch, says Dr. McCarthy, who compares types of touch to the gears in a car with manual transmission.

Gear 1: Clothes-on, affectionate touch such as kissing, holding hands, hugs.

Gear 2: Sensual, nongenital touch, clothed or undressed, such as cuddling on the couch, back rubs, whole body massage, touching before sleep or when waking up.

Gear 3: Playful touch involving any area of the body, such as taking a bath or shower together; seductive or silly touch when dancing at your house; or little, suggestive touches while watching TV, listening to music, cooking dinner, or cleaning up.

Gear 4: Erotic touch, using your hands, mouth, or rubbing to create high arousal and orgasm for one or both of you.

Gear 5: Pleasurable and erotic touch that leads to intercourse.

In good marriages, spouses regularly do at least four of these. But many couples are all-or-nothing: It's intercourse or almost no touching at all. The problem is that when a kiss on the neck or a foot rub always leads to lovemaking, couples may avoid physical contact because it means an obligation to have sex. A smarter approach: Touch when you *don't* want to go all the way. It will prime you for sex later and make you feel loved and appreciated and comforted right now. These tips can also help you explore and enjoy touch and sexual intimacy more.

Emphasize pleasure, not just the big O. "Exploration and touch without the expectation of intercourse or orgasm helps couples get to know each other's bodies and needs—you learn what kinds of touch are pleasurable as a giver and as a recipient," Dr. McCarthy says. Pleasure and affection keep you close even when you don't want sex.

Nurture emotional intimacy too. Feeling understood, supported, and valued will make you both feel closer and therefore more receptive to physical closeness.

Plan ahead. Sex-drive discrepancy? Busy schedule? Put s-e-x on the calendar. It's a fact of life: Most of us married someone who wants sex more often or less often than we do. If you wait to feel turned on before you have sex, you'll miss out on lots of great moments together. Let touching turn you on rather than expecting to feel aroused first. This may seem totally unnecessary during the hot-and-heavy exchanges of the Passion stage, but experts say it's the best way to ensure you'll still be enjoying great sex when your life is complicated by kids, a house, stress, reduced sex drive, and times of conflict.

Low sex drive? Consider saying yes anyway. "People freak out when I say this," Dr. Love confides. "But if you make time for love and romance and try to say yes when your partner wants to make love—provided you're not dealing with a compulsive or sex-addicted spouse—you will have a better sex life. Let your partner's drive get you both into bed, or wherever you'll make love, so that you can be touched and turned on. Why get into the habit of *not* doing it?"

Think of life as foreplay. "I found out early on that relational issues that seem to have nothing to do with the act of sex itself make a huge difference to my wife and to her interest in intimacy," Greg Hunt says. "I learned to pay attention to things I wasn't naturally good at. If I'm ignoring her and also not paying attention to things like chores around the house, she's not going to feel cozy and intimate at bedtime."

Don't use sex as a bargaining chip. Angry? Say something—don't grunt or "hmph" and roll over. Withholding lovemaking when you're upset turns this deep, vulnerable connection into a nuclear weapon for power struggles. Adding layers of resentment to your feelings about physical intimacy is a surefire way to make sure neither of you will be in the mood.

Are Your Passion Styles Compatible?

This quiz for couples, developed by marriage and sex therapist Pat Love, Ed.D., author of *Hot Monogamy*, will help the two of you see where you're similar—and not—along nine important components of a passionate love life, from physical desire and sexual technique to body image and communication ease. You can take it together or separately; use different-colored pens or markers.

Rank the following statements from 0 (never applies to me) to 6 (always applies to me). Answer the questions in terms of the past few months.

_____ 1. I experience sexual desire on a daily basis.

_____ 2. I experience a growing sexual interest or tension when I haven't had sex for a number of days.

_____ 3. I experience sexual desire without being physically stimulated.

_____ **Total Score (Physical Desire)**

_____ 4. I pay attention to my partner's sexual needs and desires during love-making.

_____ 5. I make an effort to learn about significant changes in my partner's sexual needs and desires.

_____ 6. I tell my partner about the lovemaking techniques I like best.

_____ **Total Score (Technique)**

_____ 7. I introduce new lovemaking techniques into our relationship.

_____ 8. I seek out information about new lovemaking techniques.

_____ 9. I am a creative or adventurous lover.

_____ **Total Score (Variety)**

_____ 10. I make an effort to feel emotionally close to my partner while making love.

_____ 11. I express feelings of love for my partner during lovemaking.

_____ 12. I am a passionate lover.

_____ **Total Score (Passion)**

▶

_____ 13. I clearly communicate my sexual needs and preferences.

_____ 14. I have a comfortable way of letting my partner know when I would like to make love.

_____ 15. I tell my partner what I enjoy about our lovemaking.

_____ **Total Score (Communicating about Sex)**

_____ 16. I am a physically desirable person.

_____ 17. I feel comfortable having my partner see me in the nude.

_____ 18. When we are making love, I am comfortable with the appearance of my body.

_____ **Total Score (Body Image)**

_____ 19. I set aside enough time in my life to make lovemaking a relaxed, sensuous experience.

_____ 20. I relax and luxuriate in our lovemaking.

_____ 21. I am a sensuous lover.

_____ **Total Score (Sensuality)**

_____ 22. I am physically affectionate throughout the day.

_____ 23. I bring an element of courtship to our lovemaking.

_____ 24. I use romantic gestures (gifts, surprises, special favors, etc.) to show my love for my partner.

_____ **Total Score (Romance)**

_____ 25. I share my feelings with my partner on an ongoing basis.

_____ 26. When I am talking, I am careful not to overwhelm my partner with too many words or too much information.

_____ 27. I maintain an open line of communication with my partner.

_____ **Total Score (Verbal Intimacy)**

What to Do Next

Compare your scores in each of the nine categories. Look for those in which you both scored high (these are your strengths) and both scored low (these are areas to work on). Then talk about areas where your scores differ widely: How can you, for example, improve communication, rev up the romance, or be more affectionate?

stage 2

realization

It's a rude awakening: After so much time cocooned in the private euphoria of Passion stage romance, you realize one day that life *isn't* all sizzle and bliss in Marriageville. Your partner ... *eek!* ... is irritating and imperfect. Your big love feels smaller. There's less *ahhh* and more *uh-oh*.

Reality settles in with a bang when your marriage enters the Realization stage. You can no longer overlook the growing heap of dirty clothes on his (or her) side of the bed. Or dismiss the unhappy discovery that your mate snores, doesn't rinse the dishes before loading the dishwasher, or expects that you'll do the grocery shopping. You wonder why your marriage isn't making you deliriously happy round the clock anymore. And you wish you were back in the paradise of the Passion stage.

"The rose-colored glasses are coming off now," notes marriage expert Patty Howell, a Leucadia, California, relationship counselor and author of *World Class Marriage—The Art and Science of Relationship Success*. "You see each other more objectively. The illusions are fading. All the hormones and brain chemicals that made early love so thrilling are wearing off. It's a fabulous time to start real relationship building—as long as you don't give in to the temptation to write off your marriage or your spouse."

As passion fades, it is time to learn each other's true selves.

Blame Mother Nature for these changes. The thrilling "love cocktail" of brain chemicals that kept you feeling happy in the Passion stage settles down within the first two years of marriage, brain researchers say. Levels of lust hormones drop. Levels of the "cuddle chemical," oxytocin, rise. This calm and cozy hormone is decidedly G-rated; it's what makes nursing mothers want to hold their babies. But it won't make the two of you rip your clothes off in the backseat of the car the way all that wild and sexy norepinephrine and phenylethylamine did. So you feel a little flat. Grumpy. Confused. Have I fallen out of love? you wonder.

Realization stage couples naturally go looking for explanations. Something's wrong, you reason. If you fix it, you can get that loving feeling back. But you look in all the wrong places. It's easy to criticize your spouse, who looks so human and so unlike Cinderella or Prince Charming now. It's easy to criticize your marriage too, as you begin to realize that it doesn't meet the happily-ever-after expectations you've been storing in your brain and heart since childhood. To make matters even more challenging, it's time for the two of you to speak up about your wants, needs, expectations, and feelings. And to figure out how to split the household chores, pay the bills, and negotiate a million nitty-gritty daily decisions that aren't very romantic but that are tied directly to your happiness as a couple.

It's a tall order, especially if you believed love alone could conquer all. "It's easy to think that you're the special couple whose love will be strong enough to solve all problems," says marriage therapist Barry McCarthy, Ph.D., a psychology professor at American Univerity in Washington, D.C. "And when love isn't enough, it's easy to make an emotional decision that you're not the perfect couple and therefore that your bond is broken."

The first mission of the Realization stage? Don't believe that your bond is broken. Understand that it's time to get down to the business of having a real-world marriage between two wonderfully human, delightfully imperfect partners who still love each other deeply.

The Shock of the Real

Couples interviewed for *The 7 Stages of Marriage* remember the shocks and surprises of the Realization stage vividly. The good news: In hindsight, they were able to laugh together about the differences that irked them early on. Their stories:

- "I grew up with two sisters—and my husband, Bill, grew up with two brothers, so we were in for a surprise when we moved in together after our wedding," says Jean Cooley of Lakeland, Florida. "What a shock to find out that this wonderful guy I'd fallen in love with had these really odd habits! Bill would leave the toilet seat up at night. I was from the Midwest, where we ate about six different vegetables. Bill liked exotic things like okra and squash—and he cooked rice the wrong way. We even disagreed about bed-making. And he was bothered by the tissues I would leave all over the house because they weren't used up yet. Bill liked to plan things out carefully, and I'm more fluid; I change my mind. We've come to see that our differences are okay, and don't mean the other person is out to get you. But it took some time!"

- "Two to three years into our marriage, the honeymoon was definitely over," says Don Howard of Blue Springs, Missouri. "There was a breaking point where we knew our communication wasn't effective. My wife, Teresa, was very assertive, and I tended to not ask for what I needed. I became resentful and frustrated and would get angry and explode or just walk away. Finally, I made a decision to become more assertive myself, and it was a real twist. We both had to adjust! It's not easy with all the other stresses in our lives—our jobs, our children, our community activities, and Teresa's graduate school work. But without good communication, a marriage is under so much strain. It's so worthwhile."

- "We made a lot of discoveries early in our marriage about our differences," says Greg Hunt of Shreveport, Louisiana. "In the early 'ga-ga phase,' we only saw how similar we were, but then came the differences, and they really grated on us. I'm a morning person, and my wife, Priscilla, isn't. I whistle before I even get out of bed in the morning. She needs time to wake up. I'm an extrovert and Priscilla's an introvert—that caused some real frustrations and conflicts. I get my energy being with people; she's energized by quiet time, a walk in the park, or staying home together watching a movie. It took us awhile to understand each other and give each other permission to be who we really are."

Realization Stage Missions

You may feel bewildered or alone in the Realization stage. You may find yourself criticizing your spouse—either internally or out loud. If you're anxious that something's gone wrong, you may pull back from your mate or cling tightly. The Realization stage can seem scary, marriage experts say, because we see our own shortcomings reflected in our spouses' actions now, just as we saw our own sterling qualities reflected in our partners in the Passion stage.

Your mission: Get in the driver's seat. It's time to make love happen instead of waiting for it to happen to you. Keep on doing the fun, marriage-building stuff we recommended in the Passion stage: Make time for sex, for romance, for checking in with each other. It's more important than ever.

When University of Oklahoma researchers studied newlyweds, they found that expressions of love and affection between a wife and husband drop by half in the first two years of marriage. British researchers who tracked married couples for 20 years found the steepest decline in marital satisfaction came about 18 months after the wedding. Perhaps that's the reason why national divorce statistics show that most marital splits occur in the first five years—and that couples married for about three years are especially vulnerable.

The rest of your Realization stage missions:

Uncover your hidden marriage expectations. We all come into marriage with a set of mostly unconscious ideas about how great things will be—expectations no human spouse can meet. "Expectations like 'Everything will be fabulous, this is my one true love, this person will make me finally happy, I'll avoid every mistake I've made in the past' put a huge burden on ourselves and our spouses and our marriages," Howell says. "We judge what's really happening very harshly when we use those standards." You'll discover how to see and understand your hidden expectations, sort the reasonable ones from the unreasonable ones, and talk about them with your spouse.

Learn to talk calmly and confidently about your needs and wants. Your spouse cannot read your mind. Many spouses report that sharing their feelings, thoughts, desires, and expectations feels scary; others just don't know how. Why it's vital: Clamming up in order to preserve the status quo will just leave you resentful and angry and keeps your spouse in the dark. Coming on too strong will put your partner on the defensive. In this chapter, you'll learn assertive speaking techniques to ensure that you'll be heard, without criticizing or blaming your spouse.

Learn to listen empathetically to your spouse. Create a safe haven where your partner can reveal his or her innermost emotions, thoughts, ideas, and expectations—without your jumping to conclusions, inadvertently criticizing your partner's vulnerable feelings, or trying to fix things when your spouse simply needs a listening ear. The combination of open, honest talk and empathetic listening fosters acceptance and deeper understanding—making the two of you feel safer and closer.

Be your real, full self—and let your spouse be himself or herself too. New research from the University of California, Los Angeles, finds that newlyweds who act as friends as well as lovers have happier marriages. Learn how to be more genuine, more empathetic, and more accepting—

friendship skills that go beyond communication techniques to bring your heart, soul, and whole being into your relationship.

Sort out the laundry...and the dishes...and the vacuuming. Housework can be an early battleground for couples. Learn how to get past traditional roles and divide the work fairly.

Become expert money managers. No subject sparks more couples conflicts than money. Research shows that newlyweds today face a new challenge: significant debt brought into marriage from school loans, car payments, credit cards, medical bills, and the wedding and honeymoon. Find out how your money personalities can work for—not against—you as you set a calm, organized course toward meeting your financial goals and achieving your dreams.

"Must-See" Love Cues

When University of Washington marriage researcher John Gottman, Ph.D., first videotaped ordinary couples having mundane conversations in an apartment "love lab," the footage was disappointingly dull. "But after a while, we finally realized that these conversations weren't as mundane as they first seemed," he says. "We were seeing how people were making bids for emotional connection with their partners and how they responded to those bids."

These tiny moments of give-and-take can make or break a marriage. Noticing your spouse's bids for love—and responding to them—is especially crucial in a Realization stage marriage, when spontaneous affection can drop by half compared to the first weeks and months of matrimony. Dr. Gottman found that husbands who eventually divorced had ignored bids from their wives 82 percent of the time; in contrast, men in secure marriages *responded* to bids 81 percent of the time. Women who eventually divorced their husbands had responded to their spouses' bids 50 percent of the time; those in stable marriages responded to 86 percent of their partners' bids.

What does a bid look like? It could be a quick kiss, a question, an affectionate touch, or a smile—anything that means "I want to feel connected to you," Dr. Gottman says. The best response? Give your partner your attention and return the bid. "A relationship is about these small moments, these bids and responses," he notes. "It is the way intimacy and trust are built."

Mission 1

Understand Your Expectations

One October morning less than three months after her marriage, Nicolle Hawthorne sat in her Jamesburg, New Jersey, kitchen holding a half-finished cup of cold coffee. The maple tree in the backyard had turned gold, the sun was shining—and she had to get ready for the long drive to her job as a newspaper reporter. *I'm married now*, she found herself thinking grumpily. *Why do I still have to work? Why can't my husband support me? I want to stay home!*

"The thought shocked me, then made me laugh," she recalls. "I loved my job and hadn't ever considered leaving it. We also needed the income. I realized that part of me wanted a very traditional marriage—and a break from the daily grind. Here I was blaming my husband for an unspoken and rather silly expectation I'd been carrying around since I was a little girl watching *The Donna Reed Show*!"

Unspoken, half-hidden expectations about married life put wives and husbands to the test in the Realization stage. These "rules" form in childhood and our teen years as we watch our parents' marriages and absorb silent imperatives about the roles of husbands and wives from society; from our cultural and religious affiliations; and from TV shows, movies, and books. Previous romances and even friendships further shape our expectations. And at a deeper level, we often believe our spouses will somehow intuit and heal our deepest psychic wounds.

These fantasies tumble out after marriage (much to the surprise of couples who've lived together for years before marrying), prompted by the promise of a safe, happily-ever-after love. But imaginary fantasies about what your spouse should or shouldn't do are dangerous, experts say. If you barely realize you're holding your partner up to an impossible standard, you may feel disappointed if he or she can't read your mind and doesn't take steps to fix childhood hurts and magically create a perfect marriage.

"When a couple is still infatuated with each other, you don't need much because you're still enjoying that chemical high," says marriage expert Pat Love, Ed.D., author of *Hot Monogamy*. "You expect very little, you feel great, and you're spending a lot of time trying to please each other. But as the relationship deepens, expectations change. And when you're not getting those needs met, suddenly your partner can do little that pleases you—everything seems annoying. Every frustration just proves that your relationship's not right, not good. You may start arguing, but not about the real issues that are bothering you."

Often that's because you don't even realize what the real issues are—or are afraid to speak up because you don't want to rock the boat. Your first step? Uncover your hidden expectations about marriage—a set of sometimes shocking, sometimes humorous, often very vulnerable beliefs. They range from who should perk the morning coffee to when you'll have children, from who makes the investments to how often you'll make love, from what your spouse should say about your new haircut to how you'll greet each other in the morning.

New expectations can arise at crucial turning points in marriage, such as when you buy a home, plant your first garden together, become parents, deal with a major illness, enter the empty-nest stage, or even in the later years of a long relationship. Building good exploration skills now will help you uncover what's really on your mind at any stage in your relationship.

Don't get us wrong. Not all expectations are unreasonable. And you shouldn't write off your expectations, either. Once you've got a handle on your personal expectations—and hopefully, your partner's done the same—compare notes with your partner. Discuss them as a way of getting to know each other more deeply, using the assertive speaking and empathetic listening skills you'll learn about later in this chapter.

Decide which expectations you can meet for each other. It's important to make an effort to please your spouse by taking actions that meet his or her needs, even if they aren't part of your personal view of the perfect marriage. And use other expectations as the starting point for personal discovery and growth: Maybe you expected your mate and your marriage to bring new excitement and adventure into your life, but things are more staid than you expected. Explore activities you can pursue on your own: A kayaking or sailing class? Jewelry making? Rock climbing?

How to begin? Do the exercise on the opposite page. Ask your partner to do it too. Then use these tips for discussing your discoveries—and for nurturing an ongoing exploration of expectations.

Accept your own expectations—and your partner's. These hopes and dreams—and even the "you shoulds"—are signs of deep needs. Your

Discover Your Hidden Expectations

Everyone comes into marriage with an invisible suitcase packed with expectations. Begin uncovering them with this list. On a separate sheet of paper, if necessary, quickly write down what you expect of yourself and your spouse in each category below. Don't censor yourself. After you've finished, read it over and ask yourself how your family of origin, your cultural heritage, your past relationships, and the TV shows, books, and movies you were exposed to affected your answers.

Your partner should consider doing the same exercise. Afterward, share what you've found—it's a great conversation starter and will get you ready for the "Your Dreams, My Dreams, Our Dreams" conversation exercise on page 114.

Common Areas of Hidden Expectations

Jobs and money	Outside interests
Sex and affection	Other friendships
Time together	Vacations
Children	Romantic times
Housing	Intellectual partnership
Housework/yard work	Excitement
Emotional needs and intimacy	Adventures
Learning from each other	Family relationships
Socializing	Coping with differences of opinion

marriage cannot meet them all, but writing them off will leave each of you feeling unaccepted, alone, resentful.

Be realistic about what you *do* ask for. Your spouse probably *can't* bring you coffee in bed each morning, prop up your self-image three times a day, or never start an argument. She probably *can* share the cooking and meal cleanup, spend more quality time with you, and learn to squeeze the toothpaste tube from the bottom a little more often. Agreeing to some realistic expectations creates a win-win situation and a buoyant feeling of success.

See what you can do yourself. Nicolle Hawthorne couldn't quit her job and laze under the maple tree with a good novel after she married, but she realized she could look for a lower-stress job that would let her enjoy her marriage. A year later, she'd changed jobs and had more time for her marriage and ultimately a family.

Grieve what you can't have. One of the toughest jobs in marriage is accepting that some items on your must-have list will never be fulfilled by your partner—simply because he or she isn't perfect, and also because he or she isn't obligated to be your personal fairy godmother. "When you really want something that is just not going to happen, you can either sulk, get angry, or do what every couple needs to do over the long term: grieve the losses that come with commitment," say University of Denver marriage experts Howard J. Markman, Ph.D., and Scott M. Stanley, Ph.D., and psychologist Susan L. Blumberg, Ph.D., in their book *Fighting for Your Marriage*. Accepting your marriage and your mate despite imperfections is a long-term practice necessary for a happy, healthy relationship.

Use disappointment as a signal of unconscious expectations. When you feel disappointed in your marriage or your spouse, pause and think about what you expected. This builds awareness of the expectations guiding your attitudes and actions. Is your expectation reasonable? Is it better met on your own?

Don't compare your spouse to other people's spouses—or your marriage to other marriages. Focus on the love, laughter, drama, and struggles in your own world. There's no perfect spouse, no perfect marriage. Resist the temptation to tell yourself "If only he were like my friend's husband" or "If only our marriage were as [fill in the blank] as theirs." Each marriage is unique, with its own highs and lows.

Mission 2

Open, Honest Talking

Couples in the Realization stage often feel they'd like to speak up—about the checking account, their plans for Friday night, a feeling they'd like to share, or a problem they'd like to solve. Yet at the same time, they don't want to rock the boat or, worse yet, start a fight. Why do anything that might discourage that elusive honeymoon feeling, which seems to come and go of its own accord these days? And why say anything at all? After all, shouldn't your one true love just *know* what's important to you?

You're bumping into all sorts of big issues, and beneath the big questions is an even bigger one: How will you communicate with each other in a way that's clear and honest, empathetic and supportive? We're here to help. A major Realization stage mission is learning the basics of good dialogue: assertive speaking and empathetic listening. (In the Rebellion stage, we'll show you how to build on these skills to solve problems and turn conflicts into productive conversations.) These are skills everyone needs and that most of us don't learn in our families of origin, from TV sitcom laugh tracks, or from romantic novels. In fact, a national survey of over 20,000 couples found that 82 percent wished their partners were more willing to share feelings, 75 percent had difficulty asking for what they wanted, and 72 percent revealed that their partners don't understand how they feel.

Learning these essential communication tools can make all the difference. When the researchers compared happy and unhappy pairs, they found that while 90 percent of blissful couples were satisfied with how they and their spouses talked together, just 15 percent of unhappy twosomes were. Just 18 percent of dissatisfied couples said their partners were good listeners, compared to 83 percent of happy couples.

Having the courage, confidence, and conviction to say what's on your mind and in your heart is vitally important for great communication. These tips can help.

Be brave—say it out loud. Don't wait for your partner to suddenly grasp unspoken thoughts, feelings, and needs hidden in your body language or in veiled hints. Example: Instead of sighing, tapping your foot, or mentioning the late hour in an offhand way while you wish desperately that your partner would announce he's ready to leave a late party, try "I'm feeling very tired. I'd like to go home in the next 10 minutes."

Focus on what you want, not on what you *don't* want. Saying what you don't want may seem more polite—after all, it doesn't put your partner on the spot the way asking for exactly what you want does. But it leaves him or her guessing about what would make you happy. Example: Say "I'm in the mood for scrambled eggs and toast" instead of "I really don't want cereal today."

Use more "I" statements and fewer "you" statements. Reveal your own feelings instead of criticizing, blaming, mind-reading, or pretending you know what your partner's feeling, says marriage expert Susan Heitler, Ph.D., author of *The Power of Two*. Don't fall into the trap of saying, "I feel that you … " It's not expressing your own feeling, Dr. Heitler says. "It's really a statement about the other person and usually sounds as though the speaker

Read My Hips: Nonverbal Communication Says It All

"I'm *not* mad!" you insist—in a gruff voice, with your hands on your hips, your eyes averted from your partner's gaze, and your brows knitted tightly together.

Which part of that mixed message do you think your spouse will believe: three unconvincing spoken words or that body language screaming, "Oh, yes, I *am* mad!"?

"Research shows that words form only 7 percent of our communication with anyone, including our spouse," says marriage expert Claudia Arp. "Tone of voice accounts for 38 percent, and body language is responsible for 55 percent of the message your spouse receives from you. That's why it's important to be honest— if something's bothering you, your body will give it away."

Five ways nonverbal communication can bring you closer:

Make eye contact. Whether you're telling your spouse you love him, asking him to check the cat's water bowl, or asking about his day, relaxed eye contact says you're truly interested and respectful.

If you're happy and you know it, smile. You'll convey the warmth and affection you're feeling.

To get closer, be a mirror. Feel disconnected during a conversation? Assume the same posture and facial expression as your partner.

Sit shoulder-to-shoulder instead of face-to-face. For a tough discussion, sitting side-by-side builds physical closeness and a team feeling and makes confrontational glares and gestures more difficult to perform—or notice.

Tune in to your own body messages—and take a time-out if you need one. If you—or your partner—notice that your heart's racing, you're sweating, and you feel your body moving into fight-or-flight mode (adrenaline starts pumping, blood pressure rises, and you may even feel a ringing in your ears), it's time to stop the discussion. Right now—even if you're tempted to make just one more important point. Research shows that physically strong emotions only lead to major fights. Stop and agree to reconvene to discuss the matter in 24 hours.

is about to deliver a criticism." Instead, say how you really feel when your partner takes a particular action. Example: Instead of "You're careless when I loan you my car," try "I feel angry. You borrowed my car and didn't refill the gas tank."

Also sidestep "You make me feel…" Instead, stick with "I feel…" This keeps the focus on your feelings and doesn't make the other person feel responsible for them. Example: Instead of "You make me feel sad when you don't call me," try "I feel sad when I don't hear from you during the day."

Be direct. When making an "I" statement to express a feeling, be succinct. Stick with a one-word description of your emotion, not a two-paragraph, nuanced report with bells, whistles, adjectives, and historical asides. Example: Instead of "I feel soooo happy and terribly excited and just wonderfully exhilarated and really very, very relieved about our plans to finally go camping this weekend!" try "I'm excited that we're going camping on Friday."

Connect the dots without blame. If you want to describe your reaction to something your spouse has said or done (or neglected to say or do), sidestep criticism and blame. Instead, employ a time-honored, matter-of-fact formula: "When you _____, I feel _____." You can also say "I feel _____ when you _____." Dr. Heitler notes, "A 'when you' phrase focuses mainly on the speaker—it doesn't intrude on the partner's turf." It shares vulnerable feelings and invites your partner to help you.

Don't presume to know your spouse's feelings. Telling your partner that you already know how he or she feels about something feels like an invasion. It also cuts off meaningful conversation, especially if the two of you speak for each other instead of for yourselves. Instead of mind-reading, ask your spouse to tell you what he or she is thinking or feeling. Then share how you feel. This invites an open discussion. Example: Instead of "I know you hate visiting my family for the holidays and that makes me feel really resentful!" Try "How do you feel about visiting my parents for Christmas?"

Angry? Cancel the floor show and use calm words instead. Resist, resist, resist (did we say resist?) the temptation to stomp, shout, slam doors, and throw plates when you see red. Same with verbal pyrotechnics. State that you're feeling angry or upset, then say you'd like to stop the conversation for now and set a time to resume later on. Use anger as a stop sign, Dr. Heitler suggests.

Avoid saying "You always..." and "You never..." at all costs. For example, "You always leave the doors unlocked at night" or "You never call me when you'll be late from work." Such definitive, categorical statements are rarely true. Even more, they breed hostility, since sweeping statements like these imply that the times when your spouse *did* do things properly didn't get noticed or acknowledged.

Mission 3
Learn Empathetic Listening

Good conversation is like a violin duet. Usually, one violinist takes the lead while the other plays supportive, harmonizing musical phrases. Think of listening as the time when you play a supportive role, following the lead of your partner and paying exquisite attention to all the details in his or her tone, phrasing, and emotions. Here's how to make beautiful music—as a listener.

Listen first for feelings... Before you jump in with a solution or pepper your spouse with questions, make sure you understand the feelings behind the words—and convey your empathetic understanding to your mate. You may find that there's nothing to fix, because your spouse simply needs to feel understood and heard. Don't worry that you're caving in to over-the-top high drama or irrational emotions or even to unwarranted personal criticism. Just *listen* for the emotions in your partner's words, tone of voice, and body language.

...and let your partner know you've heard the emotions. Eye contact along with nodding your head, a pat on the arm, or a softly murmured "Mm-mm" could be enough response to satisfy your spouse's innate need to be heard in a casual, low-key conversation. But when emotions run high or deep, be sure to rephrase what your partner's just said in a way that shows you're not just listening, you truly understand. Put the full importance of your mate's feelings into your own words. Don't just replay your partner's last statement or simply mumble, "I understand."

Go easy on yourself. No need to be defensive—your spouse's emotions aren't a criticism of you or even a request to change anything (that could come later in your discussion). If you begin feeling blamed, criticized, responsible, or even helpless when your partner describes his or her vulnerable feelings,

Every day this week, sit down together for 15 minutes and rehearse your new talking and listening skills. The first speaker chooses a topic that recently made him or her feel good, then talks about it. The listener responds. Then change roles. Do the same with a topic that triggered negative feelings in each of you.

take a deep breath and tell yourself that listening is safe and simple, Dr. Heitler suggests. Your job is simply to validate, not fix or judge.

Listen for information. Ask yourself what's true, useful, and makes sense, Dr. Heitler suggests. If you need more data, ask. You've acknowledged your partner's emotions—now it's time to respect his or her thoughts and plans. Pretend you're a TV news reporter and get the facts so that you really understand what your partner is saying.

Mission 4

Be Friends

Beyond communication skills, you and your spouse need to consistently exhibit three "friendship" attitudes to keep your marriage growing in the Realization stage: acceptance, empathy, and genuineness. "If you pump these qualities into your relationship, you'll grow a closer friendship," says Howell. "You'll have a better chance of communicating who you really are and of understanding who your partner really is."

Research confirms the power of these attitudes to help marriages thrive. "There is a pattern that emerges in the happiest and the least happy marriages," says Sybil Carrère, a University of Washington researcher who led a study that followed 95 newlywed couples for seven to nine years. "The happiest couples are speaking almost in one voice because they are so tuned in to each other's wants and desires. These people know the value of their partners in their life and know they are not out to get them. It is really beautiful music. With the unhappiest couples, there is no symmetry. There is no respect for each other. Individuals are really nasty with each

(continued on page 114)

exercise

Brush Up Your Listening Skills

For this listening exercise, each of you starts by choosing an expectation from the Discover Your Hidden Expectations exercise (page 105) or a recent experience that you reacted to with strong emotions. The speaker describes his or her feelings about the event. The listener responds attentively and empathetically. Use the listening tools listed here to help you stay on track. Experiment with the way different alternatives make the speaker—and the listener—feel.

Instead of saying "but":

I know you're tired tonight, but I wonder how you'd feel about going out to dinner.

Try saying "and":

I know you're tired, and I wonder how you'd feel about eating out.

Here's why: Using "but" negates whatever comes before it and sounds like a rejection. Replacing it with "and" indicates you're adding another thought instead of subtracting one.

Instead of immediately rejecting your partner's ideas or feelings:

It's not true that we don't spend time alone. We had lunch just last week!

Try just listening:

I hear you. It seems like we never have much time alone together. What did you have in mind?

Here's why: Telling your spouse she's wrong or shouldn't have the thought or feeling she's just expressed stops communication cold. If you're really confused, ask a question—it's supportive and gives you more information.

Instead of changing the subject quickly:

You're angry that you didn't get the new job at work? Hey, have you seen today's newspaper? I wanted to check the coupons.

Try paying closer attention—be polite if you need to veer off-topic briefly:

You must be so frustrated—you were far better qualified than anyone else in your department, and you've worked so hard! That's really upsetting! I want to talk with you more about this as soon as I find today's newspaper—Bob's stopping by to pick up a coupon in five minutes.

Here's why: Making sure your spouse knows he or she comes first and that you value his or her feelings, even when you're in the middle of something else, builds trust, respect, and security.

Instead of silence or a disinterested "Mmm-mm":
(No eye contact or response to a request or revelation from your spouse)

Try connecting:
(Stop what you're doing, look your partner in the eye, listen, and then respond.)
    Here's why: You can relax and unwind later. Letting your spouse know he or she's more important than HGTV is a small but meaningful sign of respect.

Instead of putting your mate down or getting defensive:
You never told me before that you don't like spending Friday nights with my work buddies. You're just upset because you don't know how to have fun!

Try just listening—and remind yourself that you don't have to react:
You feel bored and uncomfortable going out every Friday with my co-workers. It must have been tough for you.
    Here's why: Remember that your spouse's feelings belong to him or her— you don't have to solve them or take responsibility for them. Listening without having a negative or defensive reaction keeps feelings and information flowing.

Instead of ignoring or minimizing feelings:
You're mad that our school board candidate didn't win a seat? At least we have free and fair elections here. Why, in the Middle East . . .

Try paying closer attention to your spouse's feelings and restating them:
You're upset that our candidate lost. I would be too. You worked so hard on the campaign, and the issues really mattered in our town.
    Here's why: Ignoring or minimizing doesn't take your mate's feelings seriously. It also forces your spouse to repeat them, stuff them down, or get angry. Paying attention to your mate's big emotions won't cause a scene. In fact, experts say, it helps your spouse get past them.

Instead of responding first to the facts:
It would take months and months to find a church we both like around here. We'd have to visit for a few weeks, talk with the pastor, see if we like the times of the services, and meet some of the other members. It's a big job.

Try responding first to the feelings:
You've been feeling like something's missing because we don't go to worship services together every week. I know it's something your family did every week, and you've realized it's important to you too.
    Here's why: Validating feelings makes your partner feel supported. It doesn't mean you won't get to the facts or seek a solution. In fact, starting with feelings will help the two of you work better as a team instead of as adversaries.

other, and they struggle to find positive things to say about each other or the relationship."

Couples with a strong friendship bond didn't always agree, but they found ways to avoid destructive arguments because they genuinely liked each other and appreciated their differences. Those with weak friendship bonds felt less accepting and empathetic to their partners, leading to more disagreement. "A lot of couples neglect the friendship in marriage, and it erodes over time because of such things as career demands and having children," Carrère says. When you neglect friendship, the habit of seeing your partner in a positive light begins to fade away.

Other studies support that point. For example, a University of California, Los Angeles, study of 60 newlyweds found that partners who gave each other more emotional support early on—and who asked for more support—were more likely to feel happy in their relationships two years later. Researchers say this "friendship effect" may matter just as much as a couple's communication skills. But it is often neglected or overlooked by therapists and researchers alike.

CONVERSATION STARTER
Your Dreams, My Dreams, Our Dreams

If you haven't already, take time in the next week to talk together about your dreams and goals for your marriage—and for each of you as individuals. "If you don't have a plan, you're less likely to get where you'd like one day to be," says marriage expert Patty Howell. "If you want a life filled with satisfaction, it makes sense to have goals."

Ask each other: Where would you like to be living in 3 years, 5 years, 10 years, 25 years? If you plan to have children, when would you like to start your family? How will you raise your children? What other dreams do you have for your marriage, such as travel, vacations, a home, a jointly owned business, or joint hobbies and pursuits? Include personal goals too. "Personal goals are part of your own growth, part of your being the person you want to be and having the life that really would be the most satisfying for you," Howell notes. "It's wonderfully thrilling to have that supported by your partner. It's a way to bring about a special closeness." You'll learn more about balancing personal and joint goals in the Rebellion stage chapter.

"You have to take the mechanistic quality out of communication skills," Carrère says. "They're vital, but you can't be simplistic. We're not married to hollow automatons. Our spouses are sensitive human beings made of blood and skin and souls and hearts and minds. It's important to each of us to be genuine and to have our special humanity be understood and accepted by our partner."

This is an important point. In the pages you've just read, we provided lots of good communication advice. But none of it will do much good if you apply it without heartfelt conviction, as if you were reading a script or following directions. Howell suggests building the friendship within your marriage by responding to your mate with these essential attitudes.

Empathy. "Reflect back to your partner what they're really saying, on an emotional level," she says. "And do it in a way that uses everything you know about your partner to show that you really get it, that you know how an issue or a feeling really affects them right now. You can't do this by rote." Draw on what you know about your partner's vulnerabilities, hopes, and dreams and what's happened to them that day to show that you really *get* the significance of their message. "Your partner's level of upset might be a 4 today, an 8 next week," she says. "Your response should be appropriate to the situation; show your partner you're really working to understand them."

Acceptance. "This is where you show your partner that you don't need them to change," she says. "People thrive when their feelings are known and accepted, when they don't feel that their own responses to their lives are wrong or shameful or need to be hidden. In everyday terms, that means if your mate is completely upset with the boss, she's completely upset. It's not the time to say 'Gee, Honey, maybe the boss had a point there. You shouldn't be so upset.' It's the time to show that you understand." Accepting your mate's feelings won't encourage wallowing in self-pity or histrionics, Howell says. "It allows a feeling to pass through, rather than being bottled up," she notes. "It makes your spouse feel cared for, understood, and safe."

Genuineness. Use assertive speaking to really be yourself, Howell suggests. "It's about vulnerability instead of operating from a protected position. And what emerges isn't always pretty or convenient or instantly likeable, but it's you. And you—like me—are a complex blend! To the extent that your spouse can see this and understand it, it's deeply satisfying for you—your partner cannot accept things about you that you won't reveal."

Mission 5

Split Household Chores Fairly

When Rebecca Wiederkehr and Lee Potts married in 1986, Rebecca assumed housekeeping responsibilities despite her husband's enlightened protests. "Lee had been married previously and had lived on his own," says Rebecca, a psychotherapist in St. Louis, Missouri. "He argued with me about doing all the housework and insisted he could do the laundry and the cooking. But I turned it into a very traditional arrangement despite my beliefs that couples should share the work!" Lee earned more money; Rebecca was working at home, beginning a career as a psychotherapist. "I felt guilty," she says. "I thought I should do the wash, clean the house, and be responsible for meals, and he should take care of the cars and things outside. It was only later that I realized what I had done and didn't like it. Eventually I thought it was pretty funny. We worked things out."

The division of household chores, couples told us time after time, is one of the everyday dramas of married life in which traditional roles and modern ideals about equality clash—sometimes in surprising ways, as Rebecca and Lee discovered. Sometimes a dusty living room isn't *just* a dusty living room. For younger couples interviewed for this book, dividing the chores meant that wives as well as husbands had to give up old ideals about women as perfect housekeepers. "I work full-time and believe housework should be done by everyone who lives in the house," one woman said. "But I needed to stop feeling responsible for all the wash and vacuuming and sweeping and shopping and cooking. I had to lower my standards and let my husband do things his own way, even if it meant eating some meals later than I would like, or dinner dishes not finished till morning, or little drifts of dog hair on the steps. I needed to change, not just my husband."

Sorting out household duties matters, researchers say. When University of Virginia sociologists W. Bradford Wilcox, Ph.D., and Steven L. Nock, Ph.D., analyzed a national survey of 5,000 married couples, they found that women who reported that the division of housework was fair were happier in their marriages than women who thought that their husbands didn't do their fair share. Wives also said they spent more quality time with their husbands when they thought housework was divided fairly—either because they were simply happier or because they had more free time.

What's fair? The definition is as individual as each couple but is rarely a 50-50 split. While two-thirds of married women reported that they were happy with the division of housework, most did the majority of chores around the home. "Conventional and academic wisdom now suggests that the 'best' marriages are unions of equals," Dr. Nock says. "Our work suggests that the reality is more complicated."

Men are doing more around the house. A review of four national studies by University of Maryland researchers found that women's average housework contribution dropped by half between 1965 and 1995—from 30 hours a week to 17.5. Men's doubled, from 4.9 hours to 10 hours per week. And perhaps our perceptions haven't caught up with the new reality of who's pushing the broom across the kitchen floor: An eye-opening University of Chicago study of 265 married couples suggests husbands do *more* than their wives realize—and that while women underestimate men's contributions, men overestimate their roles.

While wives estimated that their spouses did 33 percent of the work, men thought they did 42 percent. To arrive at the truth, spouses agreed to wear wristwatches that beeped every two hours and to write down their activities every time the alarm sounded. The result? Men shouldered 39 percent of the chore burden. And while women thought they accomplished 67 percent of the work, they actually did 61 percent.

The bottom line for Realization-stage couples? Talk about your expectations, your likes and dislikes, your standards, and your time constraints when divvying up house and garden responsibilities. University of Minnesota researchers who surveyed 21,501 couples found that 49 percent were concerned about unfair division of labor at home; 44 percent weren't comfortable splitting the work according to traditional roles and preferred choosing chores based on interests. Key to success: In the happiest couples, both wives *and* husbands saw their arrangement as egalitarian. In the least happy, both saw their roles as traditional.

Here's how to achieve a happy division of labor.

Divide responsibilities, not just jobs—and give up control if it isn't your chore. If the laundry or the vacuuming or the shopping is your task, it's up to you to do it on a regular basis—without being reminded. Too often, experts note, wives hold on to housework-scheduling power, and husbands see themselves as the helpers, not the executives in charge of the tasks. Try the honor system. List all household jobs (or use our chart on page 120) and post your compendium prominently. Suggest that both of you do what you can. After a week or so, reconvene and see whether the work split seems equitable—and review the least-favorite items you've both avoided. Nobody wants to haul the icky cans and bottles to the town recycling center or vacuum the stairs? Alternate or make a deal. Keep a copy of your chore chart in the computer so you can print and display a fresh copy each week—that way, you get the thrill of checking off a completed item every time.

Do a job share. Turning a one-person chore into a two-person task—this can help motivate the partner who doesn't normally have responsibility for washing sheets or clipping straggly grass around flowerbeds. Share the work, and you'll also have time to chat while your hands are busy.

Play to your strengths. In one survey, about one in four men said they vacuum better than their wives; one in five are more proficient at dishwashing (and presumably at loading the dishwasher). Four times more women than men thought they were whizzes with the laundry. Splitting the work by areas of expertise is a good start—provided you both feel the outcome is equitable.

Post a chore chart. One couple interviewed for this book revealed that their refrigerator is now their household task headquarters, complete with a weekly rundown of who does what. They split the laundry (she does two loads early in the week; he puts the wash in late in the week), alternate dinner-wrangling and cleanup, and order out two days a week. Bathroom and kitchen floor mopping, vacuuming, dusting, and trash are also evenly divided. "It's working like a charm," the happy wife reported. "The house is always in order, and I'm not feeling frustrated and overworked!"

Don't nag, fume silently, or stage a sex strike. Women have tried countless strategies to get their spouses to assume a larger share of household duties. Tactics that are too manipulative to work include giving up and doing it all yourself (you'll just resent it); not doing anything until your spouse notices and asks about it (too manipulative); and withholding sex or home cooking or your good graces until he starts folding the towels (do you really want intimacy tied to the state of the bath mats?). A better option: Use the smart communication strategies in this chapter to make chores a subject for you to resolve together. Then try the chore exercise on page 120.

OLD THINK/NEW THINK
for the Realization stage

These myths could detour—or even derail—your efforts to build a deeper love during the Realization stage. Instead, bet on smart new thinking about the best ways to deal with disappointment, defensiveness, and that dull "honeymoon's over" feeling.

Old think: Marriage will make me happy.
New think: Marriage will help me grow—and happiness may come from our love, from my partner, or from what I do for myself. In one 15-year-long study, researchers found that your happiness level before marriage was the best predictor of happiness after marriage. Marriage won't automatically nudge your happiness set point higher, but building a deep, loving relationship can.

Old think: My spouse should change in the ways I want.
New think: Some of my expectations about marriage will be met, some will be exceeded beyond my wildest dreams, and some will never be met. That's life.
   Your partner's not perfect and isn't required to make over his or her life to your expectations. A better plan: Talk out what you expect and make a plan to please each other in reasonable ways to the best of your ability.

Old think: Luck and romance are the keys to long-term happiness.
New think: Friendship and dedication keep couples together. That means being a good daily companion, always being loyal, and actively working to improve.

Old think: If my partner's not Mr. Right or Ms. Right, I made a terrible mistake.
New think: Expecting Mr. or Ms. Right is unrealistic. Partners *always* stop looking perfect when the "honeymoon high" fades and the realities of everyday life don't match our fantasies about married life. It's a normal low point every marriage must go through—and an opportunity to build a foundation for real love, experts say.

Old think: If you love me, you'll do exactly what I want.
New think: Yes, you have the right to feel fulfilled and to expect your spouse to meet realistic needs. But your spouse can't do everything for you. Look to your whole life—interests, spiritual faith, friendships, work, and your inner life—for the rest.

Splitting Household Chores

The way your family of origin handled household chores can have a profound influence on how the two of you split up the work—*and* on how you feel about it. Use this worksheet to illuminate the household roles you learned as a child—write in which parent (or sibling) did each job in each of your families. Then note whether you love, hate, or don't really care whether you do the task. Next, talk about how you'll divvy up the work in your own household: You, your spouse, shared, or even hired out.

Happiness tip: Talk about the definition of "doing" a particular chore—must dishes be done by a certain time after dinner? What counts as breakfast—pancakes, sausage, and a latte, or a Pop-Tart and instant coffee?

	Husband's Family	Wife's Family	You Feel	Who Does It?
Daily Tasks				
Prepare breakfast				
Cook dinner				
Set table				
Do dishes				
Do laundry				
Handle pet care				
Sort mail				
Water plants				
Make the bed				
Do errands				
Buy groceries				
Buy household supplies				
Return DVDs, videos, library books				
Pick up dry cleaning				
Mail parcels				
Indoor Chores				
Manage garbage/ recyclables				
Clean the kitchen				
Clean the refrigerator				

	Husband's Family	Wife's Family	You Feel	Who Does It?
Clean the bathroom				
Vacuum				
Dust				
Change the sheets				
Replace lightbulbs				
Do small repairs				
Outdoor Chores				
Maintain cars				
Mow the lawn				
Rake leaves				
Plan/plant garden				
Do garden maintenance				
Do home maintenance				
Organize garage				
Family Paperwork				
Pay bills				
Deposit checks				
Manage investments				
Manage phone, cable, Internet accounts				
Manage insurance policies				
Make doctor/dentist appointments				
Manage charities/ volunteering				
Social				
Make weekend plans				
Arrange vacations				
Make restaurant reservations				
Send birthday and other cards				
Plan holidays				
Manage religious commitments				

Mission 6

Become a Money Team

Do money and marriage mix? As central to survival as eating or breathing, money is a supercharged issue for married couples simply because it has such complex and hidden significance. More than just dollars and cents, money may mean power or love, happiness or control, the prospect of thrilling risks or tucked-under-the-mattress security for life.

Money challenges your mathematical skills (can you really tell if your investments are performing up to par?); your organizational acumen (ever try to track all your debit-card purchases?); your optimism (wondering how to put together the down payment on a house, afford a mortgage, and still have money left over for furniture?); your good sense (hmm ... for an extra $100 per month you could lease that high-status luxury car instead of buying a hatchback); and your willpower (who can resist paging through the high-end catalogs that arrive in the mailbox almost daily?).

We love it, hate it, overspend it, hoard it, and hide it—anything but talk about it. The taboo against discussing money, experts say, is often stronger than the taboo against talking about sex. Small wonder, then, that so many researchers conclude that finances are one of the most common causes of conflict during early marriage.

A University of Minnesota study of several hundred newlywed couples found that 63 percent had serious problems related to their finances. Avoid it, and money becomes the elephant in the room—a big problem everybody tiptoes around. When one California State University researcher reviewed marriage and money surveys, he found that money ranked as the fourth- or fifth-leading cause of divorce, behind big deal-breakers such as incompatibility, lack of emotional support, abuse, and sexual problems.

"Money isn't an easy conversation," admits William Bailey, Ph.D., associate professor of human development and family sciences at the University of Arkansas and co-author of *You Paid How Much for That?! How to Win at Money without Losing at Love.* "We're brought up not to talk about money—and many couples never even discuss where the funds come from for dates and vacations and gifts before the wedding—or even how they'll pay for the wedding itself. We arrive in marriage without much financial literacy. And we come to the subject with two different sets of ingrained ideas, attitudes, and systems for handling money—one from each family of origin. Blending all of that into one system that meets your hopes and dreams and that gets the bills paid is very volatile."

And there's a new problem emerging: the double-debt couple. Utah State University researchers uncovered an unsettling new fact of life when they interviewed 1,010 couples married for just two to nine months: 70 percent of the husbands and wives had brought debt into the marriage. Half of those owed more than $5,000 when they said "I do," and some owed as much as $50,000.

The debt included unavoidable bills for medical expenses and "investment in the future" debt such as college loans. But most was not so benign. The researchers also found that 55 percent of husbands and wives had automobile debt, and 48 percent had credit card debt. The more they owed, the lower a couple's marital satisfaction. Calling it the "anti-dowry," lead researcher Linda Skrogland, Ph.D., an assistant professor of family, consumer, and human development at Utah State, noted that "debt brought into marriage was seen by the husbands and wives as the most problematic of the many difficulties they encountered during their first months of marriage." Unfortunately, she also notes, "debt never rests, sleeps, gets sick, or goes on vacation, and as long as you have debt, you will be in financial bondage."

Sorting out your finances, therefore, is one of the key missions of the Realization stage. Take a deep breath and read on. We've consulted top money and marriage experts for ways to make this easy and effective.

Your Money Personality

When Bea and Jim Strickland of San Jose, California, married 50 years ago, their money styles clashed almost immediately. "Jim believes in money as security—it buys food, a home, and provides for the future," Bea notes. "I've seen money as enjoyment, I use it to have fun. We clashed for many years, and had lots of silences and lectures, before we figured out that we see money very, very differently and need to accommodate each other. We've both benefited from the combination of our different styles. We complement each other."

Adds Jim, "I dress better and drive a better car than I might have chosen otherwise, because Bea encourages that. And I have to say, I enjoy it. On the other hand, we've saved carefully. We've used my skills and money style to be sure we've provided for ourselves. Not that it's been easy. We still have conflicts at times."

What's your money style? You most likely fall into one of these four distinct types.

- **Spender.** About 39 percent of Americans get distracted from the big financial picture by spur-of-the-moment temptations, from big cars to big vacations to another pair of shoes or high-tech gizmo. Some like the idea of saving but don't quite get around to doing it in a disciplined way. Others have simply given up on the idea of budgeting, saving, and planning for short- and long-term dreams and goals.

- **Chief Financial Officer.** About 23 percent of Americans enjoy saving their dough and making smart financial plans. They're willing to take calculated risks to make their nest eggs grow. Their goal: A secure future, low debt, and money in the bank for retirement, the kids' education, and other big things.

- **Stasher.** About 19 percent of us are so extremely careful with our money that we're hesitant to take risks. Stashers are often frugal shoppers, and savers more than investors. As a result, they may miss out on smart, low-risk strategies that could grow their money.

- **Fighter.** About 18 percent of Americans are dealing with financial setbacks so severe that they loom over most buying decisions. Setbacks include job losses, natural disasters, illnesses, and past spending excesses that keep debt high and savings low.

You may have a good guess about what category you fall into, but to help, take our money personality quiz on page 126.

The Four-Day Financial Tune-Up

Here's the plan, short and sweet: For each of the next four days, you and your spouse should have a financial conversation. Each one will require honesty, openness, and a little bit of homework. You may find it is the most productive set of conversations you've ever had.

Day 1: The Big Picture

If you've followed the advice in this book so far, both of you have written out your dreams and goals (page 114) and determined your money personality (page 126). With those results in hand, it's time to talk about the big picture: What you both want, who you each are, how you talk together about money. Keep an open mind. Listen without judgment—your spouse is the co-captain of your private, two-member investment company, bank and trust, and financial enterprise. You want respect, so show respect.

Include these conversation starters on your agenda.

Travel backward in time. Talk together about how your parents handled finances. Did your dad pay the bills in a tense, Saturday-morning session at the dining room table? Did your mom scrimp, while your dad overspent? Did they save—and proudly tell you about the power of money—or barely make it from paycheck to paycheck, regardless of income level? Most of all, how did their money management affect the way *you* handle financial matters?

Be honest about your own spending styles. Before your marriage, did you run up credit card debt or keep your cards under control? Did you save—or default on a college loan? Are you signed up for all the financial perks your employer offers, or have you figured that stuff could wait? Do

(continued on page 128)

quiz

What's Your Money Personality?

Everybody's got a money style. Take this quiz, then ask your spouse to do the same (use a different-colored pen or marker to keep your answers separate) to reveal how you compare. Choose the answer that best describes how you would act.

1. Uncle Sam's just sent you a $1,000 tax refund. You promptly:
   a. invest the money in a stock or mutual fund
   b. celebrate by buying some nice clothes, furniture, or a new computer gadget
   c. figure out which bills need to get paid first and quickly write some checks
   d. put it into a checking or savings account

2. Your monthly bills:
   a. are paid in full within a few days, often via computer, and the paperwork filed carefully
   b. sit unopened in a mountain of mail that you work through all at once every four weeks or so
   c. are quick to get opened and studied, but payments are put off until the last possible moment
   d. are nicely sorted and paid off in full by check a week before they are due

3. You've planned for the future by:
   a. building a portfolio of retirement accounts and investments, including real estate
   b. ignoring it. You've got other things to do with your money right now.
   c. doing all you can now to get out of debt
   d. putting a set amount into a safe nest-egg account each month

4. When it comes to other people and your money, you:
   a. like trading investment and saving strategies with friends, though you don't discuss personal financial information
   b. would lend a friend a significant amount of money if he or she needed it, even if you weren't sure he or she could repay you
   c. avoid talking about it because it's so stressful
   d. are very cautious. Finances are a very private thing!

5. Your attitude toward debt is:
   a. It's a tool: Used wisely for an education, auto, or home purchase, it pays off in the long run.
   b. It's a game: Use credit cards smartly, and you can maintain your lifestyle just fine.
   c. It's a burden: Debt can suck the joy out of your life.
   d. It's an evil: If you are at all capable, you should pay as you go.

6 Your charitable-giving profile is:

a. You have a charity plan that includes a targeted amount of donation cash and a list of preferred charities.

b. You give spontaneously and very, very generously, even if you're a little short of cash as a result.

c. You are happy to donate your time and energy, but giving cash is a hardship that you must weigh very carefully.

d. You wish you could give more to needy groups, but you have to think of yourself first.

7 When you shop for something major like a kitchen appliance, you:

a. first do lots of online research regarding brands, quality, and cost

b. go to lots of stores and enjoy browsing and exploring options

c. focus primarily on price: What's the best I can get for as little as possible?

d. drift quickly to the tried-and-true brands, rarely picking a new model or style

Your Score

If you mostly answered "a," you're a Chief Financial Officer: responsible, well informed, and prudent when it comes to money. You bring a talent for organizing, perseverance, and willpower to your relationship—skills that Spenders and Fighters need. If you've married another CFO, the two of you will need to work together to share financial control.

If you mostly answered "b," you're a Spender: ready to have fun with your dough. You understand that money can bring joy, happiness, good times, and help others—traits that Chief Financial Officers and Stashers need more of. Those more disciplined types can help you plan, save, and invest. If you've married another Spender or a Fighter, we suggest meeting early with a financial advisor for advice on planning, saving, and investing to meet your goals and dreams.

If you mostly answered "c," you're a Fighter: trying to bounce back from debt or another financial setback. Your determination adds strength and willpower to your money-management team. If you've married another Fighter or a Spender, see a financial planner early on so you can achieve your dreams and goals.

If you mostly answered "d," you're a Stasher: trying to create personal financial security by saving or even hoarding your hard-earned dollars. Your strength is your talent for saving consistently and not living beyond your means. But you may be overly cautious and conservative about money and investing. A Chief Financial Officer can help you with investment advice for a better return on your savings. If you've married a Spender, you might want to consider allocating a monthly allowance for each of you. If you've married a Fighter, your financial willpower could help pay down his or her debt faster, and accumulate savings sooner.

you have lots of cash stashed in a bank account, yet still wear the running shoes you got on sale four years ago? You and your spouse should be honest about your money personalities from the start. Even if they're wildly different, you can develop a spending plan that will help you make the most of your money with a minimum of fuss.

Dream big—about the long-term future. Down the road, do you want to have children, buy a home, take a trip around the world, retire at age 50, fully fund your child's college education, or start your own business? Talk about the major milestones you'd like to reach in your life together. You don't even have to agree about them yet. Just get them on the table.

And dream smaller—about the short-term stuff. Do you need a new car, living room furniture, a dishwasher, a new computer system, or do you hope to take a nice vacation in the next year or two? Talk about it. Again, there's no need to agree or disagree right now. It's more important to simply communicate all your expectations and desires.

That's enough for one day!

Day 2: The Kitchen-Table Talk

Now's the time to sit at the kitchen or dining room table with your bills, bank statements, investment statements, checkbooks, and pay stubs. You'll also need some sharp pencils with erasers, blank paper, and a calculator. (Or, if you're already a whiz with electronic money-management tools, gather around a computer and use a program such as Quicken or Microsoft Money that does the calculations for you.)

Today's goal: Do an honest assessment of the four key financial numbers: your income, expenses, savings, and debt. This takes time, patience, and stamina—so do this exercise only when you'll have at least two hours of uninterrupted time together and when both of you are well rested, relaxed, and well fed.

The ground rules: Be respectful, fair, nonjudgmental, and honest. Trade off on who uses the calculator, who riffles through the paperwork— we know it sounds touchy-feely, but you want to build a strong financial team with equally involved partners.

Step 1. On the top of a blank page, write "Monthly Cash Flow." Draw a line down the middle. On the left, write down all the sources of income you and your spouse receive each month, after taxes. If you have large investments, include monthly dividend or interest earnings. Total up the amounts so you know how much cash you have coming in each month. On the right side of the paper, list every single bill or expense you pay each month, from rent to electricity to cable TV to groceries. Look at your checkbook to see if you are overlooking anything, like payments that you make quarterly or semi-annually (car insurance? home insurance? real estate taxes?). Tally it up to see how much cash is flowing out of your house each month.

Are you spending more than you are bringing in? You're bound to see expenses that cry out to be curbed or eliminated—but it's not time to exercise the line-item veto. Your conviction that the premium cable is an obvious waste of money might, just might, clash with your spouse's need to relax with HBO on Sunday night or see the latest boxing match from Las Vegas. Do you really want to go there right now? We say, no!

Step 2. Look at your ATM withdrawals and talk about all the incidental cash spending in your daily life: The coffee and doughnut on your way to work, the lunches out, the splurges that don't quite fit any category. This could include entertainment costs like movies, a day at the ballpark, or even a trip to the garden center for a few new perennials. Some financial planners call this unconscious spending "the latte factor" and say it's one of the best places to tighten spending and free more cash to reduce debt and build savings. For now, just notice it. You're already thinking about ways to liberate that cash anyway.

Step 3. Use this worksheet to tally your current debt—including debt each of you brought into the marriage and debt you've incurred jointly, such as your wedding, honeymoon, and new furniture. We suggest considering all debt to belong to both of you, so that you can work on a joint plan to pay it down.

Step 4. Set specific goals that you can describe with dollar signs. Financial experts say that it's smart to pay down debt and build up savings at the same time, if at all possible. Work hard to pay more than the minimum on your credit cards to avoid the trap of high interest rates. (At the same time, it's fine to stick with pre-set monthly payments for most car, home, and school loans with lower, fixed rates.) Free up more cash for these good goals by trimming monthly expenses and negotiating cuts in the "slush" category (pack lunch a few days a week; invest in a cute new go-cup for your homemade coffee; spend Sundays biking together, not shopping).

Day 3: Create a Two-Person Money System

Some couples run their households from separate checking accounts for years, even decades. Others immediately close their personal accounts when they wed and then work from a single, joint account. Still others take a hybrid approach: Joint account for household expenses, personal accounts for personal spending and "mad money."

Not sure whether you need freedom and autonomy or an "all for one, one for all" system? Don't rush it. It's okay to merge your finances slowly as you gain trust and experience with each other. We recommend going slowly if your money styles are very different.

Tasks for today:

Appoint a chief financial officer. Most couples leave the execution of their financial decisions to one partner—a smart move that streamlines bill paying and investment monitoring. But it can be a lonely job. You still need regular "business" meetings to talk finances and set the course for the future. Some experts suggest doing this monthly; others say quarterly meetings are sufficient. (And both partners should be 100 percent familiar with the ins and outs of your money-management system, in case the CFO can't do the bills this month for whatever reason.)

Create a system you both can understand and use. Designate a place in your home office or bedroom for all your financial paper, including checkbooks, receipts, bills, and statements. Set up a filing system that works for you. Computer-savvy couples may decide to do this electronically as well, using financial-management software that downloads statements from your credit cards and banks, lets you pay bills online, and tracks your expenses with eye-catching, revealing charts and graphs. What's best? Whatever works for you.

Record everything. Write a simple "user's manual" for your management system—including account numbers for banks, loans, and credit cards; PIN codes for online accounts; and all the stuff you may keep in your head: direct-deposit dates for your paychecks, the month the car insurance is due, and so on.

Day 4: Protect Your Future

What's left to talk about? Your long-term financial goals. There are several questions to answer in this discussion, some of which you began to answer in your Day 1 discussion but which now need to be acted on.

- What are your home-buying ambitions?
- Will there be college educations to pay for in your future?
- How much life insurance do you need or want?
- What are your travel ambitions? (A two-week vacation to an exotic locale could set you back $8,000 these days.)
- What is the realistic long-term earnings potential of your chosen career path?
- Do you have unique, specific retirement ambitions yet?
- And finally, what do you do to make your plans a reality?

For this final conversation, we strongly recommend you involve a professional financial planner. Why? First, the stakes are truly large with these topics. Wrong moves today can have huge financial repercussions 10 or 20 years from now. Also, investing is very complicated, and it takes full-time study to stay up with the products and trends. Third, by bringing in an objective third party, it's easier to address the tough issues without personal issues coming to the forefront.

If you are loath to consult with an expert, consider taking a financial seminar together. As part of the process, order your credit scores to learn how the financial world sees the two of you. Finally, talk about your levels of commitment to smart money management going forward. Should you subscribe to a monthly magazine? Read a personal finance book together? After all, you two are wise enough to know that good money management doesn't just happen in four days! What you've just done is an outstanding start, but it is only that—the beginning of happy, smart finances together for the rest of your lives.

stage 3
rebellion

You're completely convinced: The only way to make your marriage work is *your* way. Your spouse's point of view? Obviously wrong, wrong, wrong. You're the good spouse. He or she is the bad spouse. The sooner your mate admits it and does things the right way, the better.

If you find yourself judging your marriage and your partner in stark absolutes of right and wrong, you're caught in the power struggles of the Rebellion stage. In this often dramatic phase of marriage, your relationship feels like an over-the-top opera full of fierce emotions, arguments, vulnerabilities, secrets, and threats of divorce. The two of you may fight for days or stop speaking to each other altogether, then reunite in a blaze of passion, only to argue an hour later over the tiniest thing. You want to run away—or control your spouse.

The Rebellion phase is one of the most demanding and risky in marriage. Pulling away from your partner is tempting now. This is the era of the "four- to seven-year itch," when spouses are susceptible to sexual, emotional, and Internet affairs, as well as to the new infidelities of secret spending, overwork, and lavishing too much time and attention on personal interests.

The Rebellion phase is one of the most demanding and risky in marriage.

Divorce rates peak in this stage. When Wright State University psychologists tracked 522 couples for 10 years, they found a huge dip in happiness 4 years into marriage, with another decline in years 7 to 8. Mismanaging this Rebellion phase dissatisfaction is a disaster: Centers for Disease Control and Prevention researchers who reviewed marriage statistics for 10,847 American women found that 20 percent of first marriages ended within 5 years of the wedding, rising to 33 percent within 10 years.

But hang in there. Many couples cruise smoothly through this stage of marriage without drama or frustration. The hallmark of these marriages? A healthy dose of respect, empathy, and friendship for each other and the ability of each spouse to pursue his or her interests and passions with the other spouse's consent and support. These two attributes speak directly to the main issue underlying Rebellion stage strife: a belief that you have become trapped by your marriage—by a spouse who doesn't do as he or she should, and worse, demands unfair things of you, and by a legal commitment that shuts you off from both growth and fun.

Neither should be true. Working through the challenges of the Rebellion stage not only sets these issues straight but also offers another big reward: real love, achieved by learning to accept your partner for who he or she really is. This prize is worth the struggle.

Me, Me, Me!

Behind the scenes, three forces converge to push husbands and wives from the polite explorations of the Realization stage into Rebellion.

- The first is familiar: The Rebellion stage often begins about four years into a marriage, when the glorious love hormones of the Passion stage have all but dried up. (You can conjure them up again—we'll show you how in the Cooperation stage chapter.) The result: a grumpy funk that can feel as bad as drug withdrawal. You may mistakenly blame your spouse if you lose that loving feeling, though, and accuse him or her of holding back.

- Second, a Pandora's box of needs and insecurities—often dating from childhood—bursts open now. "Power struggles in this stage push your emotional buttons," says psychologist Susan Campbell, Ph.D., a relationship expert and author of *The Couple's Journey* and *Getting Real: 10 Truth Skills You Need to Live an Authentic Life*. An example: Say your mother used to chide you about staying up too late, and suddenly your spouse is doing the same, unaware of the battles the subject caused 25 years earlier. And so you lash out, because what you want—and always wanted—was respect for your ability to choose your own bedtime. Of course, your spouse is clueless about the cause of your hostility.

  "Somehow, once a couple feels committed and secure, dark material from childhood surfaces. And without thinking about it, we expect our partners to take care of these shadowy bad feelings," Dr. Campbell notes. In a way, these needs are silly—selfish and immature. Your partner cannot possibly make amends for childhood wrongs or solve age-old insecurities. But, she says, paying attention to this old stuff is pure gold. "If you can comfort yourself, you won't need your partner to be the one who rescues you from them anymore."

- Third, and perhaps most important of all, is that partners, a few years into marriage, naturally feel a desire to pay more attention to their own interests and to re-experience some independence. Marriage experts say this is healthy. After all, you've probably spent the majority of your pre-married life focused on "I"; these past few years of "we" living were the exception, and after a while, you naturally yearn for the best aspects of your previous life.

The trick is balancing this self-interest with the needs of your relationship and your spouse. Making yourself happy will make your marriage happier. And pursuing personal goals with your spouse's blessing and support can strengthen and revitalize your bond, since it helps you grow as a person. This may include hobbies, spirituality, volunteer work, physical activity, going back to school, or even contemplating a career change. But beware: Setting your own course to spite your partner or to check out emotionally is an act of revenge or abandonment. Don't go there!

In fact, anthropologists see a link between hormone shifts and independence. In many tribal cultures, couples stay together only until their child is weaned and ready to hang out with other kids at about four years old. This coincides with a dramatic downshift in levels of phenylethylamine (PEA)—a brain chemical that gives you a near-addictive rush early in romance. In one view, a couple no longer has to stay together, because their child has achieved some independence. The bond that kept a man and woman together—to ensure that their child would thrive—is no longer necessary. It's time to move on or make another baby.

It's no coincidence that modern couples feel a pull toward independence and even divorce at the time that PEA levels naturally decline. As a result, you disagree with each other more often, feel less affectionate, partake in fewer joint activities, and blame, criticize, and even show contempt for each other. That's why marriage experts consider the Rebellion stage one of the most high-stakes make-or-break periods in your marriage.

Staying together now takes a combination of understanding and hard work—plus a generous sprinkling of fun time-outs together. Your Rebellion stage missions:

Turn power struggles into acceptance. You'll begin the lifelong work of appreciating your own and each other's true self, warts and all.

Convert conflicts into productive problem-solving. You'll learn techniques that convert standoffs and shout-downs into win-win situations that actually bring the two of you closer.

Pursue healthy personal goals—without threatening your marriage or feeling guilty.

Renew your spirituality—and share it with your spouse. Even if you do not worship together, sharing your beliefs can strengthen your marriage. In the Reader's Digest *Marriage in America Survey*, shared spirituality was a strong theme. We'll show you how to achieve it.

Recover from any infidelities. Of the one in five (or more) American husbands and wives who will have sexual affairs, many stray during the "infidelity danger zone" in the first five years of marriage, according to a national study of 3,432 married adults. Another 20 percent have emotional affairs—more or less chaste relationships that are nevertheless equally devastating for the betrayed spouse. You'll learn how to affair-proof your marriage and recover from the devastation of infidelity.

Master the art of forgiveness—not only for your partner but also for yourself. Only through forgiveness can you put the battles of the Rebellion stage behind you for good.

MARRIAGE MAGIC
Focus on You

Rebellion stage couples are quick to blame each other for difficulties. Eventually, you figure out that you really can't change your partner. But there's someone in your marriage you *can* change—right now. That's you. Treat your spouse the way you'd like to be treated, give him or her the benefit of the doubt more often, find big and little things to appreciate every day, and spend more time with your spouse without being asked. The result? A guaranteed uptick in marital happiness for you both.

Anger, Rage, and Stubborn Moments

Couples interviewed for *The 7 Stages of Marriage* admitted they've lashed out at each other during the Rebellion stage—and ultimately, worked out their differences. If you relate to the comments below, read on and do the missions!

"Ironically, we were reading a book about marriage while we drove to a conference, and as we got out of the car at a Burger King along the highway, my husband, Ed, said something that pissed me off," says Sylvia Robertson of Waleska, Georgia. "I was so mad that I back-handed him over the head with my purse. Four construction workers were leaving the restaurant at the same moment—you should have seen the shock on their faces—here were these two college professors acting like this! Ed ended up with a rivet mark from my purse on top of the bald spot on his head. We were both so mad and so sad, we drove two more exits, then pulled off and apologized. Sometimes your anger just overwhelms you."

"Jim and I are very different when it comes to making plans," says Bea Strickland of San Jose, California. "I always say yes, then think about whether I can really do it. Jim always says no—and then thinks about whether he can fit it in. We had a lot of struggles over this. One day when we were living in our first apartment, someone asked us to go on a picnic. I immediately agreed without consulting him, and he told me to never do that again. He thought he was the one in charge and should have the last word. Today, we talk things out. We're both more considerate. We don't see each other as being wrong or right anymore. We just try to see the value in each other's way of operating."

"We were quite shocked when we became unhappy with each other after our marriage," says Peggy Kinney of Durham, North Carolina. "We had read that we would fall out of love before we would truly develop love for each other, but there's no way to fully understand that ahead of time. We had a long power struggle over money because my husband, Andy, earned more than I did, and I felt he could therefore make more financial decisions and that I had to live within my own means. We gradually realized that wasn't fair, that it put us in a 'one-up, one-down' relationship. Resolving that wasn't always comfortable for both of us. But we're so much closer now."

Mission 1

Turn Power Struggles into Acceptance

Everybody's going to have differences of opinion—especially with the person they intend to share the rest of their life with. Should you fill up the car with regular or premium gas? Buy low-fat or full-fat milk at the supermarket? Set the thermostat at an economical 60° or a toasty 72°? It seems simple enough. But sometimes a seemingly innocent issue packs an emotional undertow that leaves the two of you sparring like boxers in an eight-round title fight.

These power struggles are never *really* about gas or heat or dairy products. As one of the biggest make-or-break points in the Rebellion stage, power struggles are the canvas on which you paint your insecurities and dreams about marriage. Trouble is, a couple locked in a power struggle usually aren't aware of the half-hidden vulnerabilities and expectations they're really fighting over. You simply know that something your partner has (or hasn't) done is causing you pain or tension or anxiety—and triggers thoughts of disappointment and irritation over the imperfect state of your relationship. You blame your partner, try to control him or her, and demand that he or she change. Now.

You're probably in a power struggle if an issue triggers quick anger or swift, negative judgment against your spouse. Power struggles typically go nowhere because each spouse believes he or she is right and the other, therefore, must be wrong. One spouse attacks; the other defends—then you switch roles. Nothing changes because no one's really listening. The way out? Here are a few.

Get to the *real* cause. When a fight starts, immediately pause and ask yourself if there is an underlying issue. Sometimes a dirty floor is just a floor that didn't get cleaned; sometimes a dirty floor, to your subconscious mind, links you to your childhood or is a statement about your spouse's perceived disregard for you, your time, and your shared possessions. "Look hard to find out what's really pushing your buttons," suggests Dr. Campbell. You may find an old hurt from childhood or an expectation that marriage or your spouse would rescue you from unhappiness or fulfill a long-held dream.

exercise

Whose Space Is It, Anyway?

Power struggles aren't just verbal. They can also be turf wars—territorial skirmishes that take place in the living room, the bedroom, and even the bathroom as you and your spouse vie for control of the living space in your house or apartment. Walk through your home together. In each room, stop and ask:

- Who chose the rugs, furniture, and decorations—and decided where each should be placed? Does the style reflect both your tastes or not? Do you both like the room's look and the way it functions?

- Whose personal belongings occupy the most space in this room? Whose are most prominent? Do either of you have piles of things here that really belong someplace else?

- Who controls the most space in your home for personal use and for the display and storage of personal belongings? Who has the least? Is the division of space fair or not?

- Are there areas that seem unbalanced—in terms of style, storage, or use—that you and your spouse would like to discuss and change?

Then assume responsibility for your wounds and dreams. Stop, breathe deeply, and pay attention to your feelings. "Feel the emotional pain and try to stay with your feelings," Dr. Campbell suggests. "Comfort yourself. Memories or images or words may surface from your childhood, or they may not. The important thing is to experience your own pain and take care of yourself. You're teaching yourself that this hurt won't kill you. You soothe yourself and no longer need your partner to figure out how to do that. This healing frees you to accept your partner for who he or she really is." It also stops you from lashing out at your partner as a way to alleviate the hurt.

Be compassionate to your spouse's wounds and dreams. Just as underlying issues may be causing your anger and frustration, so it is with your spouse. Rather than fighting over whose turn it is to mop, gently ask if there is something deeper behind his or her anger.

Clear up misunderstandings rather than battling for victory. So many power struggles are linked to misunderstandings about each other's intent and desires. You may believe your spouse is deliberately blocking your efforts to make your marriage more perfect, for example, when in fact your spouse doesn't know what your definition of *perfect* is. The way to get to this realization isn't through arguing but by asking questions. "What do you believe I should have done in this case?" "Should I have known this? How?" "What should I do next time in this situation?"

Untangle your dreams about your marriage. Write down what you want from your marriage at this point in your lives and why: always being home for dinner together (because your family always/rarely shared an evening meal); managing money more effectively (because your own parents were terrific/awful financial planners); or always being cheerful (because your own family was glum/exuberant). Think through whether these are reasonable expectations. If they are, take the lead in making them happen.

Mission 2

Move from Conflict to Problem-Solving

When problem-solving everyday issues becomes a tug-of-war over who's right and who's wrong, then settling even the smallest of discussions becomes a battle. "A better alternative is what I call the win-win waltz," says Dr. Heitler. "We toss information back and forth, we have an 'aha!' moment, and we come up with solutions that work very well for both of us."

This is really a win-win-*win* situation because the benefits go far beyond the convenience of working out problems effectively. You'll develop a new way of getting along together that lets both of you feel ready and willing to talk about your concerns because you know your spouse listens and cares. Mutual respect goes up, and bad stuff like hostility, coercion, personal attacks, and antagonism go down.

You'll also free yourself from the emotional and physical side effects of nasty fighting, such as feeling you've intimidated or dominated your mate—or that you've given in and given up on what you really want. You'll have fewer tense times together, and actually improve your health. Couples who learn to solve problems constructively together cut their risk for stress-related health problems including depression, cardiovascular disease, and lowered immunity.

For best results, first review our guidelines for assertive speaking and empathetic listening from the Realization stage. Then try this.

Three Steps to Effective Problem-Solving

Step 1: Describe the Problem in a Few Words—and Let Your Partner Respond

The opening round in problem-solving involves getting your overview of the issue out on the table. Don't let it smolder or expect your partner to guess!

Example:

You: "If we go to your parents' house for the weekend, I won't be able to get our tax return information together before the workweek starts."

Your spouse: "My parents have been planning for this visit for months. I don't think we can or should just cancel."

Step 2: Look Together at Deeper Concerns

This is the exploration phase. Don't try to "sell" your point of view to your spouse. And don't try to solve the problem just yet. *Do* talk about underlying worries and issues that contribute to the problem you're trying to solve. And do listen carefully to your partner's concerns. Keep an open mind. Learn all you can about your own concerns and your partner's. Your goal: See the big picture and form a mental list of both partners' concerns. This is your common set of concerns that you'll try to resolve in Step 3.

Example:

You: "I have a new deadline at work and meetings three nights this week, plus we promised to visit the neighbors on Tuesday night. The tax deadline is almost here. I'm afraid I'll be up until 3 A.M. trying to do all this during the week. I'll be grouchy and won't do my best at work, and I won't be very interested in socializing with our neighbors or contribute much to the meetings. I'm feeling squeezed."

Your spouse: "I really want to see my parents before they leave for their vacation. I haven't spent much time with them in several months. Plus, my mother invited my aunt and uncle over to see us, too. It's important to me to be with my parents for more than a short visit, and to feel at home. I'd like you to see them, too, and be with me for the big family dinner."

Step 3: Craft a Win-Win Strategy

Look for steps *you* can take to resolve the issue for both of you. This is crucial: Don't tell your partner what he or she can do, but instead say what you can do. The best solutions usually aren't your first ideas at all but may occur

Five Ways to Sidestep a Fight

These strategies can stop a fight before it starts.

- See things from your partner's point of view.
- Count to 50 before you say anything incendiary. This pause will help you calm down just long enough to think better of it.
- Don't throw verbal bombs. Avoid put-downs, personal attacks, judgments, criticism, and blaming—as well as sulking, interrupting, and stomping out of the room.
- Ask yourself if you can—and should—solve the problem on your own.
- Skip heavy conversations before breakfast and from 11 A.M. to 12 P.M. and 3:30 P.M. to 6 P.M.—because nobody should argue on an empty stomach. And ban problem-solving talks after about 8 P.M. Fatigue starts many fights!

to you after looking at your concerns and figuring out what matters most to each of you.

Example:

You: "Maybe I could stay at home on Friday night and Saturday morning and get the tax stuff organized. Then I'd join you for the rest of the weekend without any worries hanging over me."

Your spouse: "I would be willing to tell my parents you have to catch up with the taxes and can't come for the whole weekend. I'm also willing to postpone our night out with the neighbors during the week and help you get the tax information together."

These Tips Can Also Help

Decide if you've got a problem or just a difference. If an issue isn't threatening your health, safety, or financial security, doesn't work against your shared vision for your marriage, and doesn't put an unfair burden on you, then it may simply be a sign that the two of you are two different people. Perhaps you're an extrovert and love parties, while your partner's introvert personality makes him or her crave quiet nights at home. Perhaps you're great at starting projects, while your partner's terrific at sticking with it until every last detail is finished. Or maybe one of you is a morning person, the other a night owl. In that case, the solution is acceptance, not trying to change your partner. Look for the ways that your differences are marriage-strengthening assets.

Practice loving acceptance. Learning the art of accepting and valuing your partner for who he or she is—instead of grousing about shortcomings—may actually help the two of you find better solutions to problems, experts say. This loving accommodation melts defenses and motivates us to want to please each other.

Banish the deal-breakers. University of Washington relationship expert John Gottman, Ph.D., advises couples to do all they can to avoid these lethal habits: personal criticism, sneering contempt, defensiveness, and stonewalling.

Give your mate the benefit of the doubt. The next time you're feeling disappointed, hurt, or angry with your spouse, pause before jumping to conclusions. Maybe your spouse is tired, hungry, or preoccupied—or doesn't see the impact of his or her actions. Search for a benevolent explanation that will allow you to treat your mate with love and respect.

Beware of ice. A University of Wisconsin study that followed 97 newlywed couples into their third year of marriage found that spouses who give their mates the cold shoulder cause as much marital distress as those who

Three Ways to Defuse a Runaway Argument

These tension-tamers can short-circuit an argument that's getting too hot to handle.

- Use anger as a red-alert sign to stop the discussion. Walk away and use meditation, exercise, or another pleasant activity to de-stress.

- Reconnect frequently during tough conversations. Use empathy and appreciation to stay close to your spouse. And be on the lookout for your spouse's attempts to heal or avoid breaches.

- Soothe yourself and your spouse. Breathe deeply, slow down the conversation, and take a few minutes to review all the positive steps you've taken together to solve the problem already. Share your feelings. The more effectively you can soothe yourself and each other, the more productive your problem-solving session can be.

dish out scathing sarcasm and caustic criticism. Icy behavior included pouting, stomping out of the room, showing a lack of interest in a partner's emotional revelations, and more subtle brush-offs such as changing the subject, joking, or even buttering up a spouse to avoid discussing a sticky subject.

Seize the small opportunities. Practice problem-solving skills when tiny issues arise. "Moments with little bits of tension are perfect opportunities to work on your skills and experience success," Dr. Heitler says. "Talk about each of your concerns; look for solutions. The more you do this, the more the whole tone of your relationship changes. Problems become a chance to come closer together and show each other how much we care, instead of danger zones full of irritation and hurt feelings."

Be an equal-time advocate. Making sure each of you has the same opportunity to discuss concerns and solution ideas creates a sense of equality and shared power. If you tend to dominate, speak a little less and listen longer. Encourage your partner to say more. If you feel you're getting short shrift, gently hold your ground if your partner interrupts or tries to move the discussion along too swiftly.

Take time-outs early and often. As soon as one of you feels too upset or negative to follow healthy problem-solving steps, it's time to take a break. Experts say agreeing ahead of time to take a time-out if one partner becomes overwhelmed is crucial for avoiding a downward spiral you'll only regret later. Include in your agreement the understanding that you'll get back to your discussion within 24 hours.

Mission 3
Set and Pursue Healthy Personal Goals

One day, marriage therapist Patty Howell confided in her husband that she'd always wanted to be a top-notch rose grower whose flowers were perfect enough to display in flower shows and even win trophies. "Ralph agreed to support and help me," Howell says. "He dug holes for the roses, helped prune them in the winter, and helped transport the cut blooms to shows. He helped out quite a bit so that I could reach my goal."

Eventually, Howell won a national trophy from the American Rose Society for a miniature, red-tipped white blossom called Magic Carousel. "I cut the flowers in my garden in San Diego, put them in a picnic cooler, and got on a plane to Lexington, Kentucky, for that show," she says. "And when I came home, my husband was absolutely thrilled for me." Howell says following her dream gave her deep personal satisfaction. Doing it with her husband's blessing and encouragement took her marriage to a new level. "It's wonderfully thrilling to be supported so completely by your partner," she says. "Ralph was always enthusiastic and interested. He got excited when I won a trophy and never said anything like 'Oh, we can't afford to buy that special fertilizer you want.' It was a great source of closeness for us."

Setting off in your own direction for even a few hours a week, yet being married, is a tightrope walk. It's joyful and invigorating, scary and sometimes a little lonely. Yet finding your own personal bliss and pursuing it can enhance your relationship precisely because it makes you a happier person. It can also reduce conflict and frustration in your marriage by taking the pressure off your spouse for being entirely responsible for your happiness— and vice versa.

Further, it's a great way to boost self-confidence. When University of California, Berkeley, researchers tracked hundreds of couples over several decades, one pattern they found was that people who had higher self-esteem and who saw themselves as effective were happier in their marriages. And so were their partners. Individual happiness will make your marriage happier. In a University of Missouri-Columbia study analysis of 225 research papers on happiness involving 275,000 people, researchers found that people who were happy had better social relationships, including happier marriages.

The first step along this road-less-traveled? A significant and freeing shift in the way you see your mate. "Your partner is a secondary need-meeter in your life," Howell notes. "He or she cannot fulfill every one of your needs and desires and goals." It's a tough lesson to learn, and the Rebellion stage is the perfect time for it. It's easy to be lulled into thinking your spouse is the primary person responsible for your happiness. "Then we get ticked off when they're not doing a perfect job," Howell says.

In contrast, when you feel more alive in your own life, it adds joy to your marriage. These strategies can help you pinpoint healthy personal goals—playing lead guitar in a local grownup garage band, lifting weights, taking a painting class—and help you go after them with your partner's full support and encouragement.

What You Can Do about Irreconcilable Differences

Once considered grounds for divorce, irreconcilable differences may simply be par for the course in *even the happiest marriages*. That's the refreshing yet controversial viewpoint of relationship experts who say that most couples have 6 to 10 areas of stubborn disagreement that won't ever be resolved.

This breakthrough concept means you can stop fretting over the fact that your marriage isn't perfect. Unsolvable differences are normal, not a sign that you've married the wrong person or that your spouse is inflexible or selfish. Trading your partner in for a new one would simply bring 6 to 10 new perpetual problems into the equation.

What do you do with these forever conflicts? First, make sure they're not solvable. If you find yourself arguing over the same thing month after month, year after year, despite your best efforts to talk assertively, listen empathetically, and use all the problem-solving skills in this book, then it may truly be one of your unsolvable issues—at least for now. Your job: Finding a way to accommodate the issue without blaming your spouse or your marriage or storing up anger. Thinking about these questions can help.

- Have you done all you can to resolve the issue?

- Can you live with this problem as is? If not, can you take steps on your own to fix it? If so, discuss them with your partner.

- If you can live with the problem, what strategies will help you avoid anger and resentment—such as patience, humor, or tolerance?

- When will you revisit this issue together? Sometimes, seemingly impossible issues can be resolved over time as your communication skills and sense of togetherness grow even stronger.

One caveat: Not all marriage experts agree that accommodating chronic problems is healthy. The danger: You'll set your expectations for your marriage too low, live with simmering irritation, and miss out on the satisfaction that comes from successfully tackling tough issues as a team. We agree that it's smart to go back to seemingly unfixable dilemmas from time to time. But we also think it's wise to keep those problems in perspective—and give yourselves a break.

Let bliss be your guide. Perhaps you've always wanted to raise honeybees, brew beer, learn to oil-paint, or sail on a local lake. Maybe you've dreamed of taking up an instrument you played in high school, brushing up your college French, or joining a volleyball league. Think through the possibilities and listen within for the thrill that says, Yes, this is it.

Start small. Howell didn't open a rose farm; she planted a manageable garden. Once you've identified your bliss, think of a way to start small so that you can easily fit commitments into your life without stealing time from your marriage.

Talk to your spouse. Tell your partner about your interest and how you'd like to pursue it. Be honest and specific about the time commitment and what it will cost. Ask if he or she has any fears, reservations, or objections. Talk them through. You can't expect your partner to be an active participant, of course. The pleasure's in sharing your own excitement and receiving support and encouragement in return.

Reciprocate. "One of the highest goals of marriage is coming to a fuller understanding of who you are as an individual while remaining close to the person you care about most," Howell says. "This is a two-way street. If it matters to your partner that he's good at tennis, but he doesn't do anything about it, he may feel resentful or think he's sold himself short later." Partners don't let each other miss out on their dreams.

Make it a daily thing. Personal goals can be as small as having the rental DVD you really want to watch on Friday night. Picking it out is up to you; expecting your spouse to somehow guess what you'd like to see is an easy setup for disappointment.

Mission 4

Renew Your Spirituality

A sense of the divine is good for your marriage. That message came through loud and clear in the Reader's Digest *Marriage in America Survey*. It was reinforced when we talked with married couples as well as researchers about the connection between spirituality and relationships.

What is shared spirituality? Once, experts and religious leaders said it meant a union between a man and a woman who grew up in the same faith and often the same denomination. But increasingly, people are discovering

Who's Your Dream Self?

Ready for a fun, personal hobby—but not sure where to start? Sit with your spouse for 20 minutes and ask each other these questions for clues about your deeply held interests.

1. When you were a child, what activities made you happiest: exploring the outdoors, playing kickball with the neighborhood kids, dressing up and acting out stories, painting or crayoning, building things or taking them apart, or reading for hours on end?

2. If you had an extra day added onto a vacation in a foreign country, would you: relax by the hotel pool; head for the nearest big museum; visit a natural wonder; focus on great eating; find a concert or theatrical play; do an outdoor activity like golfing, hang-gliding, or biking; or immerse yourself in the regional street life?

3. If you could be a celebrity, would you be a sports star, an artist, an actor, a chef, a poet, an activist, a philanthropist, or an inventor?

4. If you didn't have to work for a living, what would you do every day? What would you never do again?

5. If you were to volunteer your time for a good cause, what would you wish to do: build houses, mentor children, teach a class, create hiking trails, raise funds, help at a church or senior home, or something else?

they can find a common spiritual ground even if their religious beliefs and upbringing are not the same. Research—and untold millions of success stories—shows that a Presbyterian can marry a Methodist, a Conservative Jew can marry a Reform Jew, a Catholic can marry a Lutheran—or any other interfaith or interchurch combination—and it can work beautifully. It just takes some talking, soul-searching, and planning.

Working out spiritual differences is more important than starting your marriage with the same set of beliefs, note researchers with Creighton University's Center for Marriage and Family in Omaha, Nebraska. "Denominational differences don't cause breakups," says center director Michael Lawlor. "It depends on what the couple does together religiously and how they deal with differences. If they can fashion a shared religious life, their marriages will be as stable as any same-church marriage."

This is especially important for couples in the Rebellion stage, when the urge to strike out on your own is so strong. Use the onset of the Rebellion stage to understand and explore your spirituality. And before you sign up solo with a church, synagogue, or mosque—and before you write off your spouse as spiritually incompatible—we urge the two of you to begin a series of soul-to-soul conversations about your beliefs. Use the exercise on page 153 to guide your discussion.

Feeling Blessed

Working out a spiritual understanding is vital. And the benefits are real, whether you belong to a traditional religious organization or embrace a more independent point of view. "I feel so gifted with my husband, Lee. He is on a path with me," says Rebecca Wiederkehr of St. Louis, Missouri. "Even though we don't follow an organized religion, we are connected. So many spouses do things alone when it comes to their spiritual world. We read books and talk about things together. We've struck a good balance. We discuss our spiritual journeys together even though they aren't exactly the same. Yes, sometimes I'd like to twist his arm to get him even more interested in what I'm interested in. But we connect so much, because we're both open to each other's experiences and ideas."

Meanwhile, Greg and Priscilla Hunt of Shreveport, Louisiana, say their Christian faith and strong affiliation with the Baptist Church has sustained their marriage since the start. "Our faith, our values, our vision of life keep our marriage strong," says Greg. "We have always had a deep conviction that God would look out for us, even when we were starting our married life. We headed off to Louisville, Kentucky, together, where I was going into the seminary. On one level, we were two crazy kids heading off into the wilderness. We had no jobs, virtually no money. But we had no anxiety because we had a deep belief that this is what God wanted us to do. We still share a common purpose."

On a large scale, researchers have documented the blessings of this kind of common bond.

- Married people are twice as likely to go to church as unmarried people—and feel happier, report University of Virginia social scientists. Their analysis of a national survey found that 72 percent of married men who attend weekly religious services say they're very happy, compared to 60 percent for married men who don't go to services. Meanwhile, 64 percent of married women who attend services regularly report that they are very happy in their marriages, versus 58 percent of married women who don't attend.

- Husbands and wives who attend services faithfully were 30 percent less likely to divorce than sporadic attenders, the same survey found.

- When Readers Digest asked 1,001 married people to describe their relationship, 29 percent said their marriages were "blessed." One in eight said their marriages had withstood major shifts in one or both partner's religious or spiritual beliefs—and most of them reported that the change was positive.

Talking about Beliefs

Even if you do not adhere to formal religious convictions or belong to a religious institution, you've no doubt got a position on God, religion, and spirituality. Whatever it may be, we encourage you to discuss it with your partner. "You may have a spirituality outside traditional systems," says Creighton University marriage researcher Gail Risch. "In this country, a lot of people question institutionalized religion, yet they consider themselves spiritual. Those beliefs can be more difficult to talk about because they don't always follow commonly accepted lines of thinking. But they're your beliefs and therefore are important. If you leave them on the back burner, you've left part of yourself out of your marriage."

Start with the holidays. You may have discussed where you'll celebrate the holidays already, as you strike a balance between observing childhood rituals with your families and creating your own. Talking about the meanings of these special days, and what in them matters most to you, is a doorway that opens into larger spiritual conversations. You may start out discussing whether you'll have a Christmas tree or a Hanukkah menorah or both; whether you'll go to midnight Mass on Christmas Eve or get up bright and early for a Christmas Day service at a Protestant church; how you'll give gifts and even which holidays will matter most in your household.

Get to the core: Talk together about the most meaningful part of your holiday celebrations. Keep the stuff that matters most and be willing to learn about your partner's cherished traditions.

Testify. Share with each other what is truly important to you as individuals in your faith life. Discuss how you can support each other's religious needs.

Find common ground. Talk about areas where the values and tenets of your faiths intersect. These are your spiritual strengths. Build the rest from there.

Don't try to convert your spouse to your beliefs. The choice to convert is your partner's alone. Don't pressure him or her to take up your beliefs.

Be honest and nonjudgmental. Talk bravely about your true beliefs and listen with an open mind and heart.

Reveal your bottom-line issues. You may feel you must celebrate Christmas with your family, or that it's important to display a religious symbol in your home, or that getting up on Saturday or Sunday morning for services is crucial. Share these must-do's with your partner and discuss ways to make them happen so that both of you are comfortable with the outcome.

Tune in to the spiritual side of your marriage. Whether you belong to an organized religious group or see yourself as a free spirit with a private spiritual practice, don't overlook the transcendent nature of your own marriage. It's mysterious—somehow you found each other and formed a committed bond. It's deeply nurturing. And marriage calls us to practice the same kind of selfless love advocated by the world's great spiritual teachers.

> ## CONVERSATION STARTER
> ### Sharing Your Faith
>
> These questions can help the two of you jumpstart a lifelong conversation about personal faith and religious observance.
>
> 1. What was your childhood religious experience? Were you baptized or christened? Did you have a ritual circumcision? Did you attend Sunday school, Hebrew school, parochial school? Did you have a bar mitzvah or bat mitzvah ceremony? A first communion? Confirmation? Did you have a "born again" experience?
>
> 2. Which holidays are most important to you? Why? What do you enjoy the most and the least? What has the deepest significance?
>
> 3. What is your concept of God or the divine? Does your religion or faith color your daily values or identity?
>
> 4. Did your parents worship together or talk about spirituality at home?
>
> 5. Do you own religious or spiritual items, such as music, art, a cross or crucifix, a menorah, *Kiddush* cup, or Sabbath candlesticks? Do you treasure these? Will you display them in your home?
>
> 6. What religious identity would you like your children to have?
>
> 7. What daily religious practices do you value, such as grace before meals or daily prayer?
>
> 8. What is there about religion in general or your own religion that you don't like?

Married love is all about radical acceptance, serving your spouse, helping whenever you're needed, healing old wounds, and sharing the wonders of sexuality and creation.

Mission 5

Recover from Infidelities

The wear-and-tear of everyday life—a busy job, the trials of raising teenagers—led Brian Bercht, 47, into an affair with a co-worker that surprised even him. "After nearly two decades of marriage to a sexy, loving woman—with whom I made love almost nightly—I came home from work one evening and told her I was moving out, leaving her for another woman," he says. "When I finally came to my senses, I was fully expecting my wife, Anne, to tell me to get lost. She had every right."

Instead, Anne Bercht sat in the same spot in her living room until the sun rose, holding a cup of cold coffee and thinking. "I fantasized about wanting to kill the other woman," she says. "I decided my marriage was worth saving. We would find a way."

The Berchts' path: A commitment to total honesty, no matter what. The agony paid off. "I needed every detail," Anne says. "It would have hurt me and been yet another betrayal if Brian hadn't told me the truth about everything. Couples fear total honesty after an affair—just as we fear it in our daily life together—but it makes all the difference in the world."

The experience was profoundly healing. "We had a good marriage before, but I like to say it was like seeing the Grand Canyon on a 28-inch color TV. Now we've moved our relationship to such a good place that it's not even like seeing it on a 51-inch plasma TV. We're standing on the very edge and looking at it. I would have never thought I'd be at this place, that we would be so open and honest. That I could feel so loved and accepted and no longer feel I have to live up to a certain level of performance that I thought was required of me. We love each other for who we are."

The affair so rocked the Berchts' world that the couple went public with their story and published a book, *My Husband's Affair (Became the Best Thing That Ever Happened to Me)*. Anne took over as director of the self-help organization for betrayed spouses, the Beyond Affairs Network, in the summer of 2006. "So many spouses think they need to keep the affair to themselves. To not ask their partners about it and not ask their friends for support," she says. "We're here to help, with support groups in 80 cities around the world."

As many as 60 percent of married men and 40 percent of married women will have a sexual or emotional affair, estimates affairs expert Peggy Vaughan, author of *The Monogamy Myth: A Personal Handbook for Recovering from Affairs*, who developed the international Beyond Affairs Network. Still more engage in one of the "new infidelities"—deceptive debt, overwork, or undue attention to outside interests—that are affairlike because they're kept secret or channel time, energy, and emotion out of your marriage.

Risk of an affair is especially high during the Rebellion stage. Power struggles, intense feelings of betrayal and disappointment, and a sense that you have the absolute right to strike out on your own are hallmarks of this tumultuous phase. At a time when the two of you are coming to terms with the confines of marriage, an affair is the ultimate act of rebellion.

What hurts the most? For the betrayed husband or wife, it's not the sex so much as the secrecy. When University of California, San Diego, researchers studied 196 women and men in relationships, they focused more on a mate's emotional infidelity than on a mate's sexual infidelity. Vaughan found a similar view when she polled visitors to her Web site recently. She asked, "If your partner had an affair, what was the most difficult part to overcome?" While 28 percent of women and 30 percent of men were most bothered by the sex, deception was considered the toughest problem by 72 percent of women and 70 percent of men.

It stands to reason, then, that the secret to healing after an affair would be the opposite of secrecy: total honesty, as the Berchts discovered.

Six Steps for the Unfaithful Spouse

Your marriage can survive an affair. Healing from infidelity is hard, painful work; both of you must be committed to repairing the damage, rebuilding trust, and reconnecting. On the agenda: The unfaithful spouse must be willing to stop the affair, provide all details honestly and completely, and take the steps necessary to prove his or her trustworthiness. The betrayed spouse must take the job of healing seriously—by not minimizing or trying to speed up the process and, at times, by setting aside overwhelming anger and despair in order to learn more about what's happened. Stopping secrecy and building a more honest union are the keys.

If you make a commitment to follow these strategies with your whole heart, your marriage has a good chance of surviving the affair—and emerging stronger on the other side.

1. **Promise to stop the affair—and to stop seeing your lover—immediately.** Agree to sever all contact. This lifts secrecy and creates a sense of safety for the betrayed spouse. Stopping an affair goes beyond no dinner dates or sex. All phone calls, in-person conversations, and quick coffee breaks together must stop. If you work with the person with whom you had an affair, keep your encounters

strictly businesslike—and tell your spouse everything that happens. Avoid private lunch dates and closed-door meetings.

It's also important to report any chance meetings with your former lover to your spouse before he or she asks about it. Talk about your conversation. If your former lover contacts you, announce that too.

2. **Answer any and all questions.** More and more marriage experts agree that couples heal better after an affair if the adulterous spouse supplies *all* of the information requested by his or her betrayed partner. In one study of 1,083 betrayed husbands and wives, those whose spouses were the most honest felt better emotionally and reconciled more completely, reports Vaughan. "I've talked with plenty of people who say with pride that they never talked about the affair," she says. "That's not healing. You need to reach the point where you can talk about it without pain. If you never, ever discuss it, you cannot recover. My own husband had 12 affairs over seven years. I'm convinced the main reason I recovered was his willingness to answer all of my questions."

It's counterintuitive—many spouses (and therapists) think that going over the details will only further upset the aggrieved partner. Truth is, willingness to talk rebuilds trust. The key? Not holding back—no more secrets. If you leave out details that emerge later, your spouse may feel newly betrayed.

3. **Show your spouse empathy, no matter what.** The single best indicator of whether a relationship can survive infidelity is how much empathy the unfaithful partner shows when the betrayed spouse gets emotional about the pain caused by the affair, according to infidelity expert Shirley Glass, Ph.D.

4. **Keep talking and listening, no matter how long it takes.** You can't speed up your spouse's healing process, and you shouldn't ever negate its significance. Be ready to answer questions at any time, even months or years after the affair has ended. And listen to his or her reactions without anger or blame.

5. **Take responsibility.** Blaming your partner for the affair won't heal your marriage. Showing sincere regret and remorse will. Apologize often and vow to never commit adultery again. It may seem obvious to

you that you'll never stray again, but your spouse may have worries, so renew your commitment to your spouse as your one-and-only.

6. **Don't expect quick or easy forgiveness.** Your partner may be in deep pain or shock. Expect tears, rage, and anger.

Nine Steps for the Betrayed Spouse

You want to scream and rail at your partner. You want all the details about the affair. Above all, you want the secrecy to stop. These strategies can help you find what you need to heal, to repair your marriage, and to move forward with your life.

1. **Ask lots of questions.** At first, you may want all the factual details: How often did you meet? When did you cross the line from friends to lovers? What sexual acts did you share? How many times? Where? How much money did you spend on him or her? Who else knows about your affair?

You've Gotta Have Friends!

In many traditional cultures, women hang out with women and men hang out with men. This segregation by sex may seem old-fashioned, but modern research suggests there's a reason we feel drawn to our women friends or male buddies and should cultivate same-sex friendships after marriage. Male bonding and female bonding not only allow us to share common experiences but also help us cut stress in ways that are tailor-made for men and women.

Stress, say University of California, Los Angeles, researchers, prompts a fight-or-flight response in men. After a tough day at work, a guy might hole up in the den to watch football or get together with buddies to watch a game—but not say much to them. In contrast, a woman under stress is more likely to take care of the kids, call a friend or relative on the phone, or even strike up a conversation with a perfect stranger. This tend-and-befriend response is triggered by elevated levels of the cuddling hormone oxytocin, which rises in women during times of anxiety.

"Men secrete oxytocin too, but the effects of oxytocin seem to be reduced by male hormones, so oxytocin may have reduced effects on men's physiology and behavior under stress," notes lead researcher Shelley E. Taylor Ph. D. "Oxytocin, along with other stress hormones, may be a key factor in reducing females' response to stress."

The tend-and-befriend pattern exhibited by women probably evolved through natural selection, Dr. Taylor believes. "Thousands of generations ago, fleeing or fighting in stressful situations was not a good option for a female who was pregnant or taking care of offspring, and women who developed and maintained social alliances were better able to care for multiple offspring in stressful times."

What it means for couples in the Rebellion stage: Cultivate your own same-sex friendships and support your mate's efforts to do the same. If the guys want to watch the game together, or the women want to form a girls-only book club, give them your blessing—and use their bonding time as an opportunity for you to spend time with folks of your own gender as well. The bonus? Close, same-sex friendships can cut the risk for emotional and sexual infidelity.

Later, your questions may shift as you think about your partner's emotions, about the reasons he or she was pushed and pulled into the affair, about whether the affair has turned a spotlight on a hidden weakness in your own marriage.

2. **Balance your rage with your need for information.** You want to scream, cry, and lash out—but big emotions may prevent your spouse from making the full disclosure that leads to recovery. To get the truth (and form a tighter connection with your spouse), be compassionate about your partner's emotions.

   "When you get all the facts, you're not obsessed anymore," Vaughan says. "The only way your spouse will be willing to answer is if you can manage not to lash out and attack every time. Spouses who've had affairs are afraid to reveal everything because they're worried it will become a marathon, with a downward spiral of out-of-control emotions." If one of you becomes upset, it's time to stop the discussion for now.

3. **Set a time limit on affair talk.** Restrict yourselves to 15 to 30 minutes. Don't let the affair take over your lives. Do ask questions as they arise instead of building up resentment and long lists of questions. "Don't let your worries go underground. Keep talking," Vaughan says.

4. **Expect curveballs.** The spouse who had the affair may become angry or even accuse you of betraying him or her. Keep the focus on the affair itself.

5. **Talk about how the affair has affected you.** Discuss your doubts, disappointments, feelings of betrayal and abandonment, anger, and sadness. As your partner builds a wall between him- or herself and the former lover, help open a window of intimacy between the two of you. Don't hold back.

6. **Don't forgive quickly or easily.** You must grapple with your pain and anger first and rebuild trust.

7. **Find support.** Reconnecting with family and friends, and even finding a support group to join, can help you feel less isolated.

8. **Spend time together without talking about the affair.** Connect as friends and romantic partners by doing the things you've always enjoyed.

9. **Forgive only when you're ready.** You'll never forget an affair, but the painful memories will fade with time. Forgiveness allows you to move past the pain and rage and to reconcile with your partner. Take this important step only when you feel ready to let go of your negative feelings, when your partner has been completely honest and has taken steps to rebuild your trust. The advice below can help.

Mission 6

Forgive Your Spouse and Yourself

Every marriage needs the grace of forgiveness. We all make mistakes, small and large: Maybe your spouse spent half of the weekly grocery money on a new pair of running shoes. Or you gave the neighbor a kiss that went into overtime at that wild New Year's Eve party back in 2001. Maybe you're nursing a longtime grudge against your spouse, blaming his or her shortcomings for your marital woes or for an irritating habit. Perhaps one of you has had an affair—or announced in a moment of anger that if you had it to do over again, you wouldn't be in this marriage.

You feel angry. Resentful. Deeply wounded. Or just terminally annoyed. Bury the hatchet? No way! Why should you let the person who's wronged you off the hook?

The truth is, forgiveness isn't a matter of giving up your soul, condoning outright bad behavior, denying a serious problem, or "forgiving and forgetting" a big betrayal. It *is* all about summoning the strength and courage to give up *your* anger and hurt.

The single, powerful constant in the continuum of forgiveness: Remembering that it will help *you* become whole again. "As we give the gift of forgiveness, we ourselves are healed," notes Robert D. Enright, Ph.D., a professor of educational psychology at the University of Wisconsin-Madison and cofounder of the International Forgiveness Institute. Forgiveness, he notes, is a paradox: "It is the forgoing of resentment or revenge when the wrongdoer's actions deserve it and giving the gifts of mercy, generosity, and love when the wrongdoer does not deserve them." The benefits for you include less anger, stress, depression, and hurt feelings—and more hope, peace, compassion, and self-confidence. In one survey of 200 married couples, those with the strongest ability to forgive also felt the least anxiety, fatigue, and depression.

The New Infidelities

Cheating on your spouse isn't just about sex anymore. These three surprising forms of infidelity are on the rise—and can be just as damaging as an old-fashioned affair.

Emotional infidelity. More and more women and men find themselves crossing the line from platonic friendship to romantic love interest, often at work or with acquaintances via the Internet. There's no sex, but it still has all the hallmarks of an affair: intimacy that belongs in marriage, secrecy, deception, and sexual chemistry. Beware: Half of all emotional affairs ultimately become sexual affairs.

Financial infidelity. Money deception can be as dangerous as adultery. It's on the rise, thanks to ready access to credit, the availability of 24/7 shopping on the Internet, an explosion in gambling opportunities, and a culture that equates consumption with comfort. Hidden financial problems can take a dramatic emotional toll on a couple—wrecking trust, derailing future plans, and undermining feelings of safety and security.

Work infidelity. Up to 25 percent of Americans may be workaholics—so focused on the job that there's little time, energy, or emotional currency left for the marriage. Workaholics may sneak away from a quiet evening at home to log in and get more job stuff done; they think about work most of the time and ignore pleas to refocus on the relationship.

Forgiveness is a hot topic these days, with over 1,200 published research studies—up from fewer than 60 just a decade ago. It has its own campaign—A Campaign for Forgiveness Research, sponsored by the Pennsylvania-based Templeton Foundation—with the goal of raising $10 million to study this seemingly simple, yet deeply complex, act. And when a University of Colorado researcher asked 150 long-married couples about the characteristics crucial for a good marriage, the ability to forgive and be forgiven made the top-10 list.

How can you forgive your spouse—or yourself? Moving toward forgiveness—and going beyond it to reconcile with your spouse—depends on the two of you and the nature of the hurt. These steps can help.

Understand exactly how you feel about a perceived wrong. Think about it and experience your feelings without brushing them aside. Take them seriously.

Promise yourself that you'll do what it takes to make yourself feel better. Forgiveness isn't just about reconciliation with your partner. It's also about making yourself feel whole again.

Put the past behind you. Even though a hurtful act in the past still stings, realize that the experience has happened and cannot be undone. This doesn't mean you should minimize the effects. It does mean acknowledging this truth: Your spouse cannot travel backward in time to change what happened.

See your partner in a loving light. Some experts say that the very first step toward forgiveness is to think of your partner as worthy of love and understanding—despite his or her flaws, wounds, and blind spots.

And remember the relief of being forgiven. Recall a time when someone you loved forgave you for something big or small. How did you feel?

Empathize with your partner's shortcomings. Put yourself in your spouse's shoes and think about what motivated his or her behavior. He or she may have acted out of ignorance, fear, or pain. Thinking this through builds your ability to feel empathy. Some experts suggest role-playing your partner's part in the act that hurt you or even writing a note to yourself explaining the problem from your partner's side.

Ask for an apology if you need one. Then accept it with grace and love. What matters is that the "I'm sorry" is heartfelt, not that it was spontaneous. After all, your partner can't read your mind. If you have to ask for the apology, that doesn't mean the apology is second-rate.

Reaffirm your loving relationship. Share with your spouse how you hope forgiveness will let you connect more deeply and intimately. Hug, kiss, make love, talk, laugh—enjoy this homecoming for your heart.

Repeat as needed. Hurt feelings can linger even after you've forgiven. You may have to bury the hatchet anew. If a wrong hurt you deeply, you may even have to forgive it on a daily basis for a while until you feel better. Forgiveness is a process, not a once-and-done act.

Big betrayal? Resist the temptation of "easy" forgiveness. Quick, "no-fault" forgiveness for a major transgression such as an affair won't help you heal or truly reconcile with your partner, because it minimizes the depth of your pain, asks nothing of the wrongdoer, and robs you of any

Pull out your day planner or switch on your personal digital assistant. Rebellion stage couples need romantic, fun dates together to escape the tension of power struggles, nurture their bond, and learn new things about one another. Try these soon.

One for you. Your partner chooses something he or she has never done before but would like to consider as a new hobby or personal interest. Your role is to support your spouse as he or she explores. You agree to go along as a cheerleader and/or fellow participant. Afterward, save time for lunch, dinner, or a cup of coffee or an ice cream cone so you can debrief about the experience. How did your spouse like it? How do you feel about it? What's the time commitment? The cost?

One for me. Same as above, except now it's your turn to check out a new interest and take your spouse along.

One for us. Revive an older, shared interest or pursue something you may have tried together once and enjoyed, whether it's kayaking, taking a cooking class, ballroom dancing, or arc-welding. It should be an activity you both truly enjoy and can participate in more or less as equals.

The no-big-issues date. If you're arguing often or even simply embroiled in big, serious discussions, you need regular time-outs so that conflict doesn't take over your relationship. Plan an entertaining or romantic date, such as going to the movies, a concert, or a special restaurant for dinner. The ground rules: Look forward to it as a special occasion—and don't talk about conflict areas. Have a no-blame catchphrase handy in case one of you strays. We suggest "Tonight, we're just lovers."

The Power of Forgiveness

Forgiveness does more than reunite you with your spouse and help you feel more peaceful and joyful. Evidence is mounting that releasing anger, resentment and bitterness has profound health benefits, from lower blood pressure and a healthier heart rate to less depression, better immunity, and even a longer life.

The mind-body link? It may be the stress hormone cortisol. In one research study of 40 couples, those in happy, untroubled relationships had lower levels of cortisol than those in difficult, contentious marriages. Levels of cortisol rose even higher when distressed couples were asked to think about their relationships. Higher cortisol levels are associated with a higher risk for heart problems, stress and anxiety, and even impaired immunity.

Forgiveness may work on two levels. First, it lifts the hostility, fear, and anger that lead to higher blood pressure and other health problems. Second, giving up grudges allows you to be enfolded more completely by the love and friendship of your spouse, family, and friends. Plenty of studies show that people with strong social networks are healthier than lone-wolf types.

---

new understanding of the role you played in the transgression. In the case of a big hurt, forgiveness requires a commitment from both spouses to work together toward healing. It can be a long road.

Understand your own weaknesses. You've made mistakes too. Work on accepting your own imperfections. Having empathy for yourself will make it easier to forgive your partner's weaknesses and irritating habits.

Then forgive yourself too. Sometimes the last person we're willing to let off the hook is ourselves. If you've wronged your spouse, it may seem easier—or more honorable—to remain in a state of self-imposed disgrace than to make amends and seek forgiveness. By feeling miserable, you show the world—and yourself—that you're doing penance. But beating yourself up doesn't leave much room for a happy relationship with your spouse. Maybe it's time to acknowledge that you too are only human and release the anger you've turned against yourself. Start by understanding how you feel, then tell your spouse about the wrong you feel you've committed. Apologize and ask for forgiveness. Then commit to stop feeling so bad about the past.

stage 4

cooperation

The calendar's crammed with work and family obligations. The filing cabinet's stuffed with household bills and statements for your retirement and college savings plans. At least one of you works at a job in which you're nearing the height of your earning potential. You've got kids now—and probably a dog, cat, parakeet, or goldfish too.

The last time you dressed up for a date with your spouse—or undressed for some leisurely lovemaking? You can't remember when.

In the big atlas of marriage, you're smack-dab in the Cooperation stage if at least two of the statements above describe your busy life. This is one of the longest, most productive, and most potentially satisfying phases of your relationship. It's the summertime of marriage, when the dreams you planted as seeds long ago come to fruition. You raise children, turn a house or apartment into a home, play an active role in civic and religious organizations, and work like mad to pay for all the good things in life, including a home, vacations, furniture, cars, clothes for growing kids—as well as saving for the future.

Being responsible is crucial in the Cooperation stage, but so is maintaining intimacy and humor.

But too often, the Cooperation stage is all about rushing, never about relaxing and being present for all the good stuff that's happening. There are simply too many big and little responsibilities to stay on top of. You've got the good life, but neither of you has a minute to enjoy it. In over half of all two-parent American families (and nearly all child-free marriages), both spouses work, bringing in more income as well as more stress, fatigue, and tension. And even in households with one stay-at-home spouse, couples report feeling as if every minute of the day is scheduled and there's still not enough time.

As a result, few couples are out playing, laughing, and loving in the warm sunshine of this fruitful season of marriage. Too often, to-do lists take precedence over truly connecting with the amazing person who's working beside you to build the miracle of your shared life.

Be careful. Taking care of business and shouldering responsibilities are important ways to demonstrate your love and commitment to your spouse and family. But the demands of the Cooperation stage can dismantle your marriage—unless you consciously reserve time and energy for your partner.

Time, Money, and Sex

Is the Cooperation stage a crisis? American marriage pundits would say so. Experts have taken to calling couples in this busy-busy stage the "harried married," sex- and love-starved victims of "super-couple syndrome." Marriage, they say, becomes a punch-the-clock business arrangement that's functional, but no longer intimate or even fun. One expert claims 85 percent of us are stuck in joyless "weekend marriages," trying unsuccessfully to cram all our needs for love, affection, and closeness into the 55 hours between the closing bell Friday afternoon and bedtime Sunday night. Another says that overwhelmed parents are a national crisis. (And any mom or dad who's spent the night rocking a sleepless infant would agree.)

When researchers at Creighton University's Center for Marriage and Family surveyed young couples about the biggest unresolved problems in their marriages, they found a surprising theme in the answers they received. "Across the board, married couples said over and over again that they didn't have enough time, enough money, or enough sexual intimacy," says researcher Gail S. Risch. Meanwhile, a University of Maryland survey found that we all feel more rushed than ever before. Using data from two national surveys, the researchers found that 39 percent of women said they always felt rushed, up 10 percentage points from 1975; 31 percent of men said they felt always rushed, up 5 percentage points from 1978.

Couples with—and without—children interviewed for *The 7 Stages of Marriage* agree. In their own way, each has fought hard to put their marriage first despite the strong forces pushing and pulling at them during the Cooperation stage.

- "We've pulled ourselves in lots of different directions, so it's a real challenge. My wife, Teresa, and I both work. We have two young sons. And Teresa's in graduate school. There are constant demands on our time and energy," says Don Howard of Blue Springs,

Missouri. "We remind ourselves all the time about what's important to us. And it's loving and communicating within our marriage and our family. The frustration and tensions of modern life put couples and families at tremendous risk. If you put all the stresses in a modern marriage down on paper, it would be overwhelming. You just have to find ways, big and little, to make sure you're loving with each other despite all of that. You have to do it for yourselves and find organizations like your church to help you. Because society isn't sending good messages about preserving your family and your marriage. Out in the world, it's all me-me-me. You have to resist that."

- "I quit my job as an industrial engineer after we had our first child," says Kimberly Jordan of Spartanburg, South Carolina. "We planned as best as we could for all the changes a baby would bring, but you can never be fully prepared. It was a big change for me. And all that fatigue with getting up to nurse the baby. We joined together in caring for him, and people were so generous giving us baby clothes and things that the early years weren't as hard as they could have been. It's beautiful, but it isn't always easy. It took a while for me to realize that my husband, Gary, needed my attention too. Eventually we let my mother babysit and we starting going out on regular dates together. That was a big shift—but a very worthwhile one. Now our sons love it when we get ready for a date!"

- "Every now and then our hyper-busyness builds to a point where somebody explodes from frustration," says Andrew Stewart of Durham, North Carolina. "My wife, Peggy, confronted me about it

MARRIAGE MAGIC
Create a Vision Statement

Writing a motto for your marriage will help remind you of all the good things in your relationship—and of what you want to be as a couple. You might use a phrase from your wedding vows or choose words that describe what's best about your partnership: "We're playful and positive." "We're always a team." "We trust each other at all times." Your vision statement isn't cast in stone. Feel free to change it as often as you want.

the other day, and we had a long talk. We had been walking together for about an hour a day, but our schedules changed and we couldn't fit it in. We felt we were losing our connection with one another because we'd lost this ritual that kept us close." Adds Peggy Kinney, "We need a half hour to an hour together to talk about all the surface stuff about our day, then move to a deeper level and then on to a deeper level. The only way to get there is to have enough time with one another. We were losing that important closeness. We had to do something."

Putting Your Marriage First

The antidote to all that Cooperation stage chaos? Simply get back to basics: Put your marriage first.

Smart couples schedule time together for friendship, fun, romance, and sex. (You've got Little League and the dentist on your calendar, why not your marriage?) They find ways to use the biggest stresses of this phase—including kids, work, and money—to strengthen rather than fray their union. And they go beyond being in the same place at the same time. The Cooperation stage can leave you too stressed out and tired to connect, emotionally and physically, with your partner. The result: Conflicts go unresolved. And emotional walls go up when the two of you are too wiped out to share what's really happening in your hearts and souls—and when you're too preoccupied to listen deeply to your partner's revelations about his or her inner life. The Rx? Putting your marriage first also means finding ways to de-stress, alone and together, so that you're truly available to your mate and your marriage.

In this chapter, we'll show you how the following four missions can keep the two of you close despite the distractions and complications of the Cooperation stage.

- **Let parenthood strengthen—not threaten—your marriage.** It's a myth that having children automatically brings a man and a woman closer together. A growing stack of research reveals something couples everywhere experience but rarely want to admit: Marital bliss plummets thanks to parenthood. Experts say having a baby is even riskier for your marriage than having an affair. Fortunately, new research also shows how couples can support and appreciate each other's parenting styles in ways that bolster their relationships, instead of giving in to blame, criticism, and disappointment.

- **Find time to settle conflicts—and connect as friends.** Airing your differences is especially challenging when you've got children in the house. Same goes when you don't have much time or energy left over after a long day claimed by work and outside commitments. But avoiding conflict isn't a shortcut to relationship harmony. Instead, it creates an emotional disconnect that can turn into icy-cold distance over the years. We'll show you how to find a time and a place for problem-solving—and how to go beyond conflict management to deepen your friendship. Deeply knowing each other is one of the keys that help new parents, and any harried couple, maintain respect, admiration, gratitude, and love.

- **Invite romance back into your marriage.** We know—you barely have time to sign your tax forms together. Where will you get three hours for a date? We'll show you how to make time for romantic moments, long and short. Keeping a playful, loving spark alive is the lifeblood of marriage. It's easy to become too comfortable together, or too tired or too time-starved to bother. Fight back—and the thrill isn't gone!

- **De-stress—and make love again.** One in three American couples are in low-sex or no-sex marriages. Why? Time's a problem, but we think stress is really getting in the way. Find out how our 21st-century warp-speed lives mute passion and frazzle human connection. Then use our proven strategies for rediscovering Eros together. And yes, you can even recapture the passion of your first months as newlyweds with a surprising, simple, and fun technique.

Your marriage will also thrive in this stage if you make use of tools and skills from previous stages: We recommend reviewing advice on deepening physical intimacy described in the Passion stage; on assertive speaking and empathetic listening skills outlined in the Realization stage; and on problem-solving strategies in the Rebellion phase. Practicing the new Cooperation stage skills in this chapter will keep your marriage a priority—so you won't be strangers or adversaries when marriage's next phase arrives.

Mission 1

Let Parenthood Strengthen Your Marriage

Diaper commercials, baby-shower cards, and your own relatives will tell you a baby is pure bliss, a heaven-sent bundle of joy, a gift worth all that sleep deprivation, all those dirty Pampers.

We *do* love our children. But what they can do to our marriages is another story.

A growing stack of research reveals that happy marriages take a nose-dive when a couple becomes a family. Thanks to sleepless nights, new expectations, and the demands of bringing up baby while holding down a job, 30 to 50 percent of all new parents feel as distressed as couples already in therapy for marriage problems, say researchers from the University of California, Berkeley. Up to 70 percent of new moms say their marital satisfaction dropped dramatically. At least one-third of mothers *and* fathers experience significant depression as they become parents. And one in eight couples separate or divorce by the time their first babies are 18 months old. Generation X parents seem to feel the parental pinch even more acutely: A recent review of 90 studies involving 31,000 wives and husbands by San Diego State University researchers found that for young couples today, marital satisfaction plummeted 42 percent further after the first baby than it did for their own parents. And with each child added to the family, happiness dipped even lower.

The shift from lovers to parents can rock your marriage down to its roots. Suddenly you find yourselves taking on traditional, stereotyped roles that may clash with your thoroughly modern expectations: A working mom trades the office, wisecracking colleagues, and the gym for breast-feeding, bottle-washing, and mountains of laundry (and after just six to eight weeks of maternity leave, often adds an office job back into the mix). A husband faithfully attends childbirth classes, spends long hours in the delivery room, and cuts the baby's umbilical cord, yet all too often feels shut out during the early years of child-rearing. Instead, he works longer and harder in his career in order to provide for his growing family, and feels more and more distant. You're both doing more, communicating less, and feeling vastly underappreciated. Modern marriage makes matters tougher: You may be having kids in your late 30s or early 40s, when the fatigue factor is higher and job pressures are bigger than they probably were in your 20s. And there's more to be anxious about than ever before in our kid-competitive society. Will your child get into a good preschool program? Can you afford this year's $800 status stroller and $100 baby playsuit? Is your wunderkind enrolled in the right art, music, and tumbling tots class?

Small wonder, then, that *Newsweek* magazine decreed parenting "The Toughest Job You'll Ever Love." Or that the National Marriage Project at Rutgers University reached the chilling conclusion in 2004 that "children seem to be a growing impediment for the happiness of marriages."

Happily, even newer research reveals something smart couples have always known: Parenthood can sweeten and strengthen your relationship. All you've got to do: Put your marriage first; appreciate each other instead of criticizing; get organized; and communicate, communicate, communicate. That's a tall order for two sleep-deprived, baby-spit-spattered, shell-shocked people (who haven't showered in days). We know. We've been there. And we're here to help—whether you're planning to start a family or have already embarked on the adventure of raising kids. Here's how.

Best Tips for New Parents

Despite all the hoopla surrounding pregnancy and childbirth, "there's not much attention to how this baby will impact you as an individual and as a couple, or the 157,250 hours of parenting that comes next," observes Pamela Jordan, R.N., associate professor of family and child nursing at the University of Washington and developer of the Becoming Parents Program, one of the nation's first parenting classes to focus on a couple's marriage, not just their child-rearing skills. Most couples, she notes, simply don't have ready-made skills to help them safeguard their marriages in the face of the overwhelming stresses of parenthood. These steps can help.

Talk about what's ahead. How will you split household chores and errands? Who's going to earn money, and who's going to stay home? What will you do for day care—and who will get baby Huey to and from the child-care center or sitter's house? Who's going to take the night shift? Who's going to wash the bottles and/or sterilize the breast pump every day? Who will shop, cook, clean, and let the dog out? How will Mom—or Dad, if the two of you have opted for a Mr. Mom arrangement—get daily breaks to recover sanity and get a hot shower? These seemingly small details can loom large in your relationship once baby makes three.

Break the silence about parenthood's downside. Yes, new babies are the cutest little bundles of joy in the universe. But caring for one (or multiples!) isn't all kisses and cuddles. Feeding, changing, bathing, and entertaining a little one 24/7 can stretch your physical, emotional, and mental resources beyond the breaking point. Find time to talk together about your frustrations, fatigue, and even moments of anger. Be specific, be supportive, and dare to be honest. These feelings are *normal*—not a sign that you're a bad parent. Admitting them, accepting each other's feelings, and working together to solve underlying problems (e.g., agreeing in advance that if one of you is overwhelmed, the other will step in and take care of the baby for a while) can keep you feeling saner—and closer.

Be frank about the losses as well as the gains. You've got the baby of your dreams, so why are you feeling so sad about your lost sex life or the elastic-waist jeans that have replaced your sleek, pre-baby size 8's? New parents often mourn silently and separately about all the ways a new baby has changed their lives, creating marital distance and even a sense of shame. For example, a new dad may feel that the new baby has taken his place as number one in his wife's affection. A new mom may feel sad or frustrated about the ways pregnancy, nursing, and the demands of child care have changed her body. These feelings are normal too. Sharing them will help you feel better and strengthen your bond as a couple.

Don't blame yourself or your spouse for marital blips. Experts say the first baby is the biggest challenge your marriage will ever face. You're both exhausted—and grappling with new identities, new expectations for yourself and your spouse, and virtually no time for personal pleasures. Your first fix-up step: Don't feel guilty or personally responsible for the downturn in marital bliss—and don't blame your spouse. It's a given. You're only responsible if you don't do anything to turn it around.

Understand the new definition of a good marriage. When Ohio State University researchers tested the co-parenting skills and marital happiness of 46 couples, they found a revealing connection: Partners who admired, supported, and agreed with each other's parenting styles when their children were babies had happier marriages $2^1/_2$ years later. Couples who criticized or even undermined each other's attempts to parent their young child were less happy with each other later on.

"It may seem that a good marriage relationship would protect a couple, but parenting can change a lot in a how husbands and wives relate to each other," says Sarah Schoppe-Sullivan, Ph.D., coauthor of the study and assistant professor of human development and family science at Ohio State University. "The issues you confront in parenting aren't typically the kind of issues you confronted before you had children. That can make a big difference in your relationship."

Dr. Schoppe-Sullivan says her study suggests that having a good marriage before a baby arrives isn't enough to ensure that your relationship will thrive afterward. New rules seem to settle in as partners judge each other's parenting abilities.

The fix? Admire everything you can about your partner's parenting. And discuss areas where you disagree, such as discipline, rewards versus punishment, bedtime, meals, and TV time.

Weave a support network. Comparing notes with other parents of children of the same age as your own can provide emotional support and a reassuring sense that no matter how busy or how crazy things are, it's probably just normal. You'll be far less likely to blame your marriage and much more likely to find solutions—and feel good about what you're doing together.

But finding support for dads as well as moms can be tricky: New moms have easier access to other women with babies or small children via mothers' groups and simply through meetings at the playground, in the pediatrician's office, or in activity groups for children. Dads typically have less access to other fathers. Look for couples' groups for new parents at your religious institution or make an effort to cultivate friendships with other couples, experts say. In one California study of new parents, those who met as a group with a psychologist to discuss child-rearing issues had no divorces, versus a 15 percent divorce rate over three years for parents who didn't meet with a support group.

Of course, you need more than emotional support. Gathering family, friends, or neighbors willing to help with meals, cleaning, errands, and child care is a lifesaver—and a marriage-saver, especially if your own families aren't available to help out. Experts say it's smart to put together a network before your baby is born, but it can help at any time. Say yes if someone offers to cook a meal you can pop into the freezer, do your grocery shopping, or watch the baby for an hour. List people who may be willing to help out in small or large ways. Don't be afraid to ask. Include one or two people whom you can count on as emergency contacts, day or night, to care for your baby in your home in case you reach a moment of desperation (it can happen to anyone!). Another option: Hire help as needed. A weekly housecleaner, a teenage mother's helper, a supermarket that will put together your grocery order for you can all take the pressure off you—and your marriage.

Expect the unexpected. No book, video, class, or tip from a friend can fully prepare the two of you for the enormous changes parenthood brings. Plan to give yourself some slack, to be surprised and even shocked. This too is normal. "I don't think you can ever say you're completely ready for it," says Kimberly Jordan, a Spartanburg, South Carolina, mother of two young boys. "We planned so much out, but you're still surprised in so many ways."

Best Tips for *All* Parents

Parenting challenges your marriage no matter how old your kids are. These expert strategies can bolster your marriage and help you put it first, whether your children are preschoolers or high school seniors.

Making Relaxation Time

Parenthood subtracts hours from your day and at the same time multiplies stress. Finding ways to relax as a couple—and individually—can improve your outlook and your marriage. De-stressing together can help the two of you reconnect. Here's how to choose a time and a place for daily relaxation, despite the demands of child-rearing. You'll need about 15 minutes for this planning exercise.

Step 1: Talk about the biggest stress points in your day—and appreciate each other's feelings.

Step 2: Identify times of day when you're together, such as the early morning, early evening, after dinner, or when baby's gone to sleep. Look for a half hour you could free up for a relaxing activity.

Step 3: Choose your stress-busting strategy. You might decide to put the baby into a sling or stroller for a short family walk, do yoga while your child plays nearby or naps, trade back massages, or even meditate after Junior goes to bed.

Step 4: Also look for ways you can give each other stress-stopping breaks during the week, such as an hour to swim, shop, socialize, or walk, or a free evening to join the bowling league, get together with your book group, or simply relax quietly at home.

Turn down the criticism; turn up the admiration. New parents often feel they're doing endless amounts of work that their partner's not giving them credit for—creating tension and resentment. Even if you feel you're the one doing the most, stop often to praise your spouse. Appreciation breeds appreciation. You'll also probably start noticing all the ways your spouse is helping out.

Kimberly and Gary Jordan realized that their styles didn't always mesh when it came to parenting their sons, Isaiah and Zachary. "I came from a single-parent family and was raised by my mother," Kimberly says. "My own brother is so much older than me that I never really saw how my mother handled parenting a boy. I'm very protective with the children, and I've had to learn to release some of that. And at times I thought Gary was being too strict, but the boys would really respond to his tone of voice when they didn't always respond to mine. I've had to learn to roll with the punches with boys, whether it was their interests in snakes and rocks and dirt or potty training." Adds Gary, "Kimberly's helped me to understand how to talk with the boys, to bring out what's going on inside, emotionally. We're close."

Go team, go! Many couples lose their essential sense of "we" when a child enters the picture—that sense of unity and oneness that is the hallmark of a happy couple. In its place, "me versus you" conflicts can take root. You each think you're right, the other's wrong, and, what's even more toxic, you're tempted to simply solve the dilemma du jour on your own. The baby won't sleep through the night? Your three-year-old shows no interest in graduating from pull-ups to underwear? Your toddler would rather guzzle milk than eat broccoli and peaches? You can't possibly get to work on time if you attend the morning tea for parents at the child-care center? You could try to solve these problems alone, but it's worth finding the time and energy to involve your spouse. Researchers say that couples who approach child-care issues with a positive attitude (less "Oh, no!"; more "We can solve this!") and as a team are more satisfied with their marriages than those who tackle problems as individuals.

Brush up on calm conflict resolution. Your marriage will benefit—and so will your kids. When researchers from the University of Notre Dame and Catholic University of America tracked 226 mothers and fathers and their 9- to-18-year-old children for three years, they found that parents whose conflicts revolved around personal insults, defensiveness, marital withdrawal, sadness, or fear had kids who displayed more depression, anxiety, and behavior problems. In a related study of 232 parents of kindergarteners, they found that parents who engaged in "dirty fighting" triggered emotional insecurity in their sons and daughters. "When the marital relationship is functioning well, it serves as a structurally sound bridge to support the child's exploration and relationships with others," says researcher Mark Cummings, Ph.D., a professor of psychology at Notre Dame. "When destructive marital conflict erodes the bridge, children may lack confidence and become hesitant to move forward or may be unable to find appropriate footing within themselves or in interaction with others. This study is a warning to strongly encourage parents to learn how to handle conflicts constructively for the sake of both their children and themselves."

The Case of the Disappearing Dad

Dads may be commonplace in delivery rooms, but most couples haven't mastered the art of weaving fathers into the everyday ups and downs of child-rearing, experts from the University of Washington and the University of California report. As a result, parenthood can open up an ever-widening emotional gap between partners. Men feel lonely; women feel overworked and underappreciated.

In a University of California, Berkeley, study, researchers tracked 100 couples from their first pregnancy through the child's first year of school. They found that the prime source of conflict during the first three years of parenthood was the division of labor. Couples expected a 50-50 split, but when women did most of the child care, their marital satisfaction fell further, faster, than men's. And moms were at higher risk for depression. "That's not a good recipe for parenting or for the couple's relationship," says psychologist Carolyn Pape Cowan, Ph.D., who, with her husband, documented these findings in *When Partners Become Parents: The Big Life Change for Couples*.

Meanwhile, University of Washington researchers found that when husbands are affectionate and understanding, new moms are happier. Understanding, they say, requires dads to play an active role in child care. "Mothers go through a profound change: The baby forces them to question the meaning and purpose of their lives," says researcher John Gottman, Ph.D. "About 85 percent of the mothers go through this, but only 35 percent of men do, and as a result they're getting less from the relationship."

What men can do: Take on more household responsibilities. Give Mom more significant breaks in the child-care routine—long enough to go out for lunch, shopping, to see a friend, or even get away overnight. Be ready to step in when your partner's tired or stressed. And find a way to help her enjoy a daily activity she's always loved, whether it's a half-hour walk, an hour to swim laps, or time to read, garden, or call friends, or simply do nothing at all.

What women can do: Hand the baby to Dad more often. University of Washington parenthood expert Pamela Jordan, Ph.D., found that men long for an important role in their new child's life—and women hold the key to inviting them into the inner circle.

Disagreement isn't the problem, Dr. Cummings says. It's how the two of you handle it. "If everyday issues are addressed in a productive or constructive way, children benefit," he notes. "I talked about the harm that destructive types of conflicts can cause. Some of the most destructive types of conflicts occur when partners withdraw from one another, stonewall, or show disrespect. Children are very sensitive to the emotional quality of the home."

Schedule a private powwow about discipline. Presenting a united front, whether it's about your 8-year-old's allotment of TV time or your 17-year-old's use of the family car, will help you avoid a major source of ongoing marital conflict. It will also help your kid feel more secure. If you find yourselves in disagreement about how to handle a child-rearing issue, work out a temporary rule and tell your child that you and your spouse need to consider the issue together before laying down the law. Then discuss the issue when you have a private, kid-free opportunity.

"We had to negotiate between ourselves about what the ground rules would be for our four children, especially when the eldest first became a teenager," says Susan Vogt of Covington, Kentucky. "We definitely had disagreements. One of us would think it was fine for our son to do something, and the other wouldn't. We weren't too far apart, but it still took a lot of debate to work things out, and the stakes got higher when they were teenagers. The positive part of working it out was that going with just one parent's viewpoint could make things too permissive or too disciplinarian. You need both opinions, melded together."

Mission 2

Settle Conflicts—And Connect as Friends

Three years after the birth of their first child, Nicolle and Zachary Johnson needed help—and found it in a classic New Jersey diner. The couple from Hightstown, New Jersey, had split their work schedules to spend more time with their new son. But the arrangement, combined with the stresses of a recent move into an old house in need of fixing up, the demands of a child who did not take naps, and the busyness of a two-career family strained their marriage almost to the breaking point. They wisely consulted a skilled marriage counselor and by chance fell into a routine of stopping for breakfast afterward at a nearby diner.

"The coffee was weak and the menu was uninspired, but food wasn't the point," Nicolle recalls. "We realized after a few months that just having time alone to talk, after we'd worked through whatever conflicts were happening, did wonders for our relationship. We felt close because we had found a time and place in marriage counseling to talk about whatever was bothering us—and then we had an hour of fun time at breakfast afterward. It was like dating again! We realized we still liked each other—and loved each other. After a while, we stopped counseling, but we kept going out to breakfast!"

The pair had stumbled upon a formula for closeness that's tailor-made for busy Cooperation stage couples. The plan: Find a time and place to deal with the conflicts and stresses in your lives. Once you've cleared the air, you can rediscover your friendship.

The beauty of this strategy: By setting aside a little bit of time on a regular basis for your partnership and your friendship, you stay connected despite the nonstop whirl of family, work, home, and financial responsibilities. Small problems get settled fast, before they can generate big tensions between the two of you. And you're freed from the fantasy that on some perfect day in the future, you'll turn your attention back to your relationship—just as soon as you've checked off every single item on your endless to-do list. Truth is, the Cooperation stage is like running a daily marathon. There are few natural breaks in the action; the only pauses are the ones you create for yourselves.

Think you can't afford to slow your pace so that the two of you can catch up with each other? You can't afford *not* to: "A lot of couples neglect the friendship in marriage, and it erodes over time because of such things as career demands and having children," notes Sybil Carrère, Ph.D., a University of Washington research psychologist who studies married couples. "When you neglect friendship, the positive perceptual filter you have about your partner begins to fail. People need to make time to nurture their marriage, just like they take time to work out, for the health of the relationship."

Here's how to make room for problem-solving and to be good to each other (opposite).

Feel Closer—Right Now

You don't have to add an extra hour to the day to find time for each other. These six fun strategies can keep you connected immediately.

Be funny. Kind-spirited humor can douse a hot argument, head off a fight, and turn the drudgery of household responsibilities and planning into something witty, smart, and hilarious. Stick with warm humor; sarcasm and snide remarks aren't relationship-builders.

Be kissy. Saluting your spouse with a longer-than-usual kiss in the morning, at the end of the workday, and before you say good night telegraphs the good news that you still find him or her irresistible and wonderful.

Be appreciative. We've said it before, and we'll say it again: You can never appreciate your spouse too much. He or she needs to hear how much you admire the way he or she gets the bills paid, organizes the kids' activities, made that tasty shrimp scampi last night, rewired the basement, cleared out three months' worth of old magazines from beside the couch, or got the trash out to the curb just in time for pickup.

Be surprising. Bring home an unexpected little gift. Get the car serviced before he changes the oil. Deliver breakfast in bed next Saturday (then pop a Looney Tunes DVD into the TV for the kids and lock your bedroom door).

Be historical. Play the songs you two loved best when you were courting. Bring out your wedding album after dinner and leaf through it together. Bring up the good times from your past—you'll both get a glow and feel lifted up as you remember your passion.

Be forgetful. Forgive your spouse's human shortcomings, then forget them. Nobody's perfect, especially under stress. (Hmmm ... could that include you?) Graciously overlooking flaws, errors, and gaffes sets a sweetly gracious tone for your relationship.

Create a friendship ritual. Find time in your day for uninterrupted connection time. It could be sharing a cup of coffee in bed before the kids are up, 15 minutes of quiet time together after dinner, or a walk before bed. Scheduling everyday time to chat will keep your marriage *off* autopilot and keep the two of you in touch, says University of Minnesota marriage expert Bill Doherty, Ph.D. The ground rules for this ritual: This isn't the time to review your to-do lists, gripe or wax poetic about the kids, or figure out logistics such as who's taking the kids to soccer on Saturday. This is friendship time. Do what you would do with a friend. Enjoy each other's company and find out what's happening in each other's heads and hearts. Admire what each other is doing. Share your feelings about your life. Have a few laughs while you are at it.

Got a gripe? Deal with it. Your husband's forgotten it was his turn to make dinner—and ordered take-out pizza for the second time this week. Your wife's borrowed your car and not refilled the gas tank, yet again. It might seem easier to let stuff like this slide by with just a raised eyebrow and a little, "Humph!" After all, you don't want to criticize your spouse in front of the kids, or you may simply have too little time together to waste it on conflict. But stuffing your reactions probably won't erase them. Instead, you may nurse a grudge until it grows up to be a big resentment.

We believe it's important to get this stuff out of the way if you are to maintain friendship within your marriage. The tools for doing this assertively, empathetically, and effectively are in the previous two chapters. The issue for the Cooperation stage: finding the time and the place to air conflict. We suggest either setting aside a few minutes during your daily reconnection ritual to ask each other about potential problems that have cropped up, or setting aside weekly time for a couple's meeting where you do business. Here you can bring up problems and synchronize your to-do lists for the week. When you've got a set time for dealing with issues, it keeps both of you from tossing little incendiary bombs during your reconnection time, your romantic moments, and the prelude to lovemaking. When you don't have a system for problem-solving, it's tempting to use any available couple time to get something off your chest.

The bonus: When you solve problems together, you feel like you're part of a winning team.

Mission 3

Invite Romance Back into Your Marriage

A funny thing happened when Kimberly and Gary Jordan made a conscious effort to put their marriage first. They felt happier. And their sons, Isaiah and Zachary, *loved* it. "I really had to get my bearings with this," says Kimberly. "I wasn't quite sure we'd gotten the balance of romance and family right until I saw our boys respond so well. It brings a sense of stability and joy. They're very interested in where we go for our dates and what we do together. When we haven't gone out for a while, they tell us it's time for a date! They love it when we kiss and hug too. And my youngest son says he cannot wait to get married! I think we've shown them a very positive view of marriage!"

The Jordans have regular dates several times each month. They take turns setting up their outings, often surprising each other with trips to unexpected restaurants. "We don't want to grow apart and then have to rediscover each other during the empty-nest years," notes Gary. "If we continue to nurture our marriage along the way, we'll be stronger for it and so will our children. They'll grow up seeing what a loving, committed, secure marriage looks like."

Keeping romance alive in the Cooperation stage takes a little planning and a lot of ingenuity. Kids, work, community activities, and the temptation to take your spouse for granted after all these years together work against the sense of the sparkly, I-only-have-eyes-for-you excitement you both need.

Schedule regular date nights. In the first year after their son Zachary was born, the Jordans went out just twice. "I was more vocal about wanting us to spend time alone together, but Kimberly couldn't seem to leave her little bitty baby," says Gary. Agrees Kimberly: "I was very focused on Zach the first year. He went everywhere with us. But by the time our second son, Isaiah, came along 20 months later, I was more relaxed. And I realized my husband was still there—and he needed my attention. I needed his too." Now the Jordans date several times a month, even if it's just a trip to a local bookstore for a cup of coffee, a chat, and time to browse the shelves.

"We need our time alone," Kimberly says. "It's a gift to be able to let my husband know he's still so special to me, that he's number one!"

Ask early and often: Do you feel loved? Don Howard and his wife, Teresa Titus-Howard, of Blue Springs, Missouri, randomly ask each other, "How's your love tank?" throughout the week. "We want to know if each other's love tank—how loved we feel—is full, half-full, or getting near empty," says Teresa. "And we do things for each other to keep our tanks filled up. It could be a card or an e-mail, a hug or a kiss. It's a quick, simple way to feel close and very, very happy with each other."

The Howards aren't shy about sharing when their tanks are dangerously low, either. "One day Teresa left me a voice mail at work, saying her love tank was pretty low. I got her a dozen roses and a card," Don says. "It's good that we do this—I could go on thinking things are just fine when my partner needs something. And I don't take it personally. Other things in her life could be draining her sense of being loved, such as the stresses of work or graduate school."

Do that thing you used to do. Revive the pastimes the two of you loved best during your courtship days or early marriage. Pull out the music you enjoyed together and dance in the dining room. Go canoeing. Play Scrabble. Wear your sexiest lingerie under a dress when you go out to dinner—and let him know. Eat Chinese food in bed. Have bread, cheese, wine, and kisses by the fire.

Got kids? Get a babysitter. A calm, mature, trustworthy babysitter is worth her—or his—weight in gold. And finding one can be as challenging as prospecting for that precious metal. Ask neighbors, friends, and relatives for leads or contact the local chapter of the American Red Cross for ways to find graduates of the organization's babysitting classes. Nervous? Test-drive a new sitter by letting her or him care for your child for an hour or two while you're nearby in the house or the yard. Branch out the next time to a short foray away from home. Find out what the local pay rate is; once you've got a solid relationship with a great sitter, reward them and cement your relationship by paying a bit more than the going rate. Even better than one babysitter: Develop a stable of two or three to boost your odds that one will be available when you need a date night.

Get away for the night ... or the weekend ... or the whole week. Quiet sex is okay. So is afternoon sex or sex when the kids are out for the

The 15-minute outing for new parents. While one parent gets baby settled for a nap or bed, the other makes tea or pours wine and puts together a plate of little snacks. Pick the most pleasant, straightened-up spot in your home or retreat to the deck or back-yard with the baby monitor. Sip, munch, cuddle, converse. You get bonus points for not talking about the baby.

The exhausted-on-Friday-night date. Take turns napping after dinner. Once the kids are in bed, pop in a video or DVD and snuggle together for a late night on the couch. Don't answer the phone or check e-mail.

The early-morning date for busy spouses. Buy frozen waffles or any other easy-to-prepare yet special breakfast food, such as frozen berries, heat-and-serve bacon, or your favorite sticky buns and special dark-roast coffee beans. Set the table the night before, then set your alarm clock for 45 minutes earlier than usual. Get up together and sneak downstairs for an early-morning tête-à-tête before the day gets away from you.

The blast-from-the-past anniversary date. Revive passion and romance with a return to an old courtship haunt. Have pizza in the park where you planned your wedding one hot summer day. Go back to the place where you got engaged—whether it was a beautiful, windswept beach or the fanciest restaurant in town. Take along a tape or CD of the songs you listened to at that time and play it in the car.

evening. But nothing beats unhurried, loud, whenever-you-want-it sex, followed by a cuddle, a nap, a shower, more lovemaking, a wonderful walk. For this luxury of uninterrupted time, you need to get away—or find a trusted friend, relative, or overnight camp so that the kids can get away. "We went to Florida last December for a running and walking marathon event," Don Howard says. "It was exciting and really helped our marriage. I was amazed by how that weekend, just two nights alone together, really recharged us."

Date at home. Don't overlook pockets of child-free time at home. Instead of watching TV, doing the dishes, or catching up on e-mail, use the hour or two while your baby naps or your older child is at school or an after-school event to get together with your spouse. Or take advantage of the natural shift in your teenager's sleep pattern (they go to bed later and wake up later). Enjoy a Saturday morning date while your teen snoozes.

What to do on your time together? Make love. Have lunch together and ban talk about the kids, the house, and the finances. After your kids go to sleep, slip out to the deck or patio for a glass of wine and a little stargazing. "One of the best things we devised when our children were at home was the home date," says Susan Vogt. "We'd strategize ways to be really awake after they all went to bed. Sometimes we'd take turns taking naps during the day so we wouldn't be too exhausted to make love. As our children grew older, the trick was figuring out how to have the whole date before they got home from their activities in the evening!"

Date on the cheap. Paying a babysitter $4 to $10 an hour can turn any date into a major financial outlay. Consider it a fixed expense and cut costs elsewhere by making the date inexpensive or even free. The Vogts took picnics to a local park and enjoyed the view of the lights coming on at dusk in Cincinnati, just across the Ohio River. They'd also surprise each other with romantic, offbeat dates; one of their most memorable involved driving to the local airport for an hour of people-watching. You could hike; bike; window-shop; swim at the local pool, lake, or beach; or even go sledding or skating in winter.

Expand your definition of a date. Dressing up for a candlelit dinner is just one option. The true criterion for a date? Anything that lets you focus on each other. That could be weeding the garden while you chat amiably, a weeklong trip to Bermuda, or 10 minutes over morning coffee. Research shows that while women tend to want more conversation with their mates, men would like to *do* something together. Find the happy medium: Combine the two in a fun activity that allows you the freedom to talk at the same time.

Keep it romantic and fun. Resist the urge to settle relationship issues or hash out problems with finances, kids, the house, or the cars. For busy Cooperation stage couples, it's tempting to use any scrap of free time together to tick something else off your endless to-do list. Don't do it! Remind yourself that this is sacred couple time. Laugh. Play. Find out how each of you is really doing emotionally. Connect. The to-do list can wait.

OLD THINK/NEW THINK
for the Cooperation stage

Believing any or all of these myths could throw your happy marriage off-course. Here's the truth about kids, work, and love.

Old think: Having kids will automatically bring us closer together.

New think: Couples need to communicate more than ever when baby makes three. While couples with children are slightly less likely to divorce than couples without children, the arrival of a new baby is more likely to bring stress and emotional distance than new happiness. Research shows that couples with a new baby are in as much distress as couples already in therapy for marriage problems. The cause: new responsibilities, no sleep, and huge new expectations for yourself and your partner.

Old think: Mom and Dad should never fight in front of the kids.

New think: It's okay for children to see their parents disagree—provided discussions are as calm and productive as possible. Seeing how grown-ups solve problems is a valuable lesson. Hearing them criticize each other, yell, or stomp out of the room isn't. Younger kids may even blame themselves. Resist the urge to escalate when the family's home.

Old think: Babies wreck your sex life.

New think: You may not have much, if any, sex for the first few months. But as you get more sleep (and for women, as your body heals and hormone levels readjust themselves), sex can make a comeback. One strategy: When the baby naps, make love. Setting aside time for intimacy can kick-start a stalled sex life.

Old think: Two-career couples are too stressed to enjoy life—or each other.

New think: Couples who are happy with their work tend to also have happy marriages. A recent Ball State University study of 107 women and men found that work didn't hurt the marriages of couples who were committed to their jobs and to their relationships. The extra income and work friendships added to their satisfaction.

Mission 4

De-Stress—And Make Love Again

Sex isn't everything. But when it's not going right—or barely going at all, as is the case for one in three American couples—there's trouble. You lose the wonderful, playful connection that inspires romance and intimacy, compassion and forgiveness, and that chases away sadness, loneliness, and conflict.

But sex is tricky for Cooperation stage couples. Pushed and pulled by the demands of children, jobs, maintaining a house or apartment, and meeting community and religious obligations, this treasure often falls to the very bottom of the priority list. In a national survey of 2,514 Americans, 88 percent said kids changed when and where they made love, 34 percent confessed that parenthood left them too tired for sex, and 30 percent confessed that sex was less romantic with kids in the next room. Meanwhile, intriguing new research suggests that women and men experience a natural drop in libido after the birth of a child; as levels of sexy hormones, including testosterone, diminish, levels of the cuddly hormone oxytocin rise. Before you know it, you've traded black lace underwear (or tasteful boxers) and satin sheets for a fleece sweat suit and flannel bed linens.

Sex is getting squeezed out like never before. More and more couples are in two-job families—and sometimes hold down more than one job apiece to stay afloat. Another trend pushing intimacy out the door: older parenthood and the fatigue that comes with raising a child in your late 30s, 40s, or 50s.

There's no time or energy for the spontaneous turn-ons that once led to hours of long, slow lovemaking. (As *Time* magazine quipped in a 2003 article about the trend toward no-sex marriage, "Sleep is the new sex!") If you've got kids, there's not enough privacy for a quickie on the couch. Couples find themselves in a sexual stalemate that's tough to break.

Don't give up. You can revive a thriving passion. In fact, you're in the best situation possible for cultivating a regular, satisfying sex life. When researchers dissected data from a national sex survey conducted in the mid-1990s, they found that Cooperation stage couples on average have *more* sex than singles. Amazingly, working parents with preschool children had more sex than single folks who worked fewer hours per week. And married women and men who worked a colossal 60 hours or more per week had 10 percent more sex than unmarried overworked folks. The reason? He or she is sitting across the dinner table from you: When you're married, you've got a steady, live-in intimacy partner.

Here's how to rekindle the flame.

Define a great sex life on your own terms. The happiest couples have sex on a regular basis, but nobody can define *regular* for you. And it's a moving target. Half of all 20-somethings in a University of Chicago survey said they made love at least twice a week—and an active 11 percent had sex at least four times. But among couples in their early 40s, just 30 percent made love even two times between Monday and Sunday. Nearly half had sex just a few times a month, but couples in this age group were the happiest—emotionally and physically—with sexual intimacy. What it means for you: There are no rules. The two of you should consider and discuss the frequency and type of sex that makes you happiest—whether it's three times a month or three times a week.

Chances are, each of you is comfortable with a different level of physical intimacy: One yearns for more; the other is happy with less. Talk about your needs and how you feel when you're at that just-right level of physical closeness. Try to reach a compromise and to find ways to build in extra intimacy so you're both happy. That could mean more cuddle time in addition to sex or simply seizing more of the thousands of daily opportunities to share a hug and a kiss.

Look sexier, feel sexier. It's easy to put off healthy eating, exercise, even haircuts. It's tempting to pull on those baggy old jeans after a long week and to fall into bed in a ragged T-shirt. We suggest making the effort to look attractive. Pull out your best jeans and most attractive tops. Dress up a little—for day and evening. Splurge on a sexy nightgown or lingerie. The payoff is as much for you as it is for your spouse: You'll feel sexier and more attractive when you look spiffy.

Take your libido for a walk. Forget weird health-food-store aphrodisiacs. Exercise is a safe, proven energy- and libido-booster. A stroll, a swim, or a trip to the gym can get you in the mood and help you enjoy sex more. In one University of Vermont study that followed midlife women for five years, those who exercised regularly reported more sexual satisfaction and stronger libidos than light exercisers or couch potatoes. And in a Harvard

University study, midlife men who ran for at least three hours per week had a 30 percent lower risk of impotence than nonexercisers. Other research suggests vigorous exercise, combined with a healthy diet and other healthy habits such as not smoking, can take 10 years off a man's sexual age. The link? Healthier blood vessels. The bonus: Physical activity helps you feel good about your body, and more likely to want to be close.

Close your bedroom door. Keep your bedroom private so that the two of you will associate it with intimacy and romance—not with late-night TV, catching up on work, or dogs and kids jumping on the bed. This "off-limits" designation also gently trains your household to respect this personal parental space—but we still recommend locking the door for your own peace of mind before lovemaking begins.

Enforce healthy bedtimes—for you and the kids. From grown-ups to toddlers, we're a sleep-deprived nation. Getting the children to bed at a decent hour not only ensures a happier morning routine (and a better school day), it also gives the two of you more quality time together when you're still awake enough to enjoy it.

Do anything—and everything—in a new way. Paint your bedroom a new color; go to an unusual restaurant you've never tried before; hit the roller rink instead of following the well-worn route to the local Cineplex on date night; read up on a delicious new sexual technique, then practice on your sweetie. Why? Novelty can trigger a rush of the feel-good neurotransmitter dopamine. That's the same love chemical that made you feel happy, energetic, and totally obsessed with your partner back in the Passion stage, says Rutgers University anthropologist Helen Fisher, Ph.D.

Add S_X to your day planner. We know. It doesn't sound erotic. Truth is, if you don't plan for sex, it won't happen very often. And it can be just as hot—or hotter—than the spontaneous version. A bonus to mapping out your sexual calendar: You'll find times other than 10 p.m. for getting together. Look for little pockets of time in the morning, at lunch, in the early afternoon. This can be especially helpful for the 23 percent of American couples who sleep in separate beds or even separate rooms due to snoring, kicking, or other sleep problems.

Make the first move. If you and your partner have reached a sexual stalemate, one of you will have to make a move. Often, one partner needs physical closeness in order to reconnect emotionally, while the other needs

Call the (Sex) Doctor!

You get your teeth checked, your car inspected, and your financial health reviewed on a regular basis—so why not consider expert help if you've hit a sexual roadblock? While most physical intimacy issues are easy to solve at home, these will benefit from professional assistance.

Hormonal swings during perimenopause (and menopause). Your gynecologist can test for changes in estrogen, progesterone, and other sex hormones that can affect libido, mood, weight, and even vaginal lubrication levels. These changes can begin as early as your mid-30s.

Health conditions that affect sexual performance or desire. Medical problems such as diabetes, high blood pressure, and hardening of the arteries can diminish the flow of blood to your genitals and erogenous zones and may even numb nerves. Depression, anxiety, and sleep disorders can zap desire.

Medications that dampen arousal and/or make orgasms elusive. Selective serotonin reuptake inhibitor (SSRI) antidepressants (including Paxil, Prozac, and Zoloft), oral contraceptives, and blood-pressure drugs can level your libido and create orgasm difficulties. Consult your doctor to see if a change in your prescription can make a difference.

Female sexual pain. Technically labeled dyspareunia or vaginismus, this sex-stopping discomfort may be the result of endometriosis, vaginal scarring, or problems with lubrication and flexibility of the vaginal walls. Gynecologists can suggest a number of treatments.

Sexual fears or phobias. Anxiety about erectile dysfunction (ED) or fears triggered by sexual trauma need understanding and sometimes medical help. For ED, talk with your doctor about diagnosis and treatment first; for fears and trauma, also contact a trained therapist. (Find one via the American Association of Sex Educators, Counselors, and Therapists (www.aasect.org) or the American Association of Marriage and Family Therapists (www.aamft.org).

Good at Stress, Bad at Love?

Stress—whether it's triggered by work, child care, outside activities, or the vagaries of life—evokes coping strategies that get us through the worst of times. But when these evolutionary responses to a bad situation become a habit, your marriage can suffer, note relationship experts Wayne and Mary Sotile, authors of the *Supercouple Syndrome: How Overworked Couples Can Beat Stress Together*. Here's how your stress coping style can backfire in your marriage.

- You go numb. You "soldier on" when there's lots to do or a big deadline looms, ignoring pleas from your mind, body, and spirit to stop. Numb's okay in an emergency, but when it becomes your default setting, the rest of your life suffers because you can't be vulnerable or empathetic. You're cut off from your own emotions.

- You work harder, faster. A big capacity for hard work's an asset in the office, but it can make you demanding and impatient at home. Your spouse may wind up feeling tense, hurt, and angry.

- You put on your game face. Being a competitor charges you up to do great things. But your spouse may feel he or she is "losing" if you're always "winning" in conversation at home.

- You see only your own needs. Stress triggers tunnel vision. You focus on only a few essentials: the work, and meeting your own needs so that you can get it done. Meanwhile, you ignore almost everything else. This is guaranteed not to be popular at home.

- You become the big cheese. Being a take-charge manager gets results—on the job. A good marriage isn't a boss-employee relationship, however. It's built on shared power.

- You multitask. Yes, doing two, three, or four things at once is efficient. But it can actually raise your stress level (and impair short-term memory, research suggests). Try it at home, and your partner may be left with the impression you don't think he or she is worthy of your undivided attention.

more emotional intimacy in order to find the path back to sexual intimacy. One way to close the distance: Combine the two. While sitting or lying with your spouse, gently hold or touch him or her. Talk about your positive feelings. (Save heavy-duty relationship issues for a time when you're not heading for intimacy.) See what happens.

Touch first. Don't wait to feel turned on to make love. Thanks to a busy lifestyle (who's got time for spontaneous sex?) and hormonal changes, Cooperation stage women and men need kissing and caressing to jump-start desire. That's a huge shift for most of us. One University of Chicago study found that 51 percent of 25- to 29-year-old men were aroused just watching their wives undress. But among men in their mid-40s, the number dropped to the 40 percent range. This change is natural and normal, experts say. Using touch—instead of overwhelming desire—as the prelude to lovemaking guarantees more and better sex. Waiting to feel turned on first, in contrast, guarantees sexual starvation.

Have a new sex talk. Your body's different now than it was when you married. So are your needs and desires. A little conversation can make all the difference. Be brave. Say what you want—and what you don't want. If your partner's ideas about what you like are obsolete, it's up to you to update him or her. Keep it upbeat by talking about what you like rather than what you dislike. And give positive reinforcement when he or she does something you adore.

Be as specific as possible. Your idea of doing something new might mean a new position; your spouse's might be to invite along something battery-powered. The authors of the 2,000-year-old *Kama Sutra*, the ancient Indian sex handbook, got it right when they said, "Though a man loves a girl ever so much, he never succeeds in winning her without a great deal of talking."

Save problem-solving for outside the bedroom. If something's not going well, wait for another, less vulnerable time to bring it up. Experts say the worst time to talk about serious sex problems is when you're trying to have sex. Emotions are too sensitive.

Dad: Unload the dishwasher—and put all the pots away! University of California sociologists who surveyed 3,563 parents and kids found that when dads did more housework, their wives found them more sexually attractive. Experts say women see the extra help as a sign of love.

stage 5

reunion

Suddenly the gallon of milk in the fridge lasts a week instead of two days. The phone doesn't ring as often; the CD player isn't cranked up to top volume. Nobody asks to wear your prettiest shoes, drive the family car, or borrow $20.

Your nest is empty. And the hectic Cooperation stage years have given way to a calm, companionable, if somewhat awkward quiet. You've reached the Reunion stage. You're here if the components of your marriage partnership that once occupied your thoughts nearly every waking minute—your careers, finances, home, community activities—have more or less settled into a routine. And the kids? They've vanished to college, to their own apartments, to travel the globe, or to live with a mate of their own. After 18 or more years of nonstop child-rearing, you're child-free.

For the first time in decades, you've got time and energy to lavish on your relationship. There are fewer distractions. It's just the two of you, free to reconnect and rediscover all the joys of your early married days, to reinvent your marriage and make it deeper, more satisfying.

You're wiser, kinder, more mature. It's the perfect time to refresh your marriage.

Just one small hitch. If you're like most of us, you've spent the last 20 years focused on everything *but* your relationship—conversations were quick exchanges on the sidelines at soccer games, dates were few and far between, and privacy at home was a rare commodity. It's understandable, normal, and even appropriate that your priorities strayed at times as you made other aspects of your partnership a reality.

The two of you have some catching up to do—and now's your big chance. The Reunion stage is the perfect opportunity to take stock of all your marital strengths and to draw on the trust, commitment, and comfort you've built through the years. It's time to talk about dreams for your marriage and for yourself. To work hard and be honest about upgrading your relationship, retooling it for the years ahead. To be vulnerable and willing to listen even when what you learn may make you feel sad or angry or defensive. And to invest in your future in ways that have nothing to do with retirement savings and financial planners—by using your marriage to safe-guard your health and your happiness.

This phase is like your honeymoon, only better. You're wiser, kinder, and emotionally mature. You have a wealth of shared experiences that make your relationship so much richer. And now you're on the doorstep of what some marriage experts call the second half of marriage. Come on in.

The Surprise Inside

Once, conventional wisdom said that this stage was full of grief (all those good-byes to the kids!). Not anymore. Don't make any assumptions about the 21st-century empty nest. Fresh research reveals what modern couples have known for a while: Not everyone grieves after saying good-bye to the kids. (And when there is grief, it affects Dad more often than Mom, some research suggests.) Sometimes you *wish* the kids would go—more and more, high school grads are staying home through the first years of college or work, leaving you in a limbo between parenthood and a sort of room-mate relationship with your semi-adult kids.

You may also be surprised to discover that the empty-nest calm you rel-ish is short-lived: Kids are more likely than ever before to move back home. At the same time, you may be called upon to take care of an elderly and/or ailing parent or relative.

Other surprises: Couples often enjoy the return of honeymoon-strength passion—at least for the first 6 to 18 months. But just as often, they're surprised by the sudden reemergence of old conflicts and old com-munication habits that had been submerged during the parenthood and partnership years. You may also discover that while you had plenty to dis-cuss about parenting, jobs, and finances, you're completely out of practice when it comes to focusing on each other in a friendly, romantic, pleasura-ble, and, yes, sexual way. You may even discover that once the busyness of the Cooperation era has subsided, the connection between the two of you is icy and distant.

Couples interviewed for *The 7 Stages of Marriage* say this stage has been anything but predictable.

"Our empty-nest years have been glorious! There's an 11-year differ-ence between our oldest son and youngest daughter, so seeing them leave was a long, long process. At times, we felt we'd *never* get the kids out of the house!" says Janell Atkinson of Georgetown, Texas. "We have total privacy. We also loved not having to sleep with one eye open wondering when our daughter would get home from a date. The transition from parenthood to empty-nesters wasn't traumatic, because we'd always maintained our own relationship. We expected our kids to grow up and leave, and we were ready to focus on each other again."

"At first I didn't feel comfortable that my husband, Ed, wanted more private time and space after our children left home," says Sylvia Robertson of Waleska, Georgia. "Ed had talked about taking one of the children's bedrooms as an office, and I would pout. Then last summer, he started spending some private time in another room at our vacation cabin. I realized I felt okay about it! Then I got curious and asked what he was doing. He said he was learning new computer skills and reading poetry. Well, I had an 'Aha!' moment. This was the expression of the guy who used to send me love letters long ago, the guy who knew all about the blue jays outside our bedroom window and the sunrises and sunsets. It was a part of Ed I hadn't thought about for years. For him, it was a rediscovery of part of himself he hadn't had time to cultivate for decades. It's been wonderful for both of us."

"In our marriage, we've encouraged each other to develop our own passions," says Andy Stewart of Durham, North Carolina. "I encouraged my wife, Peggy, to go back to school to become a social worker. And she encouraged me to quit my job as an industrial audiologist and become a health care chaplain. These seemed like crazy dreams, for adults to change jobs. We took risks. We felt scared. But we supported each other every step of the way. We had to tighten our belts and be careful with money for a while. But it's all worked out. We're happier at work, and that has produced more happiness for us as a couple. We care about each other's mental health, so taking these risks at a time when we could have just continued with our old jobs was worthwhile."

"Our empty-nest years have been like a second honeymoon. We absolutely love it! But sometimes we find ourselves settling into little ruts and routines," says Margaret Martin of Urbana, Illinois. "I sit in my chair working on a Sudoku game after dinner, and my husband, Rich, sits in his chair doing the crossword puzzle. It makes us laugh. We know you need vibrancy and vitality in marriage. You have to keep on discovering new things about each other. You have to have fun. And you have to shake things up. We did that recently when we moved from Virginia, where we'd lived for 25 years, to Illinois, where we knew no one, so that Rich could become a professor at the University of Illinois. It was a huge transition. But if you're just punching the clock in your marriage, you're going to have problems."

The First Stage of the Rest of Your Marriage

The Reunion stage can feel quite empty at first. If you've just launched your children into the adult world, you've ended an important era in your marriage. You're still parents, but it's no longer a 24/7 preoccupation. What's left to talk about? If you're at a point where your job, your home, your investments, and your civic involvements are all more or less running themselves, you may also find yourselves with little to say to each other.

Your first job? Don't panic.

"At this stage, a marriage must be held together from within—from the inner core of the relationship," says relationship expert Claudia Arp, who with her husband, David Arp, wrote the book *The Second Half of Marriage: Facing the Eight Challenges of the Empty-Nest Years*. Trouble is, you may not be communicating from your inner core to the inner core of your partner—or fully listening when your partner speaks to you. Why? The two of you may have developed very separate lives during your Cooperation stage years, simply to get everything accomplished for your busy household. You may have stopped dealing with conflicts effectively in order to maintain more peace and harmony. You may have fallen into communication routines that leave your innermost thoughts and feelings unspoken. You may even be holding on to old grudges, with resentments you'd like to air, or still have expectations and dreams you'd still like to see fulfilled. Your marriage may be on autopilot or running on parallel tracks.

Waking up next to a stranger, Arp says, is one reason that the divorce rate has grown in the past 20 years for couples married 30 years or more. Midlife is a time of crucial refocusing for couples; for your marriage to survive and thrive, it must move from the background and into the spotlight again—and stay there, even if you don't like what you see. This takes patience, gentleness, persistence, and courage. But too often, there are few guideposts to help. "In our focus on preparing newlyweds, we often forget how fast things can unravel at the other end of marriage," notes Diane Sollee, director of the Coalition for Marriage, Family, and Couples Education.

Fortunately, your shared past can serve you well. Decades spent together give you a treasure chest of memories, wisdom, stability, and humor. When University of California, Berkeley, psychologist Robert Levenson, Ph.D., tracked couples for 15 years, he found that in long marriages, partners develop a specialized emotional intelligence that allows them to read each other's feelings, use humor and affection to keep conflicts from getting too hot, and fall back on a strong sense of security that comes from having weathered all sorts of challenges together. These are your strengths, or what Dr. Levenson calls a "bank account of shared experiences." With them, you can get through just about anything together.

That's important, because there's a lot of marriage left to enjoy. Embracing the Reunion stage will set you up for decades of happiness to come. Your missions:

- **Shift your focus back to your marriage.** Renew all the reasons you're together—and celebrate all you've accomplished together. The first job of a Reunion stage couple is putting their marriage front and center—again. Experts warn that if you don't make an intentional effort to spend time together and use that time to focus on each other and your relationship (not on the kids or work or TV shows or home repairs!), your marriage could become cold, distant, or a thing of the past. Focusing on each other first is the reason why experts warn empty-nesters against jumping into lots of new activities, too fast.

- **Get off autopilot.** Now that you've made time for each other, what do you do? There are two parts to the answer. First, you'll need to release old resentments, forgive each other for human foibles of the past and present, and learn how to be intimate again. Why? Many people cope with the demands of the Cooperation stage by responding automatically, rather than authentically, to their partners. Now's your chance to override the shorthand, autopilot thoughts and reactions that got you through the crazy years and be your true selves together. Once you do that, you can also turn off the "autopilot" on how your spend your time together—and apart. Use your new freedom well! Part of this new beginning includes renewed sexuality. We'll show you the latest thinking about why natural, age-related hormonal changes you may be experiencing now needn't dim the physical fireworks, even if your libido and sexual response seem to have changed.

- **Welcome boomerang kids—without neglecting your marriage.** Adult children are moving back home with Mom and Dad in record numbers. Others are simply taking longer to leave home in the first place. Find out how to keep the momentum of your new marriage going while playing host to the boomerang "I'm back!" generation and to beloved hangers-on.

- **Use your marriage to create good health.** Your risks for heart disease, high blood pressure, stroke, diabetes, and some forms of cancer begin to rise in your 40s and 50s. Find out how to use your marriage to keep your health vibrant. Create physical and emotional well-being, together, that will pay marital dividends for decades to come.

Mission 1
Shift Your Focus Back to Your Marriage

"As long as there's a child in the house, there's a certain amount of intensity," observes Sylvia Robertson. "We had a constant stream of young folks through the house when our son and daughter were growing up. When they left home, it was very quiet. We loved our freedom! We traveled more. In fact, our children seemed more bothered by the change than we were. When we went away on trips, they would get antsy, wondering where we were and why we were doing this. It was a transition for them too."

Saying good-bye to your children and hello to your marriage in the Reunion stage can mean navigating tricky terrain. Shifting your focus isn't just a matter of making sure you're in the same place at the same time with your spouse. There's also an internal shift: paying more attention to what your spouse is really saying, offering more of your own thoughts and feelings, taking your relationship into consideration when making decisions, planning your future together. If your kids have served as a buffer between you and your spouse—allowing you to focus on parenthood rather than face issues in your marriage—the shift can be even more challenging. At the same time, the Reunion stage calls on you to craft a new relationship with your adult children.

"Your marriage has been child-centered, and one of the big challenges is to go from that child focus to a partner focus," points out marriage educator Claudia Arp. "Issues you think are long buried resurface. It's easy to be lonely and stressed out. An empty nest is a time of particular danger for an affair."

These expert tips can help you rebalance your relationships with your spouse and your kids and share the surprising range of feelings this transition can release.

Expect to grieve, or celebrate, or both. When kids move out, life *does* change dramatically—at first. Be mentally prepared for this. Empty-nest parents discover that in the first few months, sadness can surface at any moment. So can joy and relief. New research is revealing that the stereotypical grief-stricken empty-nester is often a myth. Couples in close marriages, partners who plan ahead for empty-nest years, and those who think about how they'll stay close to their grown children often have few regrets after saying good-bye.

If you are caught unawares by a wave of sadness, know that it's normal. The tiniest trigger could remind you of your faraway child: the box of laundry detergent that lasts so much longer now, the shopping cart that contains so much less, the Saturday morning with no high school soccer game to attend.

On the flip side, if you find yourself overjoyed and relaxed, well, that's normal too. University of Nebraska sociology professor Lynn White, Ph.D., has found that marital happiness often grows when the children leave home. For a year or two, many couples go through a second honeymoon. If your focus turns naturally and joyfully to your spouse in this way, seize this opportunity and enjoy it to the fullest.

Share your feelings. More surprising news: Often, the no-regrets empty-nester is Mom. Meanwhile, Dad may be feeling more empty-nest aftershocks. Talking about your experience can bring you closer.

Moms get a head start on processing empty-nest emotions and may be better prepared than dads when the big day arrives, says Wheaton College psychologist Helen M. DeVries, Ph.D. In a study of 147 mothers and 114 fathers of high school seniors, Dr. DeVries discovered that long before their children graduated, the women were planning what would come next for them, such as returning to college themselves or pursuing personal interests. Meanwhile, the dads talked little about getting ready for the empty nest and were less likely to see the change as a major watershed in their own lives. As a result, they weren't prepared for the emotional impact of a suddenly quiet, child-free house. And they had more regrets about not having been more involved in their children's lives before they left the nest. One key lesson from this research, then, is to start talking about the transition well in advance of your child's move-out date.

Look forward to a new relationship with your child. Seeing your kid set off bravely on the road to adulthood is scary. It can also bring a great sense of joy and pride for you and your spouse. Hidden benefit: Your relationship with your child may actually improve—a welcome change if the teen years brought tension to your parenting and to your relationship with your spouse. One study of young adult women and their mothers found that their relationships were so happy that the researcher called them "almost sappy." The reason: The day-to-day stresses of living together were gone. "People may worry about losing their child when the child leaves home," the study's authors noted. "In fact, they're going to have a more mature, more emotionally meaningful and deeper relationship with them to look forward to."

Free time? Hang out with your spouse. Resist the temptation to fill empty hours quickly with outside activities—even if you've always wanted to join the bowling league, dust off the French horn and toot with the local symphony, or make your mark as a volunteer. Leave empty time and space to spend simply getting to know your spouse again. Otherwise, you may be using your calendar as a tool for avoiding your spouse.

"Too often when the children leave the nest, couples move from a child-focused marriage to an activity-focused marriage," Claudia Arp says. "Community or church activities may now take up the time and energy formerly devoted to your children. Kids were buffers, and unfortunately, these activities may still be buffers to a mutual, partnership marriage."

Put yourselves on the calendar. Check the newspaper for movies, concerts, sporting events, flea markets, and other events the two of you both enjoy. Then make it a date. Sit down to at least one leisurely meal together each day. Find daily routines you can finally share without interruption. This will establish a new, closer rhythm in your relationship.

Recalibrate your conversation. Limit kid talk and look for new table topics in your own lives. Talk about *ideas* again—the books you are reading, current events, the last movie you saw together, fads, trends, what's hot or not at work. Talk like friends do, not like business partners. If there isn't frequent laughter, nodding, or smiling, it's a sign that your conversations are on autopilot, stuck in the businesslike exchanges of the Cooperation stage.

Be slow to judge, quick to appreciate. Chances are, you'll see your marriage in a new light—and you may not like everything you see. Maybe you don't have much to say to each other. Or you'll notice that you've both fallen into the habit of grumbling and complaining, or that you tend to

Rebuilding the "We"

Even if you built a strong sense of yourselves as a couple early in your marriage, chances are the stresses and demands of work, family, home, and community eroded your sense of "we." You can rebuild your unity by finding daily activities to share, by making time to check in with each other every day, and by taking your marriage into consideration when making plans. Not sure where to start? This exercise, which takes about 20 minutes, can help the two of you choose activities and times to be together.

"We" in Thought

Do This: Write down any plans you have for the upcoming week. Then note for each whether it will build, erode, or have no effect on your sense of togetherness.

Why: Often we don't consider the impact of our individual choices on our marriages. You may enjoy your Sunday morning golf ritual, but have you thought recently of the impact it has on your relationship? Will accepting overtime work mean you won't see each other for dinner anymore?

"We" in Word

Do This: Write down several "we" statements that describe your current likes, dislikes, and opinions as a couple.

Why: How often do you talk about yourselves as a united couple? Verbalizing shared values and opinions puts you into a "we" mind-set.

"We" in Deed

Do This: List activities you do daily or weekly that could be shared: cleaning, cooking, sorting mail, running errands, and so forth.

Why: Day-to-day tasks put us in routines that sometimes get in the way of closeness. Revamping routines so they include both spouses gives you time to connect and creates a sense of being a team.

---

spend your time doing separate activities all day, or that things just aren't sexy or exciting or even warm and fuzzy. Resist the urge to write your marriage or your spouse off. Don't give your mate a "shape up or else" ultimatum either. Instead, try to quietly appreciate the person who's shared his or her life with you for so long now. Think through his or her contributions and accomplishments: your kids, your home, your finances, the experiences you've shared, the trust and love he or she holds for you.

Anticipate disagreements. Your priorities are shifting now. Each of you may have a long list of projects and trips you've been itching to start once you had the time and the energy. You may also notice things about your spouse that didn't faze you in the past yet suddenly bother you. Realize that your focus has been elsewhere for the past 18 years or so. You're waking up to a new reality, and so is your partner. Don't take the bumps too seriously; do work on communication skills (and the next mission offers details).

Socialize with siblings and friends. Enjoying a social life as a couple is often a luxury for parents. Now you're free to reconnect with old acquaintances and family members. University of Indianapolis researchers who followed 66 moms and dads for 16 years found that when the kids left home, parents caught up with their own siblings. Strengthening family ties adds a new, warm dimension to your life.

Mission 2

Get Off Autopilot

Too often, marriage becomes comfortable, like an old pair of bedroom slippers. Cozy. Warm. Always there. And about as exciting as a bowl of oatmeal.

We're all for loyalty and contentment, but emotional and physical intimacy suffers when married life becomes too routine. When marriage is on autopilot, you are just going through the motions. The real you isn't there—so you stop connecting with who your spouse really is. And you end up as two comfortable people rubbing along side by side, at best a little lonely and a little grumpy, at worst cold and distant.

It's time to break out of the old routine. In the first mission, we asked you to shift your attitude about your marriage to a healthier, more unified place.

But the Reunion stage isn't merely about getting back to where you were prior to having children; rather, it is a perfect opportunity to *reinvent* your marriage for the better. After all, you've got the time, the place, and the energy. You're probably also more aware of your marriage now than you've been in years—a clarity brought to you by exiting children and a lessening of the responsibilities that kept you running 24/7 during the Cooperation stage.

Your first step? Don't ever assume you know all there is to know about your spouse. He or she always has the capacity to surprise you, as Margaret Martin has learned. "We believe we're never too old or married too long to learn something new about each other," she says. "Once, years into our marriage, my husband, Rich, found out that I know the Greek alphabet. He was really surprised. It's a small thing, but it illustrates my point. I also believe you're never at the point where you can say, 'This is as good as it gets.' It can always be better!"

Here's how to bust out of the old routine and reclaim a marriage that's full of surprises, freshness, and the potential for always getting better.

Polish your communication skills. At last! The two of you can get through a discussion or an argument without interruption. You're free to say what you want to say and what you need to say. And with more time and fewer preoccupations, you're also free to listen more deeply to your partner's point of view.

The stage is set for great communication. You may find, however, that your talents have grown rusty thanks to years of speaking in shorthand.

Now's the perfect time to unlearn dead-end habits such as criticizing, blaming, attacking, getting defensive, or withdrawing into an emotional shell. The job's more challenging than it was early in your marriage, simply because the two of you have developed your own "dance" over the years. You may scarcely be aware of it, or see only your partner's steps. But if the two of you aren't solving problems effectively, if you're arguing, or if you're not speaking freely about your thoughts and feelings and listening with acceptance and empathy, it's time to learn the steps again. The basics:

- Use "I" statements. Talk about your own feelings rather than what you think your partner is doing or thinking. And focus on what you want rather than what you don't want. Your partner will have a much clearer understanding of your desires and of what you'd like him or her to do.

The Long, Hot Summer of Love

If newlywed sex is like a fast and furious salsa, lovemaking in the Reunion stage is a slow, steamy tango. Subtle, normal mind-body shifts ease the tempo and increase the need for patience and understanding. But this careful cultivation of the erotic can bring your lovemaking to new heights, experts say.

What's happening to you at this stage? Nearly a third of women may have low levels of androgens—sex hormones, including testosterone, that the female body naturally produces in small quantities. Androgens fuel your sex drive, say researchers from Harvard Medical School.

Men's sexual biochemistry shifts too. Testosterone, the hormone that drives male libido, peaks between 20 and 30 and then gradually diminishes. The impact: In a study of 77 healthy married guys ages 45 to 74, researchers at New York City's Mount Sinai School of Medicine confirmed that when testosterone drops, so do sexual interest, desire, and activity. Meanwhile, physical changes that come with age—including the buildup of plaque in artery walls—reduces blood flow, leading to less-firm erections. The good news: Despite all these changes, the New York study didn't find any drop in sexual satisfaction with age. Here's how to adjust.

Men: Slow down the pace. Sex won't be fast and furious, but who cares? Men take longer to reach orgasm as they age, thanks to reductions in blood flow and muscle tone. In your 20s, it took 5 minutes. Now it could take 20. This can be a very happy coincidence for a woman whose arousal lasts 15, 20, or 30 minutes before her orgasm happens. Your timing's more in sync!

Women: Take the lead. Hormonal changes in their 30s and 40s leave women with more hard-charging testosterone and less estrogen, while a man's hormonal balance shifts in the opposite direction. The result: A woman may feel more assertive, and a man may feel perfectly fine about following her lead.

Make necessary mental and physical adjustments. In addition to the above changes, men's and women's orgasms may be less forceful now, thanks to hormonal shifts and a drop in blood flow. Put it all together, and you can see why it's crucial to adjust your expectations regarding the physical nature of sex at this stage.

Experiment with new positions and new products. Achy backs and fragile knees may make some of your favorite honeymoon-era positions tougher to sustain. So try something else. Keep pillows and blankets handy for support. Performing flexibility exercises such as yoga or stretches regularly can help too.

Women: Better prepare yourselves for sex. If sex hurts due to lack of sufficient lubrication, investigate personal lubricants at the drugstore. Hormonal changes can make vaginal tissues thinner, drier, and slower to produce moisture. Teach yourself Kegels, the exercises that tighten your pubococcygeus (PC) muscle. The PC contracts during orgasm and supports sex organs. Gently squeezing, holding, and releasing it several times daily builds strength and will increase sexual pleasure.

- Listen deeply. Show that you understand and accept your partner's thoughts and feelings. Rush to empathize, not to point out flaws or minimize emotions. Show you're truly on the same team. Listen first for feelings, then for information (ask yourself what's true or makes sense in what your spouse is saying). This strategy lets you focus on your partner's message and not get caught up in blame or criticism that may come flying in your direction.

- Resolve conflicts amicably with this three-step technique: First, each of you describes the problem in a sentence or two. Second, look at all your deeper concerns about the issue as well as your partner's concerns. Third, explore a wide variety of solutions that address your deeper concerns as well as the problem at hand. Experts say that when you take these core concerns into consideration, you can find a solution that lets both partners "win."

For more details on assertive speaking and empathetic listening, turn to the Realization stage chapter. For a thorough description of win-win problem solving, see the Rebellion stage chapter.

Stop making assumptions. Yes, you know exactly how your spouse likes her coffee or his hamburger. But you don't know everything about him or her. Don't assume you do—and you might be pleasantly surprised!

Find a fun joint project. You've shared a grand project—child-rearing—for nearly two decades. Why not find a new one that excites you both? "A joint project that interests both spouses is fun. And fun bonds people together," notes marriage therapist Sunny Shulkin, Ph.D., of Philadelphia. "One couple I know went out and rented an RV and made a project of driving all over the country. Each stopped and chose their favorite CDs of music that reflected something about the region they were visiting. They would play them and sing songs together. When they returned home at the end of the summer, they were well connected." The bonding time also helped them happily accept that each also needed some time and space to pursue personal passions.

Rediscover old pleasures. Go canoeing again. Travel. Revive your old interest in hiking or tennis or country line dancing. Do what you used to do. As one empty-nest husband interviewed for this book confided, "As a newlywed, I rebelled against convention by not wearing any pajamas in bed. Now I can do that again. Naked is a good thing. I love my wife's body, and I'm comfortable with mine—naked is something that's really enjoyable in the empty nest! We used to have a code word for being intimate: 'It's nice to get naked.' We're saying that a lot more these days!"

See your partner as you did when you said "I do." Think you're not attracted to your mate anymore? Rekindle passion by jolting your view of him or her out of the everyday and into the extraordinary. You've probably enjoyed this buzz of excitement if you've reunited after a few days apart. Here's how to get it without leaving town: Get a glimpse of your spouse in a public setting by planning to meet before a date at his or her job or by arriving separately at a bar, restaurant, or event. Spend a few minutes watching your spouse before you meet up; appreciate his or her good qualities. You'll probably feel a thrilling tingle when you realize, I've got a date with this man or woman!

Get a fresh perspective on your own life. Finding the time and energy to pursue a personal interest—whether it's learning a new language or how to solder plumbing, spiritual growth or windsurfing—can jolt you out of a comfortable personal rut. And in the view of Washington, D.C., psychotherapist Douglas LaBier, Ph.D., it can also bring new clarity and excitement to your marriage. Dr. LaBier calls this "constructive disengagement"—a seemingly paradoxical practice of pulling away from your marriage ever so slightly for the sake of personal growth and to create a more vibrant connection with your spouse. Create a goal and a plan for meeting it; breaking old routines also breaks old ways of seeing and reacting to your partner. The happiness and excitement of finding something new in your own life can also bring new energy and passion into your marriage.

MARRIAGE MAGIC
Switch Household Jobs

Try performing each other's usual household responsibilities for a week to gain a new appreciation for your spouse's contributions to your marriage. You may discover new chores that you enjoy too. After the week's done, sit down and discuss what you've learned. Do you want to trade any jobs? Is one of you doing the lion's share of the work? Or are you happy to return to your familiar tasks?

Let go of the past. Reunion stage couples often see each other through the sad and bitter filter of years' worth of regrets, resentments, and unfulfilled dreams. Experts say one of the keys to making the second half of marriage happy is letting go of old grudges and moving on. Let history be history, say marriage experts Claudia and David Arp. A second chance needs a clean slate. Their advice: Write down your grievances privately, then decide which you can live with, which you can fix on your own, which are worth mentioning to your mate, and which truly stand in the way of marital happiness. Forgive what you can, fix what you can, and have one discussion with your mate about issues you wish were different, then hold on only to the biggest, most important matters—such as growing closer emotionally and physically and deepening appreciation and respect.

Look on the sunny side. You've forgiven. Now what? Make a mental list of all your spouse's positive characteristics, from the way she makes the morning coffee to her kindness, from his proven commitment to your marriage to his wacky, unstoppable sense of humor.

Use conflict to learn about yourself and each other. Disagreements aren't disasters. Couples interviewed for this book, as well as experts, say that when you feel secure in your relationship, you can use problem-solving clashes to learn more about who you both really are. "Differences aren't a problem. They're the truth about us," says Peggy Kinney of Durham, North Carolina. "When we disagree and can really be vulnerable and accept what the other one is saying, we build more trust." Adds her husband, Andy Stewart, "Disagreements let us see and accept each other's differences. We share what's real about us and develop greater sympathy for each other as thinking, feeling, wanting, sensing human beings. And you learn to accept these things in yourself more easily too."

The Reunion stage is the perfect time to be this brave. You've been together for decades. You know that a difference of opinion won't sink your relationship or even your partner's affection for you. It's easier to be honest when you know that your safety net has weathered bigger storms in the past!

Look ahead to retirement. Setting a new course in the Reunion stage will help prepare you for the challenges of retirement and late-life marriage—such as the loss of your 9-to-5 workplace identity and the gaining of lots more time together. Ed and Sylvia Robertson are using the empty-nest years to practice for retirement. "We've stopped teaching summer school so

Unpack Old Marital Baggage

Old grudges, resentments, unfulfilled dreams ,and still-tender hurts often resurface during the Reunion stage. It's time to jettison the stuff that's been getting in the way. You also want to keep the *good* stuff—everything you love and appreciate about your spouse and your marriage. Use this worksheet (or a separate sheet of paper) to help you decide what to keep, what to toss. (Tip: When thinking about positives and negatives, consider these realms of marriage: emotional, intellectual, physical, social, and spiritual.)

Keep

Positive things about me, my spouse, and our marriage

_____

_____

_____

_____

_____

_____

_____

Toss

Negative thoughts about me, my spouse, and our marriage that I am better off without

_____

_____

_____

_____

_____

_____

_____

that we can travel more, spend more time together, and get used to living on a bit less money," Ed says. "We traveled some with the kids, but we didn't have quite the same freedom. There were too many schedules in the house back then. We're planning to write a marriage column for a newspaper after retirement and possibly a book, so we're getting started on that to see how we work together and to refocus away from our academic careers. We're working on our transition now, so that we don't go *whack!* and hit retirement unprepared six years from now. There will always be surprises, of course, but you do what you can."

Mission 3

Welcome Boomerang Kids— Without Neglecting Your Marriage

When Nancy and Carl Terry's son moved back into their Newport News, Virginia, home to attend a local college, his return sent new ripples through their quiet, content Reunion stage marriage. "I don't even remember any difficult adjustment when he first left," says Nancy. "It was more of an adjustment when he returned. He's a pretty mature, respectful young man. He came back for a limited time, for a definite purpose. And we didn't need many ground rules. But having a third person back in the house was a real adjustment for Carl and me. We were used to doing things on our own."

There was a bit more clutter in the house, and the Terrys found their routine was altered. "There needed to be more communicating: 'What are your plans?' 'Will you be home this evening?' He was pretty involved with school and friends, and it was a positive experience for all of us. But it was definitely a new wrinkle," Nancy recalls.

In households across America, "boomerang kids" are returning home after college in increasing numbers. Still more are delaying their first flight from the nest—living at home for the first year or two of college or while they try out their first post–high school jobs. As of the 2000 Census, roughly 4 million kids between the ages of 25 and 34 were living at their parents' homes in the United States. A more current estimate is that one-fourth of children between the ages of 18 and 34 live with their parents. Interestingly, more boys than girls are coming back home.

(continued on page 216)

Parallel Lives—or Reunited?

It's easy to think that the day your youngest child moves out of your home is the exact moment you enter the Reunion stage. But of course, it isn't. As with all of the stages of marriage, you transition slowly and imperceptibly from the intense business partnership of the Cooperation stage to the closer, easier relationship that should be the Reunion stage. Use this quiz to see whether you have already started to make a successful transition to what could be one of the best periods of marriage. Answer each question "True" or "False."

1. I've been thinking about ways I'd like our marriage to be better—and starting to talk with my spouse about them.

2. Our conversations primarily revolve around our children.

3. We're making an effort to make love more often now that our privacy has increased.

4. I would rather keep the peace than bring up a subject that I know might upset my partner or cause an argument.

5. When we go out together for a date or an outing, we look for activities and destinations that intrigue both of us.

6. We haven't talked about our hopes and dreams for the future for a very long time.

7. We've spoken openly together about how our relationship feels different than it used to, now that life is less hectic.

8. I enjoy more fun and closeness with my friends than with my spouse.

9. We've revived a hobby or interest we share or have come up with a new one that we can participate in together.

10. I find myself lonely or bored on some days.

11. We frequently eat breakfast and/or dinner together.

12. One of us makes most of the decisions in our marriage.

13 We're paying more attention to our health, and we enjoy cooking healthy meals together and/or getting exercise together, such as walking.

14 We sometimes go as long as an hour in the same room without speaking to each other.

Your Score

Tally your true and false answers as follows:

Even-numbered questions   True_____   False _____

Odd-numbered questions   True _____   False _____

If you answered "True" more often to the odd-numbered questions and "False" more often to the even-numbered questions, congratulations! You're summoning your courage, sense of adventure, and natural curiosity to move closer to your partner now. Keep it up! And if your partner is more reticent or more comfortable with old routines, draw him or her out by asking about feelings, reactions, likes and dislikes, and hopes and dreams. Help create a true meeting of your minds and hearts.

If you answered "False" more often to the odd-numbered questions and "True" more often to the even-numbered questions, your lives are moving on parallel tracks, or one of you has taken over the agenda of the Reunion stage. You need to communicate better and work harder at reconnecting. Follow the tips in the first two missions. But start small, with a small change that's easy for the two of you to make together, such as talking about something other than the kids (have some other topics ready as alternatives) or spending Saturday doing something together that you both like. Laugh, loosen up, feel free to be yourself.

House Rules for Boomerang Kids

Living with an adult child is far easier than living with a teenager—or is it? If you find yourself sticking with old parent-child roles, such as doing their laundry, preparing their meals, lending them your car, or paying their bills, it's time to take action and establish house rules. Use these open-ended questions as a starting point for a talk with your partner about what you will expect from your son or daughter. Then schedule a meeting with your offspring to hammer out the details. Everyone will benefit.

1. How should our grown child contribute financially to the household with rent and/or grocery money? If he or she has large loans to pay off, are we willing to accept a small monthly "donation," provided the rest is used to pay down the loan?

2. What house and yard jobs will become our child's responsibility? How often and how thoroughly do we expect the jobs to be done? What level of daily tidiness do we expect our child to help maintain in our home?

3. What personal care will our child assume responsibility for? Laundry? Packing a lunch? Making breakfast?

4. What rules will we set about socializing in the house? How late can guests stay? How loud can the music be? How do we feel about our child's romantic partner staying over?

Grown kids living at home is also a global phenomenon. In Italy, they're called *mammoni*, or "mama's boys." The Japanese call their not-so-prodigal kids *parasaito shinguru*, or "parasite singles." And in the United Kingdom, they go by the acronym KIPPERS, short for "kids in parents' pockets eroding retirement savings."

What's behind this important cultural shift? The trend toward later marriage is one factor. Boomerang numbers also rise whenever the economy falters; kids are more likely to come home when they can't find jobs, don't make enough to pay for apartments, or are saddled with education or credit card debt.

Most parents are happy to oblige; it's for their children, after all. Yet they do see the trade-offs. In one national survey, a majority of parents hosting grown kids said the arrangement worked out well. But they also confessed that they'd enjoy more privacy and better finances if the kids weren't there. And at a deeper level, having your kids return to the roost can freeze your evolving marriage just when you most need to focus your time and energy on each other. Another danger: If one or both of you fall back into old parental roles, your marriage could regress to the child-focused years instead of moving forward into independence, new roles, new activities, and new levels of marital connection.

When kids come home, the trick is to get on with this new life as much as possible instead of dropping everything to do an extra load of laundry or make a special supermarket trip to stock up on his favorite breakfast cereal and beer. These steps can help your marriage—and your child—keep moving toward independence.

Make 'em pay. Financial advisors are unanimous: Parents should charge their adult children rent—and require that they chip in for their fair share of the food bill, the phone bill, cable TV fees, and utilities. Kids should also expect to pay their own bills—for gas, meals out, car loans, credit card debt, car insurance, and cell phones, for example. They're grown-ups now, after all, and should know that if they incur expenses, they are responsible for paying them.

Why? You want to foster healthy independence. You also want to guard your own preretirement earnings. A recent University of Michigan survey of 6,000 young adults estimates that parents give grown kids an average of $38,000 in cash—for cars, repayment of student loans and credit card debt, etc.—between ages 18 and 34. That's a large number. Keeping the parental piggy bank shut can reduce tensions between you and your spouse and between the two of you and your not-so-prodigal child.

Share the load. You're not the maid, chauffeur, dog-walker, or laundress. A returning child should expect to shoulder one-third of the household chores. This too encourages independence and responsibility and reduces another source of potential friction in your once-quiet home.

Set ground rules. Yes, adults come and go as they please. But they don't wake up respected housemates with parties, unexpected guests, loud music, and the aroma of frying burgers at 3 a.m. Don't try to set a curfew for your grown child—the last thing you want to do is act like the parents of a teenager again. Do lay out house rules early on and expect your new housemate to comply. Make sure you and your spouse agree and will back each other up. Don't let your kid drive a wedge into your marriage by pitting the two of you against each other.

Resist the urge to regress. Babying your grown-up offspring isn't good for you or your child. He or she will either resent it or get a bit too comfortable. You'll be putting your child back in the center of your life, just when the spotlight should shift to your marriage. The same University of Michigan survey found that parents of grown kids between ages 18 and 34 devoted over 3,800 hours to helping them. That's what families are for, but don't let extracurricular parenting pull you away from your marriage partner. Avoid time-warp mothering or fathering.

Be your new self. Instead of waiting up for Junior on Saturday night, go ahead with that planned date with your spouse. Install your new houseguest in the bedroom farthest from your own so that you'll have maximum privacy for conversations, cuddles, and lovemaking. Move ahead with plans for new joint projects with your mate and for new personal plans for your free time. If your marriage is changing, don't hide it from your returning child: Kiss in front of him or her, have emotionally frank conversations, meet for dinner before heading home from work, invite friends over, and tactfully let your child know it's your private social time.

Set a move-out date. In the National Survey of Families and Households, most parents with grown kids at home said they expected their houseguests to stick around for one to three years. But many admitted that their children had no definite plans to move out. We say don't beat around the bush. Set a time limit on the stay and encourage him or her to find that great job, save the money for the real estate down payment, or pay off the mondo student loan so that independence day can be a reality.

Mission 4

Use Your Marriage to Create Good Health

A good marriage may be better than a gym membership. A growing body of research shows that married couples live longer, healthier lives than their single counterparts. "Marriage is sort of like a life preserver or a seat belt," University of Chicago sociologist Linda Waite, Ph.D., author of

FIVE PERFECT DATES
for the Reunion stage

Blasts from the past. What did you enjoy doing together as newlyweds that you haven't had time for in the past few years (or decades)? Reviving activities you once loved can make the spark of love burn brighter.

The long weekend. At last! You've got the luxury of time again! Celebrate with a weekend-long date—go to a bed-and-breakfast in an interesting region of your state, spend Saturday and Sunday at an event you both enjoy, or share an activity you cherish together. Or simply schedule a series of fun activities that will last for more than a day. It's a mini-vacation, designed for relaxation and getting reacquainted!

The bedroom makeover. Let home-decor magazines and TV shows inspire you, then head out to the local home store for paint. Shop flea markets and garage sales or your favorite store for a comforter cover, curtains, or other accents to change the look of your room. Your bedroom is your relationship's inner sanctum. Mark this important passage by making this important space reflect your hopes, dreams, and feelings about your marriage.

Look up old friends. Socializing's easier when couples aren't juggling their own calendar and their kids' schedules. Check in with friends you don't see often enough and plan good times together. The Reunion stage is the perfect opportunity to reunite your social circle!

The new dream. Make it a point to go somewhere you've never gone before—whether it's the Bahamas for a week, a big city for a day, the mountains or the beach for a weekend, or Rome for a month. Mark your independence with an adventure!

The Case for Marriage, told the *New York Times*. "We can put it in exactly the same category as eating a good diet, getting exercise, and not smoking."

Truth is, marriage helps health most when couples imitate each other's healthy habits. When Brigham Young University researchers checked up on 4,746 married couples ages 51 to 61, they found that couples mirror each other's health status: A man in his early 50s in excellent health had a very low chance of having a wife in fair or poor health. But if the man's health was poorer, the chance of his wife being in fair or poor health increased. Why? Couples live in the same environments when it comes to food, exercise, and stress reduction. They also share emotional stresses.

Healthy living is a win-win choice for married couples. You not only improve your individual health and longevity, you also create wonderful opportunities to do things together. Plus, Reunion stage couples have the extra time, energy, and motivation to bolster their physical and mental health to prevent problems down the road.

Here's how to use your relationship to give your physical well-being a big boost:

Work out together. Kimberly and Gary Jordan of Spartanburg, South Carolina, find time for a daily three-mile walk in their neighborhood. They unwind, catch up with each other, and burn nearly 300 calories each per outing. "It's such a blessing, having time to talk and walk together outdoors and unwind," Kimberly says.

Another often-overlooked couple's workout you shouldn't miss: Sex. Making love gets the heart pumping and burns about 50 calories (hey, it's not a marathon, but it will burn off an Oreo!). But that's not all. Fun in bed triggers the release of feel-good endorphins, natural opiates, and the cuddle hormone oxytocin. It increases blood flow to the brain, boosts immunity (according to some studies), and improves mental health.

Lose weight together. Ed and Sylvia Robertson recently completed a year's membership in Weight Watchers and shed a combined 112 pounds. "One of the goals we kept setting for ourselves was better health and more exercise, but we just kept flopping at it," Sylvia says. "We needed a program we could do together. We were also concerned about prediabetes." Adds Ed, "We've had that gradual middle-aged creep. Now, we're skinny again! I went from a size 49 waist to a 32! We said to ourselves that our health is important, that our bodies are worth all this effort to eat right and get more exercise."

Eat like a woman. Men reap nutritional benefits when they marry, while women's diets slide after they say "I do," concluded a recent review of 23 studies on the health consequences of coupledom. "A man's diet tends to become healthier when he starts cohabiting with a female partner, and her influence has a long-term positive impact. In contrast, women eat more unhealthy foods and tend to put on weight when they move in with a male partner," says lead researcher Amelia Lake, Ph.D., a postdoctoral fellow at Newcastle University's Human Nutrition Research Centre in Great Britain. One Australian study of 3,000 couples found that men ate more fat, salt, and sugar before moving in with a partner and less afterward—as women took over more of the grocery shopping and food prep. Meanwhile, women's intakes of fat and calories went up, as did their weights. Other research cited by Dr. Lake has found that by her 10th anniversary, a married woman is likely to have put on 19 pounds.

Bottom line? Women: Follow your healthy food instincts. Men: Follow her lead.

Exercise like a man. A new University of Pittsburgh School of Health and Rehabilitation Sciences study of 3,075 women and men ages 70 to 79 found that highly active men were three times more likely to have highly active wives. If your guy golfs, plays tennis, runs, walks, is in a basketball league, or enjoys other physical activities, go along. Play or participate if you can, or use the time to follow your own exercise routine.

Argue amicably—or practice more stress reduction. A growing stack of research links unhappy marriages with unfortunate health consequences. A study of 105 middle-aged British civil service workers found that women and men with more marital worries had higher levels of the stress hormone cortisol as well as higher levels of stress and high blood pressure—factors that raise risk for heart attack and stroke. Marital tensions have also been connected with depression, slower wound healing, more gum disease, and higher risk for stomach ulcers.

Take a vacation. University of Pittsburgh psychiatry researchers who tracked the health of 12,000 men with heart problems for nine years found that guys who took annual vacations had a lower risk of death than those who skipped these much-needed breaks. Vacations may protect health by cutting stress, by putting you in a relaxing setting with family and friends, and by giving you an opportunity to get more exercise.

Take responsibility for your health. Traditionally, a stay-at-home wife guarded marital health by cooking healthy meals and planning stress-relieving, mood-boosting activities. She probably also nagged her guy to eat his broccoli, go to bed earlier, get more sleep, and take his vitamins. An intriguing University of Chicago study found that in two-career couples, a husband's odds for good health drop 25 percent if his wife works full-time. The moral? Husbands and wives should take charge of their health, notes lead study author Ross Stolzenberg, Ph.D. Working as a team yields better results than designating one partner as head coach and nag.

Learn all you can. Healthy living can seem like a moving target: One day fat's all bad; the next, it's a miracle weight-loss food. One day, walking fast is all the rage; the next, a slow routine is touted by yet another expert as the best way to burn fat. What's right? The answer: It usually doesn't matter. The basics of healthy living are undeniable: getting up and moving most days for 30 minutes or more; eating modest portions at meals; choosing fruits, vegetables, whole grains, and lean meat as your primary foods; having a positive attitude; getting a good night's sleep; taking a multivitamin. This is simple, proven wisdom that alone can transform your health.

That said, there's value to following the health news. New research can help identify legitimately powerful new remedies and preventive measures. And great health writing is less about science and facts and more about motivating you to take action—and we can all use as much motivation as possible! But keeping up with health trends and breakthroughs takes a team. Commit as a couple to learning more about healthy living and about any health conditions you have or are at risk for developing.

Being smart about health does make a difference: In one Norwegian study of 20,000 married men, those whose wives were well educated were the least likely to be overweight or sedentary—key risk factors for heart disease and diabetes. Experts think smart spouses simply know more about health and aren't afraid to put it into practice. Our twist on this message: Husbands and wives can show their love by learning more for themselves—and each other.

explosion

The biopsy of a suspicious lump. A pink slip on Friday afternoon. The late-night phone call: *Your mother's in the emergency room.* The slow slide into depression. Even the switch from slim-fit jeans to baggy sweatpants. Quiet or dramatic, monumental or seemingly inconsequential, these explosions can rock your marriage at any time, with little warning.

Most of us never see these stressors coming. We feel strong, safe, invincible. But life has other plans. When Reader's Digest asked 1,001 wives and husbands across the nation whether a major challenge had ever tested their relationships, 94 percent answered with an emphatic *yes*. While some have been married for decades, many are still in their 20s and 30s and have been married for less than a decade. Their children are still young, their careers still growing, their dreams still in the development stage. Not the time when you expect big trouble.

Turning misfortune into triumph requires dedication and patience, flexibility and humor, affection and resourcefulness.

It is the randomness of the crises in our lives that makes the Explosion stage so different from the other six stages of marriage. Whereas those stages tend to happen in a logical, predictable order, crises that rock a marriage can and do happen at any time. Another difference: The time span of the Explosion stage is extremely variable. Sometimes it lasts a few weeks, sometimes many years. But when a crisis hits, there's no question that the rules and needs of marriage are far different than they were just a few days earlier.

The good news: We survive—even thrive—through tough times. Over and over again in our survey, husbands and wives said that coping together with the most common difficulties and disasters a couple can face—from a health crisis to a layoff, from depression to an aging parent to a major weight gain—had positive effects on their relationships. "You get a second chance when you face one of these unwanted events—a second chance to make things better in your life," says Wayne M. Sotile, Ph.D., director of Psychological Services for the Wake Forest University Healthy Exercise and

Lifestyles Program and author of *Thriving with Heart Disease*. "You have the chance or obligation to forgive and forget past problems. You do the things you've known you need to do all along to be a more loving person. It's a wakeup call that most couples heed."

Turning misfortune into triumph requires dedication and patience, flexibility and humor, affection and resourcefulness. Couples who thrive during adversity are hard-headed realists: They gather the information they need in order to take charge, experts say. They're not afraid to be vulnerable—by laughing and crying with each other and by seeking and accepting support from family and friends. And they're committed optimists who see the light at the end of a long, dark tunnel.

"A lot of the couples really turn a health crisis into a victory," says Christine Cannon, Ph.D., R.N., an associate professor of nursing at the University of Delaware who researches the ways illnesses such as breast cancer affect a marriage. "In my research, many couples have said the experience changed their relationship for the better. They were so much closer. Husbands said over and over again that they realized their wives were champions as they dealt with breast cancer. The wives saw and appreciated everything their husbands did to get them through it, and how they wanted to do even more. It's very inspiring."

"He Was My Rock"

Over and over again, couples in the Reader's Digest *Marriage in America Survey* told us how crisis forged a deeper marriage.

- "The way he took care of me when my mother died. I'll always cherish that," one woman said. "It was as hard for him because he loved her as much as I did, and yet, he was my rock. He waited a full three months to finally break down and cry his heart out."

- Another woman said she understood her husband's love for her at a new level "when I woke up from heart surgery (seven bypasses) and saw my husband standing there with tears in his eyes."

- One wife said the meaning of commitment came shining through on a very difficult day: "The day I was diagnosed with cancer. I thought he would leave me, but he was right there for me," she said.

- Husbands had similar stories. "When I became disabled, my wife took care of us and the family without any 'poor me's' and with great stamina and closeness to God," one grateful spouse told Reader's Digest. Still another found a supporting soul mate when the news was very bad: "The day the doctor said I had one year to live. We both cried and then told our kids what was going on."

What's happening? "We fall in love for good reason," Dr. Sotile says. "Then we settle into staleness or laziness or withholding the full expression of our love for a bunch of bad reasons, such as unrealistic expectations. But then something shocks us enough to remind us of what we already love. To show us that life isn't a dress rehearsal. It's the real deal, and it's time to start showing the truth of what you feel and need and want. It's not rocket science. It's discovering what you already have in your mate and in your marriage."

In this chapter, you'll read about the ways five of the biggest challenges in life can impact your marriage. We chose these because they came out on top in our survey.

- **A major illness in your own marriage**—a crisis that calls on both spouses to find new ways to stay open and intimate.
- **Depression**—an invisible threat to a couple's long-term happiness and daily life.
- **Job loss**—an economic challenge that also challenges your identity, expectations, and roles.
- **Weight gain**—a seemingly insignificant issue that in reality affects two out of three Americans and can derail emotional and physical intimacy.
- **Caring for an aging parent**—a time when the physical and emotional demands of caregiving can drain your relationship.

Of course, these aren't the only challenges your marriage might face. You may encounter infidelity (a subject we explored in the Rebellion stage chapter); sexual problems (an issue you'll find in nearly every stage in this book); adult kids who move back in just as you were appreciating your empty-nest solitude (a challenge covered in the Reunion stage); or with the day-in, day-out weariness of feeling as if there's too much stress and too much to do (a relationship-eroding problem discussed in the Cooperation stage chapter).

The Universal Needs during Crisis

In the pages ahead, we give advice for successfully weathering five of the most common explosions in marriage. But there are many others that can happen. The following attributes are key to weathering any crisis that rocks your marriage. Apply these, and chances are you'll emerge on the other side happy, healthy, and strong.

Empathy. When you truly feel and understand the struggles or pain your spouse is going through, you make it easier to stand by him or her.

Patience. Crises can happen quickly; recovering from them is often painfully slow. Know that the path ahead of you will take months, even years, to traverse, and prepare yourself for the whole journey.

Humor. No crisis is so great that you can't find a way to smile and even laugh on occasion. The ability to maintain your sense of humor is the best evidence there is that you and your spouse are coping well with adversity.

Dedication. Remember your wedding vows? Your marriage *always* comes first, for richer, for poorer, in sickness and in health. Remember that your marriage is priority number one, and you'll be sure to tend to it even as you deal with the crisis in front of you.

Intimacy. Particularly of the emotional type. The more you share your emotions and communicate your needs and struggles, the better you will support each other, and the closer you will grow.

The missions of the Explosion stage are as varied as the explosions themselves. Yet there is common ground—in particular, coping strategies that work no matter what you face. As Dr. Sotile says, these aren't rocket science. They're already at the foundation of a good marriage: communication, support, acceptance, and flexibility.

In addition, couples say that problems are more solvable when they educate themselves and are strong advocates for their own well-being. Read on to discover how to apply these strengths when life lobs an explosion into your lives.

Explosion: A Health Crisis or Chronic Illness

First comes the shock: emergency treatment for a heart attack or stroke, for example. Or the diagnosis and treatment of cancer. Or test results that reveal the presence of a chronic medical condition that will be with you—and your marriage—for the rest of your life, such as diabetes, arthritis, failing kidneys, or chronic pain.

Next comes the long haul. When a health condition travels home with you from the hospital or the doctor's office, it takes up residence in your kitchen and bedroom, on your calendar and in your daily lives, in your hearts and in your minds. "Coping with this illness will be part of your marriage from now on," notes Dr. Sotile. "There's nothing more important for living well with any chronic disease than a happy, loving marriage."

A medical crisis or lifelong health condition rewrites the script of your relationship. Your roles may change drastically. Your future doesn't look the way you'd hoped. Sex, money, work, chores, fun—they're all different now. "Managing the way an illness affects your marriage is just as important as keeping up with medications and doctor's appointments and treatments," Dr. Sotile says. "Today, most illnesses aren't short events. They're processes that go on and on and on, possibly for the rest of your lives. And both of you will need different things at different times in the process. Couples who take responsibility for this can build stronger, closer marriages despite the presence of illness."

A close marriage not only makes life easier for the two of you, it could be a make-or-break factor in the health of both the patient and the caregiver. The stress and demands of caregiving heighten the odds of the caregiver spouse developing his or her own serious health problems, as well as depression and anxiety. And marriage problems can affect you both as you cope with illness: When Israeli scientists studied 73 couples in which the wives had breast cancer, they found that when husbands were emotionally distant, their wives suffered more distress.

We're in This Together

Living well with illness means adjusting, again and again, to physical and emotional changes. It also means learning a wide, deep acceptance of the way things are while finding new ways to keep joy alive in your life and your marriage.

"One of the other things I've gotten out of my multiple sclerosis is staying focused on what's important, what my priorities are. I take having a life of joy very seriously," says Greg McGreer of Medford, New Jersey. "I don't think any of us, whether we're sick right now or not, can afford to put things off."

When Greg and Karen McGreer married just after Christmas in 1993, Greg had already been diagnosed with a slowly progressing form of MS. "I got married without any crutches or anything, but since then my ability to stand and walk have been decreased. A lot of things have been affected. I don't do as much as I used to, or I do them more slowly."

The McGreers value happiness and practicality, and they use the tools they need to get there: They recently moved to a single-story home on the banks of the Rancocas Creek and rehabbed it for easier wheelchair access. They sail their 31-foot sailboat less often on the Chesapeake Bay now, but take more trips in Greg's RV. And they maintain vibrant emotional and physical intimacy. "We've both dealt with some depression and sorrow and grief," Karen McGreer says. "It is not always easy. Being an old rehab nurse, I knew very well what the possibilities were when we married. Greg is so kind, so wise, so remarkable, so positive. We're so close in so many ways. That's what matters. We find ways to deal with the rest."

Achieving a new balance in a marriage with illness takes time and patience. It's not just a matter of caregiving, Dr. Sotile notes. "A spouse will sometimes get locked into the role of caregiving with the best of intentions," he says. "But after a while, you have to stop buffering the ill spouse from the stresses of your daily life and from your needs and thoughts and feelings. If you hold back, neither of you is fully participating in your marriage. You feel trapped. And your spouse feels less important, as if you've given up on them. You may not cry on their shoulder or be feisty in bed anymore. One of the challenges of a long-term illness is finding ways to reestablish a marriage of equals."

The two cornerstones: talk and touch. The truth is, you still need each other. And finding ways to collaborate so that you both feel cared-for and close can keep your marriage at center stage as you face down serious health problems together. We've set those as your marriage missions if a health crisis has touched your relationship.

Mission 1: Talk

After the first days and weeks of crisis and early recovery have passed, you settle into a new life together, just you, your partner, and the illness. Nothing's the same—but should you talk about it? Experts say yes. Both of you may be feeling angry, fearful, or guilty. You may worry about finances, the kids, your sex life, or your partner's future. You may be in denial, insisting that everything's really just fine, or grieving over all you've lost. Communicating about your inner experiences is key now and can set the tone for your relationship for years to come. These steps can help.

Accept your new reality. It may be painful, but accepting the fact that your partner has a long-term illness and may have limitations keeps you both from being frozen in denial. This can be especially difficult if an illness is invisible or progresses slowly. But shrugging off symptoms—or downplaying the need for treatments, doctor's visits, or lifestyle changes that keep damage at bay—can actually make the condition worse down the road. It also spells trouble for your marriage because it sends the message that one spouse's well-being isn't truly important. Recognizing reality is the first step in being a resilient, resourceful couple.

Get an education. When researchers at two Midwestern cancer centers asked 22 prostate-cancer survivors and 20 wives what troubled them and what would help most in living with prostate cancer, they reported that most couples had "an overwhelming need for information." Shock and fear often kept them from asking questions during doctor's appointments; conflicting medical opinions and confusing treatment options left them struggling to make the right decisions. Many said they were unprepared for the ways cancer treatment would affect their day-to-day lives. "Although they had been told about incontinence and impotence, health-care providers rarely spent time discussing the impact of these effects on daily lives," the researchers reported.

Learning all you can about your illness—or your spouse's—can calm your fears, open doors to new treatment options, clear up confusion, help you manage symptoms, and solve day-to-day dilemmas. You gain a much-needed sense of control. Working with cold, hard facts will also help the two of you make decisions as a team.

In fact, when Vanderbilt University School of Nursing researchers studied couples in which the wives had rheumatoid arthritis, those coping best with this painful, progressive condition knew all they could about the illness, treatments, exercises, even massages.

Best bets for trustworthy medical information? Good online sources include the National Institutes of Health, the National Library of Medicine, associations dedicated to the specific illness you or your spouse has, online support groups, and organizations for doctors who specialize in that condition. Your doctor can provide educational materials, and your local library—or the library at a local college or university—probably has a wealth of information as well.

Assemble a support team for the well spouse—pronto. In the days and weeks after a health crisis, a well spouse is at higher risk for depression and anxiety than the ill spouse, found a recent University of Kentucky in Lexington study of 417 heart patients and their spouses. Researchers found that well spouses had less support than their mates. And their emotional stress seemed to "rub off" on their partners, hurting their marriages, their relationships with friends and family, their feelings about the quality of their medical care. It even delayed their return to work.

Talking with friends and relatives can help. So can being included in medical decisions in the hospital and afterward, the researchers suggest. That way, you won't feel helpless or that you have no control over what's happening to your partner.

Talk, talk, and talk some more. "A couple needs to talk frequently about what both spouses need and how things are going," Dr. Sotile says. "What's working? What's not? What do you need more of or less of from me?" Don't hold back because you think your ill spouse shouldn't be burdened by your needs or because you think your well spouse is already doing all he or she can. It's important to be supportive and honest with each other.

MARRIAGE MAGIC
Practice Optimism

A positive attitude after illness is good for your body, mind, spirit—and marriage. Studies show links between a positive outlook and faster recovery, fewer infections, less pain, and more happiness. So do what you can to cast out the negative thoughts and focus on all that's great ahead of you.

Important questions the two of you should discuss early—and often—include:

- How can the ill spouse support the caregiving spouse?
- What can the ill spouse do to take care of him- or herself?
- What can the well spouse do to make life easier?
- What are your feelings and thoughts about the illness and how it's affecting your life, our marriage, and the future?
- Do we need more outside help and support?
- Are our coping styles in conflict? Is one of us a staunch optimist, the other a realist?
- Are we finding time to enjoy each other and life, despite the illness?

Listen—even when it's a tough job. Dealing with medical limitations can leave you feeling depressed, angry, fearful, and guilty—whether you're the "sick" or the "well" spouse. And sometimes a civilized talk won't let you or your partner really vent. Allow yourselves to express your true feelings about the illness, without blaming or criticizing each other.

Don't be the health police. The health cops are always on patrol, checking to see if the sick spouse is taking her meds, eating all of his high-fiber cereal, following through with medical treatments, and looking over test results. Trouble is, studies show that when the well spouse joins this police force, the ill spouse is more likely to resist following doctor's orders.

"Don't nag, blame, shame, monitor, fuss at, or criticize," Dr. Sotile says. "Research shows these are ineffective ways to help your spouse—they just don't work." What does work: support, encouragement, expressing concern, compassion. "It's enough to tell your spouse that you hope they'll develop a specific new health habit because you love and care about them," he says. "Leave it at that. Pushing the issue could easily backfire and hurt your relationship at the same time."

Throw negativity out; invite happiness and fun in. Often one spouse in a patient-caregiver relationship feels angry or isolated, anxious or depressed or pessimistic. "It's tough for the other spouse not to fall into the same way of thinking," Dr. Sotile says. "It's vital that the other partner continue to express love, concern, and care while refusing to participate in this form of misery. Joining in can lead both of you into anger, conflict, and worry. If you both burn out on negativity, it's not going to help either of you."

The antidote? Declare periods of time when you don't talk about the illness—it could be for an hour, a day, or a weekend. Do whatever you can still enjoy together. "If you used to go country dancing, and now one of you can't dance, think about everything you enjoyed about that experience and try to re-create as much of it as you can," Dr. Sotile says. "Don't throw it all away. You enjoyed the music, seeing friends, dressing up, getting out of the house, laughing. There are other ways you can still have those parts of the experience."

Likewise, spend time appreciating small pleasures together: the sun on spring leaves, a CD by your favorite musician, a new movie.

Don't do it all—or sideline the sick spouse. "You both need to feel necessary," Dr. Sotile says. "We all need to feel needed, including someone who has a health condition. Letting the patient be a source of strength and encouragement helps everyone."

Mission 2: Touch

Physical affection is a powerful stress-reduction tool for married couples—and the better your relationship, the stronger the power of touch. In an intriguing University of Virginia study, 16 married women agreed to be zapped with very mild electric shocks while researchers studied their brain activity with magnetic resonance imaging (MRI). Each woman in turn held her husband's hand, the hand of a male stranger, or no one's hand.

The results? Chalk up a victory for marriage. When husbands reached into the MRI machine to clasp their wive's hands, activity in the part of the brain that registers the anticipation of pain quieted down significantly for the women. They said that they felt less distress. And brain images also showed less agitation in the hypothalamus, the area of the brain that controls the release of stress hormones. Women who were most satisfied with their marriages got the most benefits. In contrast, holding a stranger's hand cut stress only a little.

"We can't see what our spouses are doing to our brains and emotions until a stressful event arises, but it's going on all the time," noted lead researcher James Coan, Ph.D., soon after the study was published. "When a wife holds or caresses her husband, she is really reaching into the deepest parts of his brain, calming down the neural-threat response."

Touch is second nature in a close marriage. But when one spouse is sick, that can all change. Experts suggest that couples make it a point to stay physically close and even resume their sexual relationship. But pain, muscle weakness, surgical scars, breathing problems, medication side effects, and worries about stamina or the effects of a physical activity like sex could make you both feel wary. The ill spouse may not feel attractive. The caretaking spouse may not want to overtax his or her mate. Your instinct may be to wait, but how long? This advice can help you both get the affection and love you need—safely.

Shower each other with physical affection. Hold hands. Hug. Kiss. Touch whenever possible. Learn how to perform a simple foot, hand, or back massage—and trade massages. The more touch, the better. It's soothing, cuts stress, and makes you feel closer and happier. If you have surgical scars or feel self-conscious about your changing body due to weight gain or loss, spend time holding each other while you are dressed. Dr. Sotile suggests gradually letting your partner see surgical scars or changed parts of your body, then gently rubbing them with lotion or touching them.

Have fun. Your mate is still your partner, so don't forget physical flirting and fun even if it doesn't lead to intercourse or an orgasm. Tease each other. Tickle. Fool around. Get to second base and linger there.

Make love when you're both ready. Physical love triggers the release of the bonding hormone, oxytocin, in women—you feel calm and happy. It also lowers blood pressure, protecting against heart attack and stroke. Men also experience a fivefold increase in oxytocin just before orgasm. The health benefits of regular sex for men? In a study of 1,000 guys from Northern Ireland, those who had sex three times a week or more cut their risk for a heart attack or stroke by 50 percent. Frequent orgasms lowered risk of death to one-half that of sexually inactive men, say researchers from Queen's University in Belfast. Maybe that's why long-married men live up to five years longer than their unmarried counterparts.

And yet, you may be worried about sex—and that's normal when illness visits your marriage. Eighty percent of heart patients, for example, are scared to make love for at least six months after a heart attack. Sex may not be the same—and it's wise to talk with your doctor first for advice on whether you're in the small minority of heart patients for whom sex may be risky, if your medical condition causes pain, or if you take medications that

What Men Want, What Women Need

When illness strikes, marriages adjust. But researchers are beginning to see that the most crucial adjustments depend on who is the caregiver and who is the patient. Our traditional roles may keep us from getting the help we need most— or giving our partners what they really need. These tips can help you overcome this gender gap.

When a Wife Is the Patient

Men: Stop being Mr. Fix-It. When a wife is the patient, a husband may jump to show his love by offering solutions for every symptom, large or small. Often what a woman really needs is a husband who simply listens attentively to her feelings— and shares his own emotional responses to being the caregiver. Miss this, and your wife may feel very isolated or criticized by your take-charge approach. You also raise your own risk of burnout.

Women: Look for extra support. If your spouse is overwhelmed or under-equipped to listen to your feelings as much as you'd like, you may need more supporters. Ask a friend or two to hear what's on your mind and in your heart. And give your husband credit for showing his love by trying his best.

When a Husband Is the Patient

Women: Don't suffocate your spouse. Trying to do everything, without telling your partner how you're feeling or what you need, can make an ill husband feel weak, useless, and frustrated with both of you. Talk together about what you do for each other and what your spouse can do for himself. And if your partner frequently snaps, "I can do it for myself!" then pay attention. He probably can.

Men: Ask your wife if she's getting enough support. You don't have to provide it, but you can listen with compassion. If your partner seems overwhelmed, now's the time to suggest some practical fixes: Can she ask a friend to take the kids to the movies? Could the family have take-out pizza on Friday nights instead of a home-cooked, full-course dinner? Could fellow church members or a laundry service take care of the pile of sheets and towels in the wash basket?

have dampened your libido or sexual response. Take it slowly. Enjoy the full experience of touching, tasting, feeling.

Need a little help? Ask your doctor. Steer clear of health food–store and online remedies for low sex drive or orgasm troubles. Some may be dangerous; others are simply ineffective. Still others could interact with medications you take and produce unwanted side effects. Both men and women experiencing arousal or orgasm difficulties after a brush with a major illness may boost sexual pleasure with a little pharmaceutical help, Dr. Sotile says. Viagra-type pills and creams that enhance blood flow in your most erogenous zones may be worth exploring.

Your doctor may also be able to adjust other medications you're taking or suggest other strategies to improve your sex life. If talking about your sex life with your doc makes you uncomfortable, pave the way by writing down your questions in advance.

Redefine intimacy. Don't give up if sex isn't what it used to be or is simply not an option right now. Embracing, hugging, touching, and kissing count too. Even if you can't manage intercourse, spending time together touching and talking can bring you deep, satisfying intimacy.

Explosion: Depression

When one spouse is depressed, a marriage is depressed. This illness erodes emotional and sexual intimacy and suffuses a relationship with pessimism and resentment, anger and isolation. Even the sunniest, most capable partner can be pulled into depression's strong undertow: You may be overwhelmed by extra household chores that your partner is too lethargic to finish, resentful because your spouse won't just snap out of it, or feel that you're somehow to blame for the illness itself. You may feel alone yet unwilling to tell anyone there's depression in your household, or you may simply wonder when the sparkle and joy, the humor and fun seeped out of your relationship.

Meanwhile, a depressed spouse may believe these sad, empty, tired feelings will pass, that it's not a big deal—or is all the fault of the well spouse, the boss, or life circumstances. Or that depression must be kept secret.

If there's depression in your marriage, it's time to act—for your partner and yourself. Waiting increases the chances that your relationship won't last;

depressed couples are nine times more likely to divorce. And trying to fight or make peace with this often misunderstood illness on your own raises risks for both of you. The longer a nondepressed spouse lives with a depressed partner, the higher his or her own risks for depression. The deeper a depressed spouse sinks, the tougher it may be to finally treat the depression—and the greater the risk for alcoholism, drug abuse, violence, and even suicide. The stakes are high, but the odds are that things will improve.

Remember, you're not alone. An estimated 19 million Americans are currently going through depression. In the Reader's Digest *Marriage in America Survey*, 42 percent of respondents named depression as a major challenge in their relationships. It's not surprising that most said this insidious illness had a negative effect on them. But there was an unexpected ray of hope: One in four said depression had a positive outcome for their marriages. "Getting diagnosed and treated makes all the difference," says Emily Scott-Lowe, Ph.D., an assistant visiting professor of social work at Pepperdine University, who leads workshops across the country about depression and marriage with her husband, Dennis Lowe, Ph.D., a psychologist and director of Pepperdine's Center for the Family. "Just 33 percent of people with depression seek and get help. But when you do, your chances for significant improvement are 80 to 90 percent."

In a University of Colorado study of 774 married couples, researchers found that when depression entered a relationship, *both* partners became unhappy with their marriage. That's no surprise for the Lowes. Their struggle with depression began many years into their marriage and surprised them both: "I was never someone that anyone considered most likely to become depressed," Dennis Lowe says. "In fact, I was voted 'best smile' in my high school yearbook." His depression isolated his family and strained his marriage, yet it took years to diagnose, even though he and his wife are both mental-health professionals.

"There's a bias that says women get depression more often than men, but it may just be that men don't ask for help or realize what's wrong, or respond to depression by abusing alcohol or becoming aggressive or violent," Emily Scott-Lowe says. "And often with men, there's more agitation than lethargy. A man may seem worked up. He may have frenetic, restless energy that doesn't fit with the typical picture of someone in bed with shades down and the sheets up over their head."

The battle won, the couple now present workshops about depression's impact on couples and families based on their own experience. Their advice? See depression as an unwelcome guest—it's an illness, not a shortcoming. Get help and support together.

Mission 1: Fight the Depression

Depression isn't a choice or a little case of the blues. It's a physical illness as serious and life-altering as diabetes, heart disease, or arthritis. A depressed spouse can't just "snap out of it" or "get on with life." The reason: Depression is marked by dramatic shifts in brain chemistry that alter mood, thoughts, sleep, appetite, and energy levels. Genetics usually make many of us susceptible to depression; any number of factors can trigger the slide, including prolonged or severe stress, financial problems, a big loss or change in your life, the birth of a child, parenthood, and even some health conditions and prescription drugs. Marriage itself even raises your risk: Up to 1 in 10 brides experience "postnuptial depression" in the months after the wedding. And up to half of all women and men in unhappy marriages may be depressed, perhaps due to marriage problems (though some experts suspect that undiagnosed depression is behind the problems).

If you think your partner may be depressed, your first step is to pay attention to the clues—and help him or her get a diagnosis and treatment. These steps can help.

Be alert to small changes. Depression can come on slowly, almost imperceptibly. "You look for all types of other explanations—we just had a new baby, it's a tough time at work, it's a phase," Emily Scott-Lowe notes. "It can take a while to see the pattern or to be ready to accept that depression might be the cause."

Often it's up to the nondepressed spouse to take the lead: The illness itself often prevents depressed people from recognizing that something's wrong or seeking help. They may feel too lethargic or withdrawn or may think they can fix it alone.

If you notice that your spouse isn't acting, feeling, or thinking as he or she normally does, ask yourself if it could be depression, but don't stop there. Depression may be the reason your spouse is working extremely long hours, drinking too much, using recreational drugs, or looking for thrills in risky activities. It can also look different in men and women.

Don't wait for your spouse to hit bottom. Letting a depressed person sink low before offering help is an old-school approach borrowed from the early days of alcohol- and drug-addiction treatment. But the reasoning behind it is flawed and dangerous. Long-term depression is harder on your marriage, tougher to treat, and more likely to recur, and it leaves its victim in despair. The most chilling risk: It leaves open the very real possibility of suicide. About 60 percent of people who attempt suicide have major or minor depression or another mood disorder—and depressed men are four times more likely than depressed women to take their own lives.

Break the ice gently yet firmly. If you suspect your partner is depressed, don't blurt out a layperson's diagnosis: "You're depressed!" or announce: "You better get help!" In order to begin the process of healing, approach your spouse with concern and with an action plan. You might say, "I'm concerned about how feeling tired and losing your appetite are affecting you. You deserve to feel better. Our doctor may be able to help you, and I'd like to arrange a time when we can meet with him. Next week, I can go on Wednesday or Friday. What's good for you?"

Get a diagnosis—together. Dozens of health conditions—including heart disease, diabetes, lupus, viral infections, and chronic pain—can trigger the same symptoms as depression. So can scores of prescription medications, including some birth-control pills and drugs that treat acne, herpes, high blood pressure, high cholesterol, and cancer. Your family doctor can rule out underlying causes and decide whether or not it's really depression.

Ask your spouse if it's okay for you to attend this evaluation. "When you're down that low, you may not be able to express what's going on or even realize what all your symptoms are," Emily Scott-Lowe notes. "And you may not be able to concentrate on the treatment recommendations your doctor is making. You need an ally in the room."

Know that the odds are in your favor. As we noted, the success rate of depression treatment is as high as 90 percent. Usually the road back is relatively simple: antidepressants, counseling, or a combination of the two. That said, recovery may take time and patience. There may be an initial trial-and-error period while you try various antidepressants or see whether various therapy techniques, such as cognitive behavioral therapy and interpersonal counseling, are helpful. The results are worth it.

Find a mental-health counselor for the two of you. Depression affects both of you—and your whole family. The Lowes suggest finding a therapist or counselor who has worked with depression in couples. "You may have issues to deal with individually as the depressed person, and the two of you may have issues to deal with that stem from coping with depression," Dennis Lowe says. "We found it very helpful to have a counselor we could see together at times and separately at other times."

Be alert for relapses. About half of all people who suffer a bout of major depression will have a relapse; 75 percent of those will have another relapse; and 90 percent of those will have yet another. Once a first episode passes, many doctors prescribe a maintenance dose of antidepressants to prevent a relapse. Both spouses should also stay alert for signs that the illness is returning.

Mission 2: Protect Your Marriage—and Yourself

Caring for a depressed spouse can be lonely, overwhelming, and emotionally draining. You may blame yourself, feel helpless, grow pessimistic, lose your sense of humor, and even consider leaving. It's easy for the nondepressed spouse to become angry and frustrated with an irritable, lethargic mate who's pessimistic and critical, who can't unload the dishwasher or get the kids ready for bed anymore—let alone make love, ask how you're doing, or acknowledge that you've been holding things together for weeks, months, or years.

"This starts a cycle that burns you out and doesn't help your partner at all," Emily Scott-Lowe notes. "I did this with Dennis—I would become extremely angry with him. Then I would feel really guilty and try to make up for it by taking on more and more around the house. Then I would get angry all over again. This wasn't helping Dennis, of course, and it was wearing me out emotionally and physically."

These steps can help the nondepressed spouse stay well—and protect your marriage and your family while helping a depressed partner.

Admit that you cannot cure your partner's depression. Your spouse needs your love, support, and concern. But these important qualities can't reverse depression any more than they can control blood sugar, ease arthritis pain, or clear out clogged arteries. Just as you wouldn't rely on love alone to cure a medical condition—or withdraw love because it didn't—don't expect that your feelings or attention will be able to alter your spouse's off-kilter brain chemistry. Use your love to get help and to remind your partner of his or her intrinsic worth during this challenging time.

See depression as an intruder in your marriage. Like any other illness, depression is an outside force—an unwelcome visitor wreaking havoc with your spouse's health, your marriage, and your home life. Seeing it this way can allow both of you to talk about its effects without blame or shame. "Once we started talking about it as a third party—as 'the depression'—we could express our frustrations constructively," Emily Scott-Lowe says. "If Dennis was really doubting his worth, I could say, 'That's just the depression talking. It's not you. When you're not depressed, you don't think this way. It's feeding you lies.' "

This shift in thinking can clear the air. "It was a relief for me," Dennis Lowe says. "I felt Emily was walking on eggshells sometimes, not wanting to tell me how she was feeling. Depression was the elephant in the room that no one wanted to talk about, and I felt even guiltier. Seeing it as the intruder was an accurate perspective. It helped me see why I felt the way I did and let me accept reassurance because it acknowledges what's going on instead of denying it."

Find support. Admitting there's depression in your marriage can be tough. So can accepting help. Choose a trusted friend to confide in—preferably someone who's experienced depression in their own life or within their family. And if you're overwhelmed by extra household duties because your spouse can't do his or her share, say yes when others offer assistance. "At one point, I was crying at church, when my friend shook me and said, 'Emily, people here at church are lined up waiting to help you.' I kept saying we didn't need help until she shook me into reality. We had people bringing us dinner several nights a week. One neighbor took our sons to spend the night, and it was so nice to know they were having fun. Depression can suck the energy right out of a household."

Monitor your own moods and thinking. Enduring barrages of negative comments, holding the household and family together, and losing the sweetest, most supportive aspects of your marriage isn't easy. Over months

(continued on page 244)

Are You "Catching" Your Partner's Depression?

Caution: Depression can be contagious. To see whether your partner's depression is affecting your own mental health, read each statement below and check those that apply to you right now.

- I feel overwhelmed by all the housework, child care, bill-paying, and yard work I've taken on because my spouse can no longer handle them.

- I try to learn all I can about depression because it helps me cope and may help my spouse recover.

- I wonder sometimes if I'm to blame for my partner's depression.

- I make a point of eating healthy foods, exercising, and staying on top of my physical and emotional health, even if I'm feeling rushed or blue.

- If my spouse doesn't want to do things on the weekends, I sometimes go out with friends. There's no point staying home, bored and miserable.

- My spouse's lethargy and negative attitude make me very angry sometimes. But I feel really guilty when I get mad.

- I have told at least one close friend about my spouse's depression because I need emotional support.

- I haven't confided in anyone or asked for support as I cope with my spouse's depression.

- Since my spouse can't shoulder his or her share of the household responsibilities, I've tried to simplify my own life—I've hired help, enlisted the kids, and/or changed routines so less needs to be accomplished.

- I feel ashamed that my spouse is depressed. It seems like a weakness.

- I try to see my spouse's depression as an illness rather than something he or she can control or that I may have caused.

● Nothing I say to my partner ever seems right—he or she becomes angry or critical or withdrawn or even threatens to leave our marriage.

● I've been drinking more, working longer hours at my job, or taking recreational drugs in order to escape from what's happening at home.

▲ I try to talk with my spouse about how the depression affects me and our marriage, instead of bottling it up.

● I've thought seriously about separation or divorce because my spouse's depression is too difficult to live with.

▲ My partner has acknowledged his or her depression and sought help.

● I haven't gone out and had fun—with my spouse or with other friends—for a very long time.

▲ When my partner sees his doctor and/or therapist about the depression, I sometimes sit in on the appointment and add information.

Your Score

How many of each shape did you check off?

Circles _____ **Triangles** _____

If you tallied more triangles than circles, good work! You're working hard to maintain your mental health despite the daunting challenges of living with a partner who's depressed. The key factors: a willingness to talk about the illness, both at home and with friends and experts; taking steps to find personal support; learning more about the disease; and working hard at maintaining your own life.

If you tallied more circles than triangles, chances are your own mental health is suffering due to your spouse's illness. It's time to take a deep breath and resolve to make your own health and happiness your top priority—for your own well-being and for the future of your marriage. Reread the two missions to find out what to do. But most of all, realize that you are not to blame for your spouse's situation. Depression is a biochemical illness. Seeing it as an unwelcome intruder rather than someone's fault will release many of your negative feelings, freeing you to get support and make time for your own health and happiness.

and years, the nondepressed spouse may give in to confusion, self-blame, demoralization, and resentment, notes Anne Sheffield, author of *Depression Fallout: The Impact of Depression on Couples and What You Can Do to Preserve the Bond*. You may conclude that you must leave to save yourself. If this sounds familiar, get help for yourself—and insist that your mate do the same. "Depression separates couples with surgical skill and is a major home-breaker," Sheffield notes in her book.

Conquer depression before you try to work on your marriage. Depression can wreak major havoc in your marriage. You may be tempted to fix what seem like smaller issues before tackling the illness head-on (it may be easier to ask your partner to communicate more effectively than it is to say "It's time to get help," for example). It's reasonable to ask your spouse to help all he or she can around the house, to be responsible and treat you well. But looking for major changes while your spouse is under the influence of depression may simply create more frustration. Focus on lifting depression first.

Respect your own needs. If your spouse has depression, you still deserve everyday niceties—a neat house, regular meals, a calm family environment—as well as friendships, a social life, and time to pursue meaningful interests. As much as possible, pursue these things. It's easy to spend your time dealing with your spouse's needs and issues. But don't sacrifice your own joys and goals needlessly. As we noted, you are susceptible to depression too. Pursuing your personal pleasures will not only help prevent that but also better prepare you for aiding your spouse.

Explosion: Job Loss

You lose more than a paycheck when you lose a job. Whether you're downsized or flat-out fired, the financial stress and embarrassment of being unemployed, plus the anger, worry, and lowered self-esteem that can go with it, can strain even the most solid marriage. Money's tight. Household routines change. Expectations shift.

"Money is the most psychologically loaded topic between partners these days. It's what sex was 50 years ago," says psychologist Stephen Goldbart, Ph.D., founder of the Money, Meaning & Choices Institute in

Kentfield, California. "It's resonant with power and esteem and identity." Losing the part of yourself that brings home the bacon conjures fears about making the next mortgage payment. It can also trigger deeper doubts and discomforts about your own worth—and what you and your spouse expect from your marriage.

Job loss rocks millions of American marriages each year. The national unemployment rate was 4.6 percent at the time this book was written—relatively low by U.S. Department of Labor standards. Yet it meant 7.6 million of us were out of work. Many face the grueling prospect of long-term unemployment: Nearly one in five were jobless for over six months. The impact? In the Reader's Digest *Marriage in America Survey*, 47 percent of respondents said that a layoff or job loss was a major challenge in their relationships; about half described the experience as negative. "Looking for a job is harder than having a job for most people," Dr. Goldbart notes.

But there was also a surprising bright note: One in three said that the outcome was ultimately positive. "If you can survive a life-changing crisis such as job loss that impacts your spouse and your family and that you really can't control, you can survive just about anything," says Damian Birkel, founder of Professionals in Transition, a North Carolina–based national support network for downsized employees. "You learn the depth of your relationship. We've survived two job losses and three downsizings, and I can honestly say I'm more in love with my wife, Donna, now than when we got married 30 years ago."

Beating the Pink-Slip Blues

Nearly three-quarters of jobless Americans say family stress is greater since they lost work, according to a survey by the New York City–based nonprofit National Employment Law Project. One in three said they interrupted their own or a family member's education, and one in four had to move to make ends meet. Joblessness can cancel plans to start a family, delay retirement, force one spouse to work long hours, and create a host of unexpected challenges on the home front. An unemployed spouse may feel lonely or depressed; a partner may resent taking on extra hours at work or feel hemmed in by the sudden round-the-clock togetherness. The balance of power can shift. And issues like who takes the trash out and who makes dinner can become battlegrounds.

When British researchers surveyed 24,000 out-of-work women and men in several countries, they found that unemployment had a deeper effect on well-being than divorce or widowhood. "Many days, I felt that I had 'Loser' tattooed on my forehead and 'Will Work for Food' tattooed on my chest," says Birkel. "But relatives and friends and all others couldn't see my tattoos because they didn't really exist!"

Your marriage can be a source of strength during unemployment. These steps can help you navigate the pitfalls, focus on the true values of your relationship, and stay close after a pink slip.

Mission 1: Set a New Budget—And New Priorities

When Dr. Goldbart counsels worried couples who've lost jobs or fortunate pairs who are suddenly wealthy, he advises the same starting point: Step back and look at what money means to you. "Any financial transition is an opportunity for a couple to look at the core operating principles that guide their decision-making about money. It works for people with oodles of money and those who must tighten their belts. It's very eye-opening."

It's also essential. "If a couple isn't on the same page about money, they'll be all over the map about what to do when one partner loses a job," he says. Perhaps one of you is comfortable with short-term debt and wants to use credit cards for necessities, while the other partner will cut spending as much as possible to avoid debt and hold on to savings. Perhaps one of you feels that continuing to go out for the occasional date—even if it's just for pizza and a second-run movie—is worth the expense, while the other thinks it should be the first budget item to cut. Maybe one of you wants to cancel the kids' planned stay at summer camp, while the other believes that's too important to let go.

"People think the first step is coming up with a budget to make their money last. But a budget is just a tactic," Dr. Goldbart says. "It only works if you expect the same things from your financial decisions, if your values are similar. If you haven't had that conversation, getting through unemployment will cause a lot more stress and conflict. Often the real stress of unemployment isn't working with a limited budget, it's dealing with the way it changes your life and takes away things you had expected from your marriage." The following process can help you sort out—and agree on—common financial goals during a financial crisis.

1. **Set aside a few uninterrupted hours.** Have your conversation when you're well rested, well fed, and you don't expect any distractions.

2. **Take turns talking and listening.** Describe for your partner what you most want in life that money will buy—and what you most fear about losing the power to have those things. Listen without judging when your partner does the same. You might look through your checkbook or credit card statements to jog your memory. "Your partner shouldn't try to agree or disagree at this point," Dr. Goldbart says. "The goal is to get everything out on the table." Talk about what money means to you: Fun? Security? Power?

3. **Set common goals.** Assemble a list of concerns and values the two of you share strongly, plus a list of important goals that you may not share. Talk about how you'll accomplish them with limited resources: What's most important, such as paying the mortgage? What's least important, such as a pricey vacation you'd been considering? What can you accomplish, in some form, without spending any money?

4. **Come up with a budget.** Don't assume you'll land a new, equally lucrative job within a month. Expect to be unemployed for at least six months and plan accordingly. How long will unemployment checks and, if you're lucky, your company's severance package last? What savings can you draw on? What emergency funds could you tap as a last resort? Look at your spending over the past few months and figure out your financial bottom line: Which of your bills are fixed costs, such as your mortgage or car payments? Which could you trim if need be, such as switching to a cheaper telephone plan or cutting the hours in your cell-phone plan? Can you negotiate with any of your creditors?

5. **Check in with each other.** End the discussion by asking each other how you feel about your decisions. Thank each other for the sacrifices you've committed to making, as well as the compromises you agreed to reach. Commit to a follow-up session a few weeks down the road to make sure things are progressing comfortably.

Mission 2: Support Each Other

If ever there was a time for good partnership and communication, it's when one of you is searching for new work. Here's how to work together in the best way possible.

Agree on the job-search parameters. If a better job becomes available in a different city or state, would the family be amenable to moving? What if a potential new job is a night shift or requires frequent travel? Is it essential that your next job provide health-care insurance? It's best to talk about the parameters of what sort of job you should—and shouldn't—pursue right at the start. In particular, moving your family for a new job can be traumatic if everyone isn't in agreement that it's the right thing to do.

Agree on whether it's time to go solo. More and more people today are independent contractors working out of their homes. If this appeals to you, talk it through thoroughly with your spouse. Is there space in your home to set up shop? Can you earn enough to compensate for the salary and benefits you'd get working for a company (remember too that independent contractors pay much higher taxes)? Is it realistic to think that you can make it work? Is your personality suited to this type of lifestyle? Can the family handle it if you need to spend 80 hours a week getting established or traveling more frequently?

Agree on a job-search strategy. Coming home to find an out-of-work spouse curled up in front of the TV, playing computer games, or otherwise goofing off could make a working spouse feel angry or resentful. Questioning an out-of-work partner frequently about what he or she is doing, how many résumés he or she is sending out, and how many phone calls he or she has made today could easily trigger the same feelings in him.

The answer? Come up with a job-search strategy. Talk together about how the out-of-work partner will look for work, how much time he or she will spend on it each day, and how much time he or she will spend on other activities, such as exercise, relaxation, and household chores.

Don't nag or interrogate. It's easy to let rising worries about money and the future erode the good feeling between you. Couples dealing with unemployment need each other's support and encouragement—and each other's resourcefulness—more than ever. Yet you may instead find yourselves locked into a fruitless communication pattern, with the unemployed partner becoming more and more defensive and even depressed as the other partner badgers him or her with questions about the number of résumés sent out, the number of want ads answered.

If your spouse is working hard to find work, trust him or her. If something's getting in the way, it's time to approach the issue with a gentle touch. Find a

Who Washes the Dishes Now?

If your spouse is suddenly home all day, it makes sense for him or her to pick up more of the chores, from laundry to vacuuming, from cooking to ferrying the kids around after school. Or does it?

"There can be pitfalls," says California psychologist Stephen Goldbart, Ph.D. "First, if you're out there looking for work or trying to create work, you should be busy. You won't necessarily have more time for housework. And the other issue is gender roles. Despite modern views of shared housework, in the deepest parts of ourselves, we're still where we've always been when it comes to who does what."

Even in the 21st century, old-fashioned sex roles can tangle an out-of-work spouse's efforts to help out more around the house. A jobless wife may find that the amount of housework grows and grows and grows to take up the whole day as she takes up traditional jobs she may have watched her own mother perform or that her kids and husband subtly expect of her. ("How about a meat loaf tonight? You've got time to make one now.") An unemployed husband may feel "feminized and emasculated and disempowered," Dr. Goldbart says, especially if his identity was strongly aligned with his professional life.

The best solution? A soft approach. Talk with your job-seeking partner about how the household situation has changed. Discuss which tasks you'd like to keep doing. Ask which ones he or she would like to take on. Trade off on the rest or negotiate a 50-50 split.

quiet moment and talk about what you've noticed: "I notice you haven't talked about your job search lately. What's going on?" Ask your partner how he or she is feeling. If your spouse is feeling stuck—either by lowered self-esteem or because he or she has exhausted all job-hunting prospects—it's time to brainstorm new tactics. Maybe a part-time job, regardless of the pay. Perhaps it's worth investing funds in a career counselor or head-hunting service.

Hold a weekly job update meeting. Birkel suggests setting aside a specified time each week to review what's happening on the unemployment front. This frees the two of you from the grind of discussing it on a daily basis. This meeting is also a good time for both partners to talk about the household budget and about any changing emotions. Both of you need a chance to share fears, worries, anxiety and, any brainstorms you've had about the experience.

Hunt for the silver lining. Sometimes job loss is a real opportunity. We're not being Pollyannaish here. Everybody knows at least one person who's been through the test of job loss and emerged saying, "It's one of the best things that could have happened." Got kids? Unemployment could provide a chance to stay home with a young child or to be in the house when a teenage son or daughter gets home after school. Losing a job can also give you the time and the push you've needed to get out of a less-than-ideal work situation or to explore a whole new field.

Ask how you can help. An overenthusiastic offer to help may simply seem kind and practical, but an unemployed spouse may easily infer that you wish they'd just get moving. It's sure to backfire and create tension. Instead, approach your partner as you would a friend or a colleague: Let him or her know that it's okay to turn down your offer to pick up the résumés at the copy shop. Ask what your spouse would like you to do—if anything—to help. This approach leaves your partner in control.

Maintain your optimism. Two intangibles that vanish when a job is lost: positive work feedback and a feeling of accomplishment. The spouse of a job seeker can replace some of those good feelings by staying positive about the job seeker's prospects; reaffirming that he or she is deeply loved; and emphasizing all the enduring, nonfinancial contributions he or she makes to the marriage, the family, the household.

Mission 3: Stay Positive

Your job and your income weren't the only things that made your family love you—or that you and your spouse enjoyed. Fight cabin fever and reconnect with positive feelings with these tips.

Get out of the house. Staying home will only induce cabin fever. Don't forgo all pleasures: Instead of a night out at a fancy restaurant, go for pizza—or take a picnic to a beautiful local park. Birkel recommends couples and families focus on abundance whenever possible, instead of deprivation. "I remember a Saturday while I was out of work when my family needed to get away from other problems," he relates on his website. "We were short on cash, so we packed a picnic lunch and went to a neighborhood park. My wife, daughter, son, and I enjoyed the scenery, munched our sandwiches, and took turns flying a kite that we'd never used before. It turned out to be one of the best days I can remember."

Count your blessings. You didn't marry your spouse just for his or her paycheck or the status of his or her job. Take a step back and gain perspective about the good things in your life: your marriage, your kids, your home, your health, your sense of humor. Just as you don't need money to have a good time, you don't need it to measure a good life. Consider keeping a daily list of things you're grateful for.

Remind yourselves that this is temporary. You will find a job. This is a short-term situation—and so are all the tensions that go with it.

Exercise more. Getting out of the house for a walk or finding some private time to lift weights or work out will release stress, boost your mood, and help you feel you've accomplished something.

Explosion: Weight Gain

Love and marriage, the old song says, go together like a horse and carriage. But today, weight deserves a place in that lyric too.

In the age of the obesity epidemic, a dangerous combination of too much sitting and too much snacking have made serious weight gain a fact of life for two out of three American adults, according to the Centers for Disease Control and Prevention. Marriage itself may be to blame: Studies suggest that married women and men gain three to four pounds within three months of saying "I do" and 16 to 19 pounds by their 10th anniversary. We gain because we meld our eating and activity habits and fall for temptation if a spouse prefers cheese fries to carrot sticks or TV to taking a walk.

But the extra weight doesn't create a healthy bond. Instead, it gets in the way of emotional and physical closeness between a man and a woman. Among participants in the Reader's Digest *Marriage in America Survey*, one in four said that they or their spouses had put on significant weight since saying "I do." The added pounds had a negative impact on half of these couples.

"Weight doesn't have to define who you are as a person and as a spouse. But all too often, it has a big effect on relationships," says Martin Binks, Ph.D., a clinical psychologist and director of behavioral health at the Duke University Diet and Fitness Center. "Society teaches us to hate our body if it's not the 'right' shape and size. That, more than the weight itself, can lead to relationship issues."

Dr. Binks's pioneering research has uncovered a wide variety of ways in which weight can literally mute a couple's sex life. Some effects are physical: Increased body fat seems to interfere with arousal and sexual response for men and women. Others are emotional: In his research, an overwhelming number of women and men said they no longer want to be seen undressed. The good news? Opening up your feelings about your body can help you gain body confidence and reconnect with your own desires, he says. And losing just a small amount of weight can boost libido and free your ability to enjoy sex again.

Take Back Your Marriage

That leads us to an odd twist in the weight-and-marriage story: Sometimes weight loss itself can come between partners. In our Reader's Digest survey, one in eight participants who named overweight as a marital challenge also reported that big weight loss *caused* trouble.

"Announcing that you're going on a diet can make your spouse think you're judging them or their weight," notes Aaron Larson, founder of the National Healthy Marriage Institute based in Provo, Utah. "Your mate may be worried that you'll love them less or even leave if you become slimmer." Restocking the pantry and refrigerator with new, low-calorie foods—and tossing out family favorites—may anger a partner who isn't on a diet.

Larson knows what he's talking about. Extra pounds crept up on him slowly, until the bathroom scale sounded the alarm. "I got up a lot at night when my two children were very young, and I'd reward myself with a treat. I didn't really notice how much weight I was putting on until I was on the borderline between overweight and obesity, and I said to myself, It just isn't healthy to have this much fat on my body."

Larson's next challenge: losing pounds without imposing a carrot-sticks-and-exercise regimen on his wife or family. "My wife has always maintained a healthy weight," he says. "I didn't want to punish her by taking foods out of our household. And I didn't want to set myself up for overeating 'forbidden' foods later after I'd lost weight."

His strategy? "I never gave up ice cream. I just cut back from a big bowl to a four-ounce serving in a little drinking glass, and I ate it with a baby spoon. It lasted a long time that way because I had just as many bites as I'd had before—they were just smaller bites." It worked. Larson lost 50 pounds in five months while enjoying ice cream and chocolate almost every day.

If overweight is an issue in your relationship, we suggest you tackle two important marriage-saving missions: First, feel good about your body right now—don't let the artificially "perfect" bodies of air-brushed magazine models and surgically enhanced movie stars set the standard for your life. Second, lose weight without throwing your marriage off-course. Here's how.

Mission 1: Feel Good about Your Body

"Weight doesn't have to define you," Dr. Binks says. "Even if you're trying to lose pounds for health reasons, it's important to try to overcome limits we put on ourselves based on the number on the scale, giving yourself permission to go ahead and have the life you want right now, regardless of your size or shape." These tips can help you keep weight from becoming a barrier to closeness in your marriage.

Talk about your body and your feelings. "Too often, people are afraid to talk about weight and about sex," Dr. Binks says. "If self-conscious feelings about your body are getting in the way of sexual intimacy, have a conversation about it. Even if you're just feeling a little self-conscious, it's worth sharing it. Breaking the silence can open up broader conversations—about intimacy, about how you're feeling about yourself and your relationship, about what you like and don't like in your sexual relationship."

Enjoy yourself and your relationship *now*. "Most often, relationship difficulties related to overweight start with the overweight person, not with the spouse," Dr. Binks says. "Society teaches people you have to hate your body if it's not at the right weight or shape. So people stop enjoying life. They put off all sorts of things they'd like to be or to do and plan only to start if they can lose weight. It doesn't have to be that way!" Remind yourself that it's not only okay to accept yourself as you are right now, it can also be a first step toward going on to achieve a healthier weight.

Adapt your sex life to your changing body. Extra weight may be making your accustomed sexual positions uncomfortable or even painful. Or they may simply leave you feeling so self-conscious that you can't focus on pleasure. "You may find there's great enjoyment to be had by making some shifts in where your body is," Dr. Binks says. "Sexual intimacy should match what your body can do comfortably."

Some ideas: Buy lingerie that looks and feels attractive yet gives you some coverage if you're feeling self-conscious. Set the mood with beautiful sheets, music, candles, even incense. And try out some new positions for sex that are more comfortable for each of you.

Finally, be a receiver, not just a giver. It's tempting to hide from receiving affection or sexual pleasure if you're uncertain that your body "looks right." Fight this temptation! Sexual intimacy is only intimate when it's mutual. Your partner wants to please you!

Mission 2: Lose Weight and Keep Your Mate Happy at the Same Time

If your spouse has ever sulked when you chose fruit salad over Chubby Hubby ice cream, inadvertently (or intentionally) sabotaged your diet by loading your plate with French fries, or given you a very dirty look when you suggested that he or she might want to join you at the gym, then you've walked into one of dieting's biggest traps. Losing weight, experts say, can make your spouse feel threatened, judged, jealous, or simply inconvenienced.

"Dropping pounds is a big lifestyle change," Larson says. "You're not eating the same way. You may choose to exercise instead of watching TV. This can make your spouse feel uncomfortable. It can even lead to attempts to sabotage your efforts." Your partner may feel anxious that you'll change when you're skinny, or that you'll judge him or her harshly, or that you'll seek greener pastures. He or she may also simply be annoyed that you dumped a favorite ice cream and replaced it with frozen banana slices.

Don't let your spouse's fears derail your efforts to drop a few pounds. Weight loss is good for your health, your sex life, and your self-esteem. Here's how to accomplish it without jeopardizing your marriage.

Set a modest goal. Duke University researchers recently found that women and men who lost just 10 percent of their body weight saw big improvements in their sex lives. "Feeling good about yourself and feeling in control are so important," Dr. Binks says. "But we think the positive change reflects even more than that. Research shows that losing just a small amount of weight improves lots of health conditions—it helps with blood pressure, blood sugar, and heart health. The health of blood vessels improves, so you have better blood flow—a factor that can also make sex more enjoyable for men and for women."

Reassure your mate. Tell your partner that you accept and love him or her as they are and that you don't expect him or her to lose weight because you are. "It's also important to do this nonverbally," Larson says. "Try hard not to send disapproving glances if your spouse has second helpings at dinner or orders the large ice cream cone. This can be very difficult, but it's very important for your marriage relationship."

Lead by example—not by nagging. "As excited as you are about learning to lose weight, we recommend not trying to convince, coerce, or even motivate your spouse to lose weight too," says Larson. "If you do, you'll only end up damaging your relationship."

That smart advice can be difficult to follow, Larson admits. "When you find something that works for you, it's only natural to share it with the person you love the most—especially if they're overweight too. But people are a lot like donkeys—when you try to force them to do what you want, they just dig in their heels. Resentment builds up and spills over into the rest of your relationship." And if you're an emotional eater, the resulting marriage woes could send you back to the cookie jar, reversing your hard-won weight-loss success.

A better strategy: Be like India's visionary Mahatma Gandhi by *being* the change you want to see around you. "We're wired to mimic what we see around us," Larson says. "Eventually your spouse may decide on his or her own to take steps like yours. Then their motivation will be internal. Their lifestyle changes are much more likely to stick. And you won't have conflict over weight loss."

Find a weight-loss partner—outside your marriage. When University of Massachusetts researchers studied 109 dieters, they found that those who were the most successful had supportive weight-loss buddies. "If

MARRIAGE MAGIC
How to Talk about Dangerous Weight

If your spouse is ignoring weight-related health problems such as high blood pressure, type 2 diabetes, or heart disease, you can make a difference. Instead of lecturing, tell your spouse how much you love him or her and *ask* how you can help with sticking to a special diet or exercise plan and/or remembering to take medications.

your spouse simply can't be supportive about weight loss, we suggest getting your support elsewhere," Dr. Binks says.

Keep buying, cooking, and serving the same foods. Yes, you read that correctly. Contrary to the advice of most major weight-loss programs, Larson suggests that you do not disturb your home food environment: Leave the ice cream in the freezer and the chips on the shelf for the rest of the family.

Explosion: Caring for Aging Parents

Long ago, they nurtured you. Now it's your turn to care for your aging mother or father. It's an honor, a duty, a necessity. But it's not simple. Finding the time, facing the emotional ups and downs, and navigating complex health-care systems and insurance rules is tough enough. Caregiving while holding down a job, raising kids of your own, and sustaining your marriage can be an impossible mountain to climb every day. And modern medical advances that boost longevity may add to the burden as people live longer with increasingly serious physical and mental conditions such as heart failure, arthritis, or Alzheimer's disease.

Caregivers say they feel squeezed on all sides: Often it may seem that your spouse and even your siblings won't help out enough—or an elderly parent doesn't live close by. Coping with your own fears, worries, and anger is compounded by the need to take care of your parent's emotions too. All this leaves little in reserve for your own relationship. Small wonder, then, that in one national survey of 514 women and men, nearly one in three said elder-care duties strained their marriages. And when the Web site caregiving.com asked its visitors how caregiving impacted their marriages, 81 percent said it tested their relationships in ways they had never imagined.

And yet, many also say it can make a marriage stronger. In the Reader's Digest *Marriage in America Survey*, one in four said a parent's prolonged illness or the need to take responsibility for a parent was a major challenge for their marriages. But more than a third of these caregivers said the experience had a positive effect on their relationships.

That's no coincidence, experts say. While caregiving can impact your relationship, your relationship is a lifeline when you're called on to take care of an aging parent. "It takes both spouses to make caregiving work," says psychologist Terry Hargrave, Ph.D., a professor of counseling at West Texas A&M University and author of *Loving Your Parents When They Can No Longer Love You*. "Otherwise, the burden is almost too much to bear."

The Realities of Love

Within just a few years after Ed and Sylvia Robertson's son and daughter left home for good, both of their mothers needed help. Sylvia's mom even moved from Florida to live with them in Waleska, Georgia. "It was part of our obligation, and we accepted it lovingly," Ed notes. "We also learned more about the reality of health and memory in older age as a result. We now say to each other, 'I will love you for as long as I remember,' instead of, 'I love you forever.' It doesn't sound as joyful as 'forever,' but it's realistic and true and inspires us to live zestfully right now, in the present."

Caring for aging parents can change your marriage emotionally and geographically, as Nancy and Carl Terry discovered. "We had lived in the same house, in the same neighborhood in Newport News, Virginia, for 25 or 26 years," Nancy says. "We had so many close friends, jobs, and a church we were very involved in. But my parents, who lived in North Carolina, were not in good health, so we moved to Raleigh to be closer to them and to see them through aging and illnesses. My father has since died, and my mother has Alzheimer's disease. It was a major move and a major change for us, but our marriage survived beautifully."

Not everyone's so fortunate. Caregivers often burn out as they attempt to juggle so many responsibilities and so much emotion. More subtle marriage stresses include fatigue, guilt if one of you worries you're not spending enough time with your parent, financial worries, lack of time for your relationship, and less emotional energy for your spouse. And inviting an older parent or other relative into your home may create new power struggles. You're in charge, but your guest is accustomed to being the head of the household. In one survey, half of all caregivers said they worry more about the people they take care of than they do about their kids, jobs, partners, or their own health.

"Just when the total freedom of the empty-nest years arrived, parents came back into our lives," Ed Robertson notes. "It changed things for a while."

There are many wonderful books, websites, organizations, and support groups that can help you master the art of caregiving. You'll find them in the Marriage Resource Guide. Less is written, though, about how to nurture your marriage while fulfilling this important responsibility. Your marital mission? First, work together to make caregiving work. Second, find ways to focus on your marriage. Here's how.

Mission 1: Make Caregiving a Team Effort

These ideas can help you stay connected and share the responsibilities of caregiving.

Name a designated caregiver and a designated support person. Dr. Hargrave suggests that when possible, one person should be the primary caregiver, an arrangement that can comfort an aging parent and keep care coordinated. "It makes sense to have one person running the show," he says. But this approach can also lead to burnout—unless the caregiver's spouse becomes head of the caregiver's support team. Most often, the wife may be the caregiver, and the husband would then be a very active support person. But the roles could be reversed.

"Being the primary support person, in charge of the support team, is a big responsibility," he says. "Caregivers typically don't take care of themselves, so the support person has to be very active. At times, you'll have to step in and find someone to take the caregiver's place so that he or she can take a break, get a massage, get other things done in his or her life."

Assemble a caregiver support team. Put together a list of people the support person can call on for help as needed. This could include siblings and in-laws who can help with care, with the caregiver's household chores or childcare responsibilities, or with insurance paperwork. It could also include friends and neighbors who can be available for social activities and emotional support too.

While most caregivers have at least one sibling, a national poll found, a whopping 60 percent said their brothers and sisters did little to help out. Call a meeting or schedule telephone time to discuss what you need and explore reasons why your closest relatives are holding back. Suggest specific tasks they can take on that will lighten your load, such as spending time with your parent, accompanying him or her to a scheduled medical appointment, or agreeing to shoulder a portion of the cost of care.

Scope out local resources. Government agencies, local support groups, and national organizations can all offer support and assistance. So can local adult day-care groups, home health services, nursing homes that offer short-term respite care, private care aides, and your local Agency on Aging. Put together a file folder with descriptions of various organizations and contact information so that it's ready when you are.

Debrief each other every week. Set aside time to review how caregiving and the support effort are going. Is the caregiver getting what he or she needs? Which jobs seem like too much? Talk about how the previous week unfolded. When was the caregiver stressed? When did he or she have too many duties? And look at the week ahead to find trouble spots, such as a doctor's appointment and a child's high school band concert on the same evening. Look beyond schedules. Find out how the caregiving spouse is feeling and how well he or she is sleeping, eating, and handling the demands of work, family, and friends.

The support spouse should get a turn in the spotlight too. Discuss how support efforts are going: Does this spouse have the help he or she needs? Is the caregiver accepting help and support? Does the support spouse have enough early warning of potential trouble spots so that he or she can step in? Are there areas where you both can improve your communication?

As you talk, give yourselves permission to express any emotion that comes up. Bottling up sadness, grief, or anxieties can trigger the brain chemistry that leads to depression—and cut you off from upbeat feelings.

Monitor yourself for burnout—and ask your spouse to watch out too. Check in with yourself once a day. How are you feeling? Do you notice any signs of burnout, such as overwhelming fatigue, irritability, or depression? Are you turning more to alcohol or medication to keep yourself calm? If you or your spouse notices changes, talk with your doctor or a mental health professional. Cherish yourself!

Integrate your parent into your family. If he or she is living in your home and is able, give him or her some household responsibilities—even if it's just folding towels and matching socks. Everyone wants to feel needed and make a contribution.

Mission 2: Enjoy Your Marriage

Skip the guilt. Finding time for yourselves and feeling joy together isn't a luxury now. Your marriage can be a source of strength, courage, and renewal, buoying you up. These steps can help.

Spouses: Be Alert for Burnout

If your partner is the caregiver for an aging parent, one of your biggest responsibilities is to help watch for signs of burnout. Often the caregiver is one of the last to realize he or she is physically, emotionally, and mentally exhausted. If you spot any of these signs, arrange for your spouse to take a break—and explore ways to lighten his or her load on a regular basis.

- Withdrawal from friends, family, and other loved ones
- Loss of interest in activities previously enjoyed
- Feeling blue, irritable, hopeless, and helpless
- Changes in appetite, weight, or both
- Changes in sleep patterns
- Getting sick more often
- Emotional and physical exhaustion

Protect your privacy and your couple time. Don't put off dating or time together, and try to move ahead with shared interests. If you can afford it, hire someone to be with an infirm relative so you can get out together. Or take friends, neighbors, and relatives up on their offers to help you out.

Make a social investment. Feeling guilty about taking time for your marriage or for other friendships? Truth is, feeding your relationships is an investment in your own future. Your duties as a caregiver may last only a short time. What will be waiting for you afterward?

De-stress together. Take a daily walk, join a nearby gym, try a yoga routine on DVD. Relaxing together is an example of healthy multitasking: You're doing two important things at the same time. Combining stress reduction with couple time may even yield a neat bonus: After a while, just seeing your spouse could evoke your body's natural relaxation response.

Support each other's efforts to stay healthy. Stock the fridge and pantry with ready-to-eat produce such as baby carrots, cherry tomatoes, and bananas. Opt for higher-fiber, whole-grain breads, cereals, rice, and pastas. Try to keep overeating in check. Make it easy for your spouse to make healthy lifestyle choices (don't nag!) by "modeling" them yourself and by keeping temptations out of the house.

You've made it—at last! Like the kid who's found the prize in the cereal box or the football team that wins the Super Bowl trophy after a tough season, the two of you have arrived at the sweetest, most well-earned stage of married life.

The journey required hard work and patience, love and determination. Defying the odds, you've built a relationship. A home. A family. A life. Was it all worthwhile? For most couples, the answer is a resounding *yes*: Experts, surveys, in-depth research studies, and real-life husbands and wives all agree that marriage happiness soars with time. If you've hung in there, you know that your relationship is sweeter, deeper, and richer now—so many years after you first said, "I do." The rewards of a Completion-stage marriage can be huge: Studies show that couples in enduring, stable marriages have more joy and meaning in their lives. They're healthier and live longer too.

While some stages of marriage arrive with a bang, the Completion stage emerges quietly. The lifestyle changes of the Reunion stage have become routine, career issues ebb, and you discover a comforting warmth in your marriage. You *know* each other, deeply. You realize that life is good and that deep down, you are truly happy. It is an extraordinarily good feeling.

> There's no question that the years after retirement can be the best of your life.

Some couples reach this blissful, culminating stage of marriage earlier than others. But for most, its arrival coincides with another major shift in your life: retirement age. It's a perfect pairing.

"There's no question that the years after retirement can be the best of your life," says Stephen Treat, D.Min., the director and CEO of the Philadelphia-based Council for Relationships and an instructor in psychiatry and human behavior at Jefferson Medical College in Philadelphia. "You've got wisdom, you're more self-accepting, you've gotten rid of insecurities over the years. You know your spouse very, very well. Now you have the time to enjoy all that you've accomplished, all that you are."

Conventional advice says to focus mostly on money and health as you prepare for retirement—and both are deeply important. However, research shows that the keys to *happiness* in the Completion stage lie elsewhere.

When Harvard Medical School researchers tracked the health, wealth, and happiness of 824 women and men from their teens through their 80s, they discovered that inheriting "good" genes and salting away a big nest egg *weren't* the major predictors of bliss late in life. The real keys: the ability to adapt to changing circumstances and capacity for enjoying the moment, friends, and a loving spouse. When researcher George Vaillant, M.D., looked more closely at 150 retired men from the study, he found that three attributes distinguished the happy guys: They knew how to play, they had a sense of meaning and purpose in their lives, and they valued their marriages and their friendships.

"Getting ready for retirement means much more than financial planning," says Dr. Vaillant, a Harvard Medical School psychiatrist and author of *Aging Well: Surprising Guideposts to a Happier Life from the Landmark Harvard Study of Adult Development.* "The factors that make later life satisfying are a sense of play—the capacity to enjoy life for its own sake. Finding meaning and purpose in your life. And having a good marriage. In the years before you retire, it's as important to work on your relationship with your spouse as it is to put money into your retirement account."

Shifting Gears

The biggest shock—or reward—of retirement? A sudden plunge into deeper intimacy with your partner. Now you're together for much of the day. You no longer have a job (or young children) to give you something to do, a sense of identity, a purpose—or a buffer to keep the two of you occupied but a little distant from each other. For better or worse, it's just the two of you now. "The biggest issue for retired couples is that all of a sudden, there's a whole new level of intimacy that wasn't available when you were both working," says Dr. Treat. "Couples usually aren't ready for it. It feels awkward, even threatening. Husbands and wives haven't practiced just *being* with each other, just sharing time together and being intimate. They've got the concept of *doing* down pat—that's what people do when they're working and raising a family, when you're fulfilling obligations and expectations. That's what our culture values. But just *being* becomes more and more important as you age. And it's very difficult to do if a couple isn't used to being together in an intimate way."

After decades spent working, raising children, building a home and financial security, the sudden quiet of the Completion stage can be unsettling. Couples interviewed for this book candidly reported feeling a void, a lack of identity and purpose, at first. They said they were surprised by new conflicts with their spouses—over household chores, over how much time they would spend together and apart, and even over how often they would make love.

There's good news too. Some felt their marriages blossom anew as the ease of retirement let them relax and experience a honeymoon phase. And the happiest were often the bravest: They grappled with the missions of the Completion stage for months or even years. It wasn't always easy, they said, but it was worth it. "There are very few days when we don't acknowledge that this is a wonderful time of our life," one husband told us. "We're grateful to have arrived here together. So many of our friends have divorced or separated or even passed away by now."

Couples told us that creating a good Completion stage marriage means working out new day-to-day roles (who cooks? who cleans?), finding new sources of meaning and creativity, and accepting the fact that time together is a precious, limited resource.

- "The most recent challenge to our relationship was retirement six years ago," notes Hollie Atkinson of Georgetown, Texas. "A lot of our identity was bound up in what we did for a living. We thought we had considered this challenge very carefully, but it turned out to be more difficult than we had imagined. For one thing, I tried to take over the kitchen, and my wife, Janell, didn't want the kitchen taken over!"

  Janell Atkinson adds, "Hollie first mentioned retirement when we were in our late 50s, and I felt, Is it here already? We're not that old. But there was so much we wanted to do with our lives. The transition was difficult—more difficult for me than I had expected. I didn't see the glorious part that was ahead. I knew these were supposed to be the golden years, but I thought, My goodness, where are they? Now the shadows have come apart, we both made adjustments, and I'm glad we're here."

- "Retirement put new demands on my time," says Jane Turner of Marion, North Carolina. "I was looking forward to doing my own

CONVERSATION STARTERS
for the Completion Stage

1. How much of each day and each week should we spend at home doing things together? How much private time would each of us like to have? How much time would each of us like to spend socializing or pursuing interests (hobbies, classes, volunteering, a part-time job) on our own?

2. Should we continue doing the same household and lawn/garden chores we've always done? Is it time to redivide these jobs since we're both at home now? Are we interested in swapping—to take a break from a task we don't like or to try something we've never done on a regular basis, such as lawn care, cooking, grocery shopping, filling out insurance forms, tending to investments, or keeping the social calendar?

3. What do we expect of our children now? How often would we like to talk with them on the phone, to write to them, to e-mail, to visit? Has our relationship moved from parent-child to friendship? How can we foster a close relationship without imposing?

4. What kinds of activities and commitments can we make that will give our lives meaning and purpose? What causes or issues are most important to each of us? What creative interests would we each most love to develop? What about learning—is there a new skill or subject area we'd like to study, either by taking a class or learning from books, workshops, and seminars?

5. How has our marriage grown in the years leading up to the Completion stage? What strengths have we developed? What qualities of our marriage, and of each other, most inspire and comfort us? Are we both satisfied with the way we communicate, with our emotional closeness, sexual intimacy, shared spirituality, and sense of fun? What would each of us most like to see happen in our marriage in the next 1, 5, and 10 years?

thing, but I felt more responsible to my husband because he was home now. I think that's a stress a lot of couples may feel but don't know how to verbalize: Now we have to meet all our needs through each other. We realized we could end up with a huge void in our lives, and we thought about what we could do to keep ourselves growing. I started taking art lessons. My husband, Clay, started doing pottery. And we put up an antique log cabin beside a trout stream in the mountains of western North Carolina, on 80 acres down a two-mile-long gravel road. We love our new life."

- "When the children are gone and you're back together as a couple, your whole marriage changes. Then when you retire, everything changes again," says Bob Richter of Orange City, Florida. "The big thing is, you don't fuss about things that aren't important. There's so little time left."

- "I remember exactly where we were when Lee told me he was thinking about taking an early retirement," says Rebecca Wiederkehr of St. Louis, Missouri. "We were driving through northern Missouri. I was panicking inside, thinking about what it would mean financially and what it would be like having him at home all the time. It frightened me so much. It took Lee several years after that to retire, and it went really well. I did have to adjust to him having more free time than I did, but in so many ways it's been really great for him and for us."

The missions of the Completion stage can help you navigate this new world and reinvent—or reinvigorate—your marriage.

Keep your marriage growing. Retirement itself can rock your marriage as one or both of you cope with the loss of identity, friends, and a sense of purpose related to your work. You're suddenly home all day together. What will you do? What will you talk about? And as the years go by, physical limitations can change your relationship too. Your first mission: Being more open, accepting, and appreciative than ever. Having a marriage that's alive and growing is never more important than now.

Play—and be in the moment. Kids can do it. But somehow, adults lose the childlike ability to simply be, to simply enjoy what's happening right now. This is the time to revive this important skill: Research says it can be as important as a well-stocked retirement account for ensuring well-being in the years ahead.

Share a new sense of meaning and purpose. In the Harvard study, men who were happy during the Completion stage were three times more likely than unhappy guys to say they'd found meaning and purpose in their lives. Sure, you can catch up with daytime TV, hit the golf course, and lunch with your friends, but after a few months, we guarantee you'll be wondering, Is that all there is? Passive leisure pursuits won't keep you or your marriage happy. So why not explore new meanings, new purposes together?

Reorganize your time, your territory, your tasks. The nuts-and-bolts issues of sharing a home and a schedule aren't really so small. Dividing household chores equitably, balancing "we" time with "me" time, and even reorganizing your home so that both of you have space for hobbies and privacy can make all the difference. We'll show you how real couples met this challenge—and what the experts say you can do to make a success of this important but often overlooked aspect of the Completion years.

Mission 1

Keep Your Marriage Growing

Happy, long-married couples interviewed for *The 7 Stages of Marriage* weren't shy about reporting that they didn't see eye-to-eye on everything—even after 40, 50, or even 60 years together. And they didn't expect to! Despite their shared history, partners said they felt they were still changing and learning new things about themselves and each other.

"We're not the same two people who got married as a 19-year-old and a 20-year-old," says Hollie Atkinson, married to Janell. "We're still growing and getting to know each other all over again. The surprising thing is, when we change as individuals, things that we thought we'd conquered and put to bed years ago as a couple can come back again. You deal with it, learn from it, and move on."

Michael Hoxsey of Cincinnati, who has been married for 48 years, told us he thinks spouses should *always* see themselves as "engaged" to each other rather than settled down once and for all. "Throughout your life and your marriage, you keep on resolving the questions 'Who am I?,' 'Who are you?,'

Risk and Safety

Establish a deeper, more secure sense of trust and openness in your relationship with a "risk and safety" exercise suggested by Stephen Treat, D.Min., director of the Council for Relationships in Philadelphia. This is a great way for Completion-stage couples to open up and talk about emotions and thoughts you may have been holding on to for a long time. It's also a great way to share all the new feelings you're having about this new phase of your relationship.

For this exercise, set aside about a half hour.

Here's how it works: Both of you agree to listen thoughtfully and without judgment to whatever your partner has to say. You'll take turns being the speaker and the listener.

The speaker's role: Talk about something that's emotionally risky. It could be a feeling you've never shared with your partner, or one that makes you feel a bit overwhelmed. You might discuss how you think your marriage is going, whether you're satisfied, and what you'd like to do about it. You might also discuss your thoughts, fears, and hopes about retirement.

The listener's job: Ask questions. Rephrase and reflect back the speaker's message. (The speaker can add information or gently correct the listener's understanding of the message if it's not quite accurate.)

Once the listener is finished asking questions and reflecting what he or she has heard, switch roles.

and 'Who are we?' The engagement period, when a couple is creating their whole reality, should never end," he says. "Marriage shouldn't stop your individual growth or your growth as a couple."

As his wife, Joan, sees it, "Marriage is a sacrament. We marry each other every day. It's an ongoing experience, not something that happened once."

How to deal with the inevitable conflicts of daily life? The fundamentals still hold true, says Barbara Christensen of Newport News, Virginia, who's been married to husband, Chris, for 56 years. "We have genuine respect for each other. Sometimes we do become irritated or angry at each other, of course, but we have learned to use the tools we learned long ago. We talk it out and become one again," she says. "We compromise. We agree to disagree. We honor the other's right to their own opinion. We decided long ago that divorce is not an option for us. So we work every day on our relationship."

After retirement, Completion-stage couples are often surprised to discover that indeed, they don't know all there is to know about each other. You may discover that the two of you have different plans and dreams for this important time of life. Or that you have very different ideas about how to run the household. Or that your marriage needs a tune-up in order to fulfill long-hidden needs and desires. These tips and exercises can help you nurture a growing marriage now.

Open up a little more. Moving into the "third age" of your life and your marriage can stir up a rainbow of feelings, from euphoria and relief to fear and anxiety. Don't bottle them up!

"A couple becomes more intimate when partners take risks," Dr. Treat says. "That requires being emotionally honest and making the relationship safe for taking those risks. When you're both emotionally honest, you don't collect grudges and negative feelings over the years that fester and fester. You stay current with each other and connected."

Sharing your feelings and thoughts can be especially important if retirement leaves you feeling as if you've lost your identity and sense of purpose—a risk for anyone who felt strongly invested in a career or demanding job. Losing your work identity can lead to feelings of depression. What helps: A spouse who understands that this loss is big, a marriage that lets you express your feelings, and a plan for finding new purpose (keep reading!). If depression persists, consider seeing a counselor or therapist.

Appreciate each other. Most of us are guilty of taking our spouses and marriages for granted; that's why we've woven this piece of solid-gold advice into just about every marital stage. Veteran couples were unanimous in saying that appreciating each other is key to a happy Completion-stage union. "I get so much energy when someone appreciates me," Michael Hoxsey says. "And yet, it's so easy to forget to give appreciation or to hold back because you don't want someone to get a big head. But why hold back— especially with your own spouse? Why not give them a greater sense of their own personal strength and value to you?"

Feeling appreciated can be life-giving. In one study from Finland that tracked 206 women and men ages 80 and older for 10 years, researchers found that those who had the strongest sense of emotional closeness, belonging, and reassurance of their worth were 2.5 times more likely to be alive at the end of the study than those who didn't receive the same reassurance and nurturing.

Reconnect. You're spending hours and hours together, but that doesn't mean you're pouring out your heart and soul to each other 24/7. (Nor should you!) Setting aside a few minutes each day to focus on each other can keep you feeling close and clued-in to each other's feelings and plans. "We have a sharing time of about 10 minutes a day to get 'in touch' with each other on our thoughts and feelings for the day," says Barbara Christensen.

Laugh. "Since 1997, I have had nine major operations, and Chris has almost died twice in the last two years due to his diabetes, heart surgeries, and organ shutdown," Barbara says. "All of these things have put a huge strain on our relationship for weeks at a time. But we use a lot of humor in all of these situations. We do tend to look on the 'up' side of life, and we have a great sense of humor about our lives and our circumstances."

Laughter works even if you weren't born with a funny bone. "Chris is a natural pessimist, so he has had to teach himself to find the bright side of things," she adds. "We believe that we can meet any challenge to our relationship by digging deeply and finding a bright side to things happening to us. We use humor constantly."

Don't sweat the small stuff. "My husband, Bob, and I have been married 60 years," says Bette Richter. "At this point in our lives and in our marriage, you don't fuss about little things. " Adds Bob Richter, "We've learned how to listen to one another, to compromise, to let whoever is the best at doing a certain thing be the leader. That's something we would have argued about in the past. We still have issues—we're still growing and changing as people and as a couple. But instead of arguing or being stubborn we say: In five years will it really matter? The answer is usually no."

Savor your past. Take time together to reminisce about wonderful moments in your own history. Reliving times of closeness and love rekindles warm and even passionate feelings. For Joan and Michael Hoxsey, the memory of a mis-mixed honeymoon martini sends them back to the earliest days of their long marriage—and evokes lots of giggles. "Just after we got married, we were supposed to go on a cruise, but we missed the boat," Michael recalls. "So we stayed in our Seattle apartment for four or five days

A Couple's Appreciation Journals

A year after the death of their son Jamie, Joan and Michael Hoxsey of Cincinnati began keeping daily journals to record their gratitude for one another. "We feel you get back what you focus on. If you look at what's good, you'll get more of it," Joan says. "We each take about 5 to 10 minutes in the evening to write and share what we've written."

Simplicity is key to their journal project's success. Making an entry is not a requirement. If you skip a day, a week, or a month, it's okay. "We tried keeping a more formal journal a few years ago, and it didn't work. This time, we decided it had to be motivated by free will," Joan says. The journals themselves (they each keep one) are from a local dollar store. "We didn't want to make it gorgeous and expensive, just everyday," she says.

The results? Wonderful beyond words. "I think we've said things to each other in these journals that we've probably wanted to hear for more than 40 years," she says. "We've written appreciations that we thought the other never noticed." And the benefits spill over. "It makes me more appreciative the next day, because I'm looking for all the ways I really do appreciate Joan," Michael says. "Sometimes I find something wonderful in the most amazing, irrelevant place or event in our lives."

The couple shared recent entries with us: "On January 30, 2006, we must have had trouble with the computer," Joan notes. "I wrote, 'My dearest Michael, I love you, Mikey! You are the dearest person in the whole world, my heart's desire … you certainly handled your frustration in an even-handed and calm way today … thank you … quiet time together … it has been a good day despite the electronic struggles … I love you forever, Joan.' "

Michael's entry for the same day: "Darling Joanie, I want this to be the best year yet. You well and well-rested. Me well, us sharing the life we have, the best yet."

with really nothing to do. Joan cooked our first meal in our home. It was fried chicken. And she offered me a martini—mixed with four parts vermouth and one part gin instead of the other way around. It was delicious! I'll never forget it."

Joan Hoxsey giggles softly as she adds, "I was a 19-year-old bride, and with all the confidence in the world I handed him this martini. All I knew was that it had to have an olive in it. After all, I've seen it in the movies! That memory really does take us back to the beginning of our marriage!"

Adapt to new limitations—but hang on to physical intimacy. Bob and Bette Richters admit that a variety of health problems have intruded on their lifestyle in recent years. "Between the two of us, we made 17 trips to doctors, clinics, and drugstores in the past month alone," Bob notes. "Things come along when you're older, including the fact that I fell out of a tree I was trimming recently and fractured three vertebrae."

Bob's injuries have made it difficult for him to walk long distances. "My knees bend just fine, but my legs just won't keep going," he says. But that hasn't ended sexual intimacy, just changed it a little. "You learn to adjust your intimate relationship," he says. "We're still sexually active. There have been brief times when we weren't due to illness, but we always resume. If intimacy has been good all along, if you've worked to keep it going, then you don't have to give it up. Lots of older people do, but we don't think they really have to. It makes such a difference." Adds Bette, "I think good sex is a strong tie for a marriage. And so is affection. We kiss and hug frequently. When one of us is leaving the house, it's almost a law that we kiss. We'll kiss when we pass each other in the hallway. And we scratch each other's backs. We're affectionate in many different ways."

MARRIAGE MAGIC
Have an Adventure

One morning this week, read the events calendar from your local newspaper out loud. Choose something to do together, just for the heck of it. Then go and make sure you enjoy yourselves together. Developing the ability to make your own fun together is crucial in the Completion stage.

Barbara and Chris Christensen keep the romance in their lives by cuddling, hugging, giving each other shoulder and neck rubs, planning little surprises, and "always kissing hello and goodbye," Barbara says. "Due to Chris's medications and physical ailments, we have not been able to have the intimacy that is such an important part of a loving relationship, but we've found ways to make up for it. We know of many couples in our age group who stay married even though they can no longer have a sexual relationship, and they grow distant from each other as they live more or less like brothers and sisters. We don't want that."

Sexual intimacy in long-married couples isn't unusual—it's just that nobody says much about it, notes Dr. Stephen Treat of Jefferson Medical College. "The whole issue of sex and libido is not talked about in older age," he says. "We certainly know that many older couples in their 70s and 80s are sexually active and content. Their sexuality may have changed from intercourse to touching, kissing, holding, but there are many, many couples that have very alive, very meaningful sexual relationships."

Mission 2
Play—And Be in the Moment

When Dr. George Vaillant, the Harvard Medical School psychiatrist, caught up with 150 retired men whose health and happiness he'd been tracking since they were teens, he made a surprising discovery about living the good life in the Completion years. More than money or good health, it was the capacity to play—to enjoy their marriages, their children and grandchildren, and their hobbies—that predicted which guys felt the most satisfied.

But play is not an easy skill for a grown-up to master. "We're wired from age 20 until age 65 to do things that other people will find valuable—that's how we get paid and how we get our own sense of worth," says Dr. Vaillant. "All that has to change in later life. Men in my study were happiest when they could do things simply because they enjoyed them, not because other people would like what they did."

Attaining this in-the-moment, who-cares-how-good-I-am bliss can be tricky. Dr. Vaillant suggests taking lessons from little kids: "Fourth-graders know how to play. They don't have to be important. They don't get upset if their phone calls aren't returned. And they don't have to be paid for what they're doing," he says. He also holds up Winston Churchill as a good example of a guy who knew how to trade in drive and ambition, in favor of pleasure and fun, at retirement. "Churchill was always looking for other people's esteem. He wrote beautifully and won a Nobel Prize in Literature," Dr. Vaillant says. "But as soon as he retired, he stopped writing and took up watercolors. It was simply something he enjoyed for himself."

Being in the moment is a great marital skill too. It's the only way to fully experience your partner—and yourself. To embrace who you both are right now and to enjoy flashes of the young woman and young man you once were. "Right now is all you have," observes Joan Hoxsey. "You just don't know what tomorrow or the next hour will bring, but you do have time to enjoy one another right now."

And it's all the small moments—such as sitting in bed talking in the morning sunlight, holding hands as you take a walk, bringing your beloved a cup of tea after dinner, listening to a well-loved song that serendipitously plays on the radio—that most touch our hearts and stay in our memories. "It's all the little things that are the most important, we find," Joan notes. "It's not the special outings—the big vacations and fancy dinners—though they are fun. It's the unplanned, personal moments together that count most. They're the little tiny moments of just feeling like this person really holds me in such love and esteem that I could do anything, could be anything, as long as we're together."

Here's other guidance on regaining your sense of play and being in the present.

Slow down! Instead of answering e-mail while chatting with your wife or catching up on today's newspaper while having breakfast with your husband, focus on a single thing: your partner. Turn off the TV, the computer, even the radio. Close the magazine or book, fold up the newspaper. In a world filled with 24/7 entertainment and news, concentrating on your own everyday life may seem boring, unnecessary, even unworthy of your full attention. Remember the old contest line "You must be present to win"? It applies to your marriage too. If you're not present, you'll miss the small, special moments and connections that can happen only when you're really there with each other—even if you're just talking and laughing as you crunch on spoonfuls of high-fiber cereal and skim milk as the sun rises.

Zen and the Art of Now

Enjoying the present—and all the richness this moment, right now, can offer—is one key to Completion stage happiness. Being here, now, helps you fully experience your own feelings and thoughts, listen more deeply to your spouse, and respond with your whole heart and soul. These strategies can help you appreciate and stay in the present moment:

Watch your breath. Feel your attention drifting away? Take a moment to pay attention to your breathing. After a few breaths, also notice how your body feels. This technique can also help you relax.

Just feel it. The next time you hold hands, kiss, or make love, focus your attention on the physical sensations you're feeling. If you find yourself getting distracted, gently return your attention to the physical world.

Put your cares on an ice floe. The next time you and your spouse do something enjoyable together—whether it's sharing a meal, heading out for a date, or taking a walk—banish distracting worries ahead of time. Beforehand, sit quietly for five minutes, close your eyes, and relax. Think about the things that worry or preoccupy you and that could divert your attention during your outing. Then imagine loading your cares onto a drifting ice floe in the Arctic Ocean for the next hour or so. Promise you'll come back to reclaim them later.

Relax together. Barbara and Chris Christensen spend time together each day doing something they hadn't had time for in decades. "We sit down at the game table with a board game or cards for a half hour most days," Barbara says. "That time seems to renew our energies to tackle whatever else is waiting for us."

Let go of the past. It's easy—hey, it's only human—to hold on to old, unfulfilled dreams. "But if you cling to old dreams and goals that haven't been completely fulfilled, you can become very bitter," Dr. Treat says. "You can feel a lot of despair later in life if you're still living off an original dream that never came true, such as being made vice president of your company. When you do that, you see your life as a failure. And you can't spend your time thinking about reality—about all the good things that have happened in your life. The goal is to keep changing, to look at yourself in new ways, and to change your dreams as you move forward in life."

Focus instead on every single good thing that's happened to you so far. Your job. Your marriage. Your family. Your home. Your hobbies, civic or religious involvements, or other contributions. "Look at all the successes you've had," Dr. Treat says. "Then cast off old dreams and refocus on dreams you can fulfill in the months and years ahead. Every so often, review your goals and dreams. Don't be afraid to switch several times. It's practical and healthy."

In particular, focus your efforts on dreams that truly mesh with your unique strengths, abilities, personality, and what you enjoy most.

Explore new ways to have fun together. Dance! Travel! Garden! Tune up the dusty 10-speed and go for a spin!

"Having a good time together really energizes our marriage," says Jane Turner. "We took weekly dance lessons before our sons left home, so that we'd have a fun activity to fall back on when there were no sons at home at all. I was tired of sitting on the sidelines at events, watching everyone else dance. And Clay had danced early on in our marriage—our first really romantic date was at a sorority convention in New Orleans, and we danced, but then we never danced again for 25 years." Now the Turners are adept and graceful. "We love tango because it's so sexy, the waltz because it's so romantic," Jane says. "You never catch us sitting down when there's dancing."

On the shores of Lake Erie in the upper corner of Pennsylvania, Shirley and Terry Snyder are indulging a newfound love of gardening, biking, and travel. "Terry's great at just going up and talking to people when we travel," Shirley notes. "In Boone, Iowa, we saw a railroad museum, but it was closed for the winter. The next day, we saw some older men at the museum and struck up a conversation. They showed us a really neat steam engine. We look for little things like that, meeting different people and experiencing new things."

Support each other's dreams. Jim Strickland of San Jose, California, took up the banjo a few years after he retired. He's now president of the San Jose Banjo Band and plays with them every Tuesday night. "He told me he'd always wanted to play the banjo, and I surprised him with one on his birthday," says his wife, Bea. Adds Jim, "I never on my own would have started spending money on banjo lessons. That's something Bea would do easily. Bea's great at getting things started. My strength is sticking with it. That was a good combination for getting my banjo-playing under way. I'm not all that musical, and I still don't play well. I'm a hack—but I love it!"

Volunteer Together!

Thousands of organizations have volunteer opportunities for older Americans. Here are just a few that couples can do together and that take advantage of the unique contributions that only a Completion stage couple can bring, including wisdom, compassion, common sense, and free time.

- Mentoring
- Tutoring
- Being a museum docent or guide
- Sharing your professional skills with a nonprofit group
- Service travel: Building homes, schools, and clinics and fostering educational opportunities around the United States and the globe
- Working at a local library, community center, or historical society
- Coaching youth sports or Special Olympics
- Championing a local environmental cause
- Joining the board of a local organization whose work you believe in, whether it's your church, an athletic club, a botanical garden, or a local orchestra
- Playing with kids at an after-school program
- Playing with animals at a wildlife rehabilitation center or pet shelter
- Feeding the hungry—collecting food or organizing inventory at a local food bank

Still not sure how to start? Go to the website VolunteerMatch.org and enter your Zip code to find a volunteer opportunity near where you live from its huge database of listings.

Bea Strickland follows two of her passions each summer when she takes up residence in London for four weeks to immerse herself in archeological museums and conferences. "Jim doesn't want to travel that much, but it's okay with him if I go. I love learning, I love conferences, I love the British Museum," she says. "Yes, I miss Jim. And we talk on the phone a lot. Going to London lets me fulfill my own dreams, with my spouse's support."

Clay and Jane Turner decided to take up new creative pursuits late in marriage. "We'd read about creativity and aging research, and we had known about so many people who died after retirement. They had nothing to do, nothing to engage them. We had a lot to live for and wanted to be there for each other." Clay became a master gardener and a potter—and even built a studio beside the creek at their North Carolina mountain home. "I use creek water to turn the pots," he notes. Meanwhile, Jane developed her drawing and painting talents. "We didn't want to have a huge void in our lives," she says. "We wanted to do all we could to keep ourselves growing."

Mission 3

Share a New Sense of Meaning and Purpose

Reinventing your life and your marriage means looking beyond leisure and searching for meaning. In Dr. Vaillant's study of retirement-age men, the happiest had ready answers when asked what gave their lives meaning and purpose. They watched their grandchildren. Played the piano. Volunteered or pursued a creative project. Men who said their retirement years were satisfying were up to three times more likely than unsatisfied guys to report enjoying their relationships, doing volunteer work, and having hobbies or other interests. In contrast, the least happy said nothing gave their lives purpose—or they tended to spend their time in passive pursuits such as watching TV.

Following your Completion stage bliss in a purposeful way could mean making a commitment to help raise your grandchildren. To build a new relationship with your grown children. To volunteer in your community or halfway around the world. To take up a cause that is near and dear to your heart. To nurture a marriage truly based on love, honor, and respect. To develop a personal interest or talent that's always called to you. To keep on learning. Here's how veteran couples, and experts, suggest tackling one of the Completion stage's biggest opportunities.

Look for new meaning in your marriage. Now's the time to reconsider what you want from your marriage—and what you've always wanted to give your spouse as a marriage partner. More joy? More affection? More laughter? More moments shared in special activities you both enjoy, whether it's walking in the woods, reading out loud together, touring distant lands, or simply feeling a deep, peaceful connection? Talk together about these marriage dreams and about small steps you can take to make them happen.

Step into a new role in your family. By the time you reach the Completion stage, your kids are too old for unsolicited advice. "One of the powerful things about moving up the ladder of life is making the transition in families from parent to peer," Dr. Treat says. "When parents don't make that transition, they still try to parent grown kids and alienate them. No adult needs unsolicited advice about running their own life, especially from a parent. That approach backfires. It pushes kids away from you. But instead, if you figure out how to become peers, you can develop a whole new friendship and a new, close connection."

Moving from parent to peer means opening up and being vulnerable. You're not all-powerful Mom or Dad. You're a fellow human being experiencing pleasures and annoyances, ups and downs, every day. Chat. Share your experiences. Ask about theirs. Laugh. Ask for advice as you would with a friend. (Don't be afraid that you'll seem dependent. Your kids will be thrilled.) "Opening up this way creates real family unity," Dr. Treat says.

Look up old friends. One of life's greatest satisfactions is a circle of close friends—something many of us find and cultivate on the job. What now? Reconnect with old friends you've lost touch with over the years. You have a shared past and shared affection. "When we're old, our lives become the sum of all whom we have loved," Dr. Vaillant says. "It is important not to waste anyone. The task of living out the last half of life is excavating and recovering all of those whom we loved in the first half." The benefit for your marriage? A happier you, a more fulfilling social life, and less pressure on your mate to be your 24/7 playmate.

Rewrite Your Business Cards

Two of the biggest questions for spouses in the Completion stage are "Who am I?" and "Who are we?" You're probably no longer working full-time in your chosen profession. You may have moved to a new place. Your children left the nest long ago. You may be left with an unsettling feeling that psychologists call the "Who am I without my business card?" phenomenon.

To help you reinvent your identity, practice rewriting your personal business cards—and one for yourselves as a couple. Stumped about a new title? Dream big, and don't hesitate to change your "job description" as often as you'd like.

Wife

My old business-card title would have been:

_____

_____

My new title is:

_____

_____

Husband

My old business-card title would have been:

_____

_____

My new title is:

_____

_____

Couple

Our old business-card title would have been:

_____

_____

Our new title is:

_____

_____

Keep your hand in at work. Many retirees maintain relationships with their former employers by working as consultants. Others find part-time jobs in related fields, or take low-stress part-time positions to earn extra cash and to maintain working lives. Still others step up to the challenge of starting home-based businesses. Forty-four percent of retired women and men interviewed for the Cornell Retirement and Well-Being Study reported that they worked for pay at some point after retiring. As more baby boomers get their gold watches, expect the number of still-working retirees to rise—both as a pragmatic hedge against fears about the future of Social Security and company-backed pensions and as a way to keep doing what they've always done.

If you loved your job, continuing to work may give your self-esteem and your marriage a boost, says California psychologist Betty Polston, Ph.D., author of *Loving Midlife Marriage*. "Anything that replenishes a healthy sense of self will also make your marriage happier," she says.

Give back to your community. Join the school board, the town council, the planning board, or the library board. If you're a longtime member of a civic organization—from the Rotary to the Girl Scouts—step into a leadership role or spearhead a special project that's always been close to your heart. You've got the time, the wisdom, and the expertise—now use them. One husband interviewed for this book got elected to the local school board soon after the youngest of his four children left home. His wife has worked on presidential campaigns in several states. "We have discretionary time, and we want to put it to good use, doing things we believe in," he notes.

Consider volunteer work. When University of Wisconsin researchers looked into how volunteering affected the self-esteem of 373 retired women and men ages 65 to 74, they made an encouraging discovery: Giving of yourself can fill the gaps left in your life—and in your identity—when your role as a worker or active parent ends. Volunteering restored a sense of purpose and joy and helped retirees sidestep the unsettling feeling that they'd lost a big piece of their identity when they left the workforce.

Hollie and Janell Atkinson have taken this route, tutoring Spanish-speaking teens in conversational English. "We work with 14- and 15-year-olds who will need better English at school and in the work world," Janell notes. "It's fun, and we feel we're giving back this way."

The benefits go beyond feeling good. A recent survey of 600 older Americans found that volunteering gave them a chance to feel valued, to make a difference in the world, to use their wisdom for a good cause. Volunteers felt physically active and intellectually stimulated. Meanwhile, a University of Michigan study of 884 older women and men suggests volunteering may help you live longer too. The key: feeling you can still make a contribution to the world around you.

And yet, fewer than one-third of retired people do volunteer work. Time to change that for the better! Don't be shy about shopping around for a volunteer activity that you'll enjoy. You'll stick with it longer, get more out of the experience—and probably bring more to it—if you like the cause. If you'd rather walk dogs at the animal shelter than wash dishes at the soup kitchen, don't feel guilty. Follow your natural inclination.

Deepen your spiritual life. "When I retired, I knew I was going to do something about my wayward spirituality," noted a retired Harvard University financial aid officer in a recent issue of *Harvard Magazine*. She's always done yoga and meditated but has since joined a church as well. Studies suggest that people who have ongoing religious lives or private spiritual practices feel greater well-being, have less depression, and lead fuller and happier lives.

Mission 4

Reorganize Your Time, Your Territory, Your Tasks

At home together all day, Hollie and Janell Atkinson discovered something that made them mad and then made them laugh. "After we had both retired, Hollie tried to teach me to load the dishwasher—and that did not go over well with me," Janell recalls. "He was suddenly in the kitchen wanting to help and wanting to take control."

Over the next five years of their retirement, the Atkinsons worked out a new system for doing chores and preparing meals: Hollie makes breakfast. "I make lots of different kinds of eggs: scrambled, fried, omelets, breakfast tacos," he says. "And if I'm really pressed hard and the weather's cold, I'll make oatmeal. Janell enjoys that." They've split kitchen cleanup, laundry, and housecleaning too. "We had to learn what chores were ours individually and where there was room for give and take," Janell says. Adds Hollie, "I have a little bit of compulsiveness to my personality. I have certain ways to do things; sometimes they don't match with the way Janell does things. That's all part of the give and take."

Clay and Jane Turner discovered they needed to rebalance their schedules. How much time would they spend together all day? "For couples in retirement, the issues of solitude and connection are critical," Clay says. "Fortunately, Jane and I love similar things. She gets as much thrill out of seeing the first wildflower of spring as I do. We also have individual private things we enjoy apart from one another. That's part of our emotional framework: the rhythm of solitude and connection."

That adjustment wasn't easy. "At first, I felt I was giving up my time to myself," Jane says. "We had to learn how to talk about it and keep a sense of humor. Now I can simply say, 'I'd like to go do something by myself for a few hours.' We've learned not to hurt each other's feelings."

Just as newly married couples must carve out agreements about how much time they'll spend together, how they'll divide the space in their home, and how they'll split up the chores, Completion stage couples face the same questions all over again. This time, the important question is: Will we do what we've always done, or is it time for something new? Here's how long-married partners, and marriage researchers, suggest you approach the question.

Shuffle the housework. Redividing chores inside and outside the home can be crucial to your happiness because it maintains a sense of fairness—and keeps you from stepping all over each other's toes, Dr. Polston says. Both are important. Studies show that unless couples make a conscious effort to reshuffle housework, they stick to the preretirement status quo. The result: In most cases, women spend significantly more time on the housework, while their spouses get more time to relax. Not a recipe for happiness. In a study of retirement-age couples, Dr. Polston found that husbands helped more after retirement in 60 percent of happily married pairs. "The importance of this can't be overstated," she says. "Splitting responsibilities more evenly contributes to well-being and fulfillment." It also prepares both spouses for a time when they may need to take on all the chores, solo.

Dividing the work also lets the two of you sidestep power struggles brought on when one spouse seems to "invade" the other's traditional domain.

How to get started in your marriage: Someone has to initiate the conversation about chores, says Dr. Polston, and often it's the wife. "Women often not only run the house, they also do the emotional probing in the relationship. So a wife may have to sit down with her husband and talk about dividing the work. Realize that people don't change tremendously, but just little shifts in behavior, in cooperation, can be wonderful. Partners should realize that even these little shifts set the tone for the relationship in this new stage—how you handle yourself in renegotiating who does what and how you take on new roles."

Balance solitude and connection. Some couples spend every waking minute together. Others fill their hours with personal hobbies, outside interests, and even part-time jobs just to keep their distance from each other. "There should be private time and couple time," Dr. Treat suggests. "You don't want your later years to turn into a process where two people merge. If you hold too tightly to your partner, it's going to cause resentment and anger. If you're completely separate, you'll both be lonely and disconnected. You need balance. So you have to talk about how you'll achieve that."

The right balance? It's different for every couple. "Having a conversation about time can be difficult, but it's important for both partners to process those feelings out loud," Dr. Treat says. "You should not be accusatory or judgmental—ask the difficult questions, but do it in a loving way. You could say something like, 'How are we going to be as individuals, and how are we going to be as a couple?'"

Barbara and Chris Christensen have achieved the balance that works for them. In addition to daily rituals that keep them close—including about 10 minutes for a daily check-in and about a half hour of relaxation time—they each maintain separate interests and friendships.

"We have found that we need time apart," Barbara says. "I have a group of women friends that I have known for the last 30 years. We have dinner out once a month. We women also have slumber parties and weekend or weeklong vacations as a group at a beach or somewhere. Chris, a former fighter pilot, has many aviation-oriented groups and friends and also a penny-ante poker-playing group of our friends. I may be with him during the poker night, but I don't play, and the wives usually watch a 'chick flick' DVD or something while the poker group has an evening of fun. We have found it important to have separate time as well as together time."

FIVE PERFECT DATES
for the Completion stage

The learn-something-new date. Choose a topic that interests you both and spend a day immersed in it. Check local colleges, museums, organizations, stores, and special-interest clubs for classes and workshops in your chosen topic, whether it's learning more about French Impressionist art, developing the skills to retile your bathroom, canoeing techniques, or delving into your cultural heritage.

The catch-up-with-siblings-and/or-cousins date. The Completion stage is a great time to renew close relationships with your brothers, sisters, and cousins. After all, you've got the time, the maturity, and a wealth of shared experiences to draw on. Get together for an afternoon, for dinner, or for a weekend reunion.

The trading-spaces date. Chill a bottle of wine or a pitcher of iced tea, arrange some nibbles on a platter, and go on a tour—of your own house. Your objective: to see whether your living arrangement matches your current lifestyle and your plans for the future. Does one of you need more space for a hobby or for a private relaxing, reading, or thinking spot? Jot down your ideas, then head out to a home store, furniture shop, garage sale, or secondhand treasures store to hunt for new furniture, if needed.

The who-cares-about-time date. You're not on the clock at the office now—and your times together as a couple don't have to be time-limited either. Plan a midweek overnight date somewhere you've always wanted to go.

The build-a-better-marriage date. A weekend or weeklong marriage workshop can help your relationship grow and sparkle. Check the Marriage Resource Guide and chapter on marriage enrichment programs–Getting Help–to find one that interests the two of you.

quiz

Ready for Your New Future?

Longevity experts are coining new phrases to describe post-retirement life because old truisms about "the golden years" don't apply anymore. We're living longer, staying healthier, working harder, and expecting more from ourselves and our relationships. (No more sitting on the couch waiting for the kids to call!) Are you ready for the third age of life—and the Completion stage of marriage? Take our quiz and see. Choose the answer that best reflects your current thinking.

1. If I have to describe myself, I:
   a. Talk about my former career or grown children.
   b. Talk about my hobbies, volunteer work, or other current passions and pastimes.

2. The best way to handle home and garden chores after retirement is:
   a. By reorganizing tasks more fairly now that at-home time has increased.
   b. The way we have been handling them for so many years.

3. On a lazy Saturday afternoon, I'm happiest:
   a. Just enjoying myself doing things I find fun.
   b. Finding a project and getting something accomplished.

4. When I think about my unfulfilled dreams and goals, I:
   a. Accept that not everything works out the way you plan.
   b. Feel bitter, frustrated, or embarrassed.

5. In my opinion, getting ready for the "golden years" means:
   a. Saving money, staying healthy, and planning new activities with my spouse.
   b. Financial planning. Without ample resources, retirement will be lousy.

6. If I can afford to stop working, I'd like to spend most of my time:
   a. Learning new skills and getting active with new pastimes and goals.
   b. Relaxing. After decades of work, I deserve to sit a little.

7. In our marriage today:
   a. We talk a lot about our emotions and goals.
   b. We are established enough in our relationship that we don't require deep talks.

8 When I look ahead to the next 10, 20, or 30 years, I worry about:

   a. Not having enough time for everything we want to do.

   b. Boredom.

9 When I think about the aches, pains, and serious physical limitations that aging will bring, I feel:

   a. Upbeat and optimistic. My spouse and I have a good support network and a can-do attitude.

   b. Helpless and scared.

10 The thought of being at home all the time with my spouse makes me feel:

   a. Happy. We've got a lot of catching up to do.

   b. Worried. We'll be stepping on each other's toes all the time.

Your Score

Tally up the number of "a" and "b" answers.

   a. _____

   b. _____

More "a" answers: You're on the right track for a healthy, happy, satisfying Completion stage marriage. Unlike past generations, couples heading into the new golden years may have 10 to 30 years ahead of them. You'll thrive if you seize this opportunity to reinvent yourself and your marriage—by replacing old identities and unfulfilled dreams with a new vision of yourself and your goals, by taking on meaningful and creative new projects, and by working to deepen marital intimacy. At the same time, the Completion stage calls on couples to rediscover a sense of play and the ability to simply enjoy life.

More "b" answers: You haven't broken free of your old identity as a worker and/or parent—or from the hard-driving, goal-driven ethic of your working years. It's time to pause and let yourself experience the profound transition to post-retirement life—and to get in touch with dreams and interests you've never had time to realize until now. It's also the perfect time to focus on creating a deeper, more satisfying marriage.

PART THREE

extra wisdom

premarriage

smart relationship steps to take
before you say "i do"

The price tag for the average American wedding has climbed to a stunning $26,800. But while you're looking for ways to trim the tab for the dress and the tux, the caterer and the cake, here's one expense you should *add* to your budget: A premarriage education class.

"Love alone won't guarantee the success of a marriage. Neither will living together first," says psychologist David H. Olson, Ph.D., a University of Minnesota marriage expert and developer of one of the nation's most widely used marriage-education programs, PREPARE (Premarital Personal and Relationship Evaluation). "More and more couples know that marriage isn't easy. Many have been married before and know firsthand that it can be very difficult. They've seen their friends and relatives and parents having problems. They're not sure what to do—so they're scared."

One solution: setting aside a little time and laying out a little cash (programs typically cost from $250 to $2,400) for a relationship class before you tie the knot. Research studies and enthusiastic reviews from couples say these programs can calm your fears, teach important skills, help you know your spouse better, cut your risk for divorce by half or even more—and make your wedding day *and* your future brighter.

We had never really talked about things that seemed so far in the future, such as retirement and where we would like to live...

Once, many premarital programs were just a short meeting or a few sessions with the pastor, priest, or rabbi who would officiate at your wedding—or nothing at all. In the late 1990s, surveys showed that 73 percent of married couples admitted they'd had no premarital counseling—and 12 percent said they'd simply met with a pastor or other religious leader once or twice. The one exception: Couples married in the Roman Catholic Church have been required for decades to attend Pre-Cana marriage classes that are, in some parishes, quite extensive.

One warning: Many traditional programs that focus on teaching the "true nature" of marriage have been shown to have little benefit. What works better, research shows, are courses that teach the skills and behaviors that are highly predictive of marital success. These findings are so exciting that lawmakers in at least five states—Florida, Arizona, Tennessee, Maryland, and Minnesota—have passed legislation offering financial incentives to couples who sign up for classes before they say "I do." And Congress in 2006 set aside more than $100 million a year to promote community-based marriage education programs.

The goal? Lowering a divorce rate stuck at nearly 50 percent and improving life for millions more couples who stay together, albeit unhappily. So far, it's working. In 122 counties across the United States where religious institutions adopted "community marriage policies" including required premarital classes, divorce rates dropped 17.5 percent over seven years, according to a recent study from the Utah-based Institute for Research and Evaluation. Proponents are so confident about the strengths of these classes that they call them "insurance policies" against divorce.

And many couples agree. "We had never really talked about things that seemed so far in the future, such as retirement and where we would like to live, and even how we would like to take care of our parents when they get older," says Sandra Sullivan of Asheville, North Carolina, who took a four-week class with her husband, Ed, shortly before their wedding in 2003. "Our classes showed us what our strengths and weaknesses were as a couple and as individuals. We were pleasantly surprised in some areas and learned new skills in others, such as talking about finances. I think we enjoyed our wedding a lot more because we were on a much firmer footing."

School for Brides and Grooms

Hundreds of organizations across the nation offer prewedding classes in most every conceivable setting: churches, synagogues, mosques, community centers, childbirth and healthcare clinics, courts, military bases, high schools, colleges, HMOs, EAPs, 4-H extension offices, and businesses. The time commitment ranges from single sessions lasting 4 hours to a weekend to a series of classes that meets every week for 4, 8, 12, or even 28 weeks.

No matter the length or setting of the class, its success is based primarily on whether it adequately teaches the skills that will improve a couple's odds of marital harmony. Successful courses teach that disagreement is a normal part of marriage no matter how well you have courted or whom you

Polish Your "MQ"

Marriage researchers have identified dozens of factors that influence the future success and happiness of a couple bound for holy matrimony. Many of these "marriage quotient" factors can be improved if you work on them. Here's a shortlist of traits that predict marital satisfaction—and dissatisfaction.

Your odds for a happy marriage are higher if you are:

- Outgoing
- Flexible
- Good at assertiveness, communication, and problem-solving
- Self-accepting
- Age 20 or older
- From an emotionally healthy family
- The child of happy parents
- Well educated or trained for your career

Your odds for a happy marriage may be lowered by:

- A tendency toward anger and hostility
- Difficulty dealing with stress
- Impulsiveness
- Anxiety
- Self-consciousness
- Irritability
- Being under age 20
- Feeling pressured to marry

As a couple, your chances for a happy marriage go up if you share:

- Similar values
- A long history of friendship
- Good communication skills
- Good conflict-resolution skills and style

As a couple, these shared traits may lower your odds for a happy relationship:

- Mismatches on important values, such as religion or roles in marriage
- Knowing each other for just a short time
- Premarital sex
- Premarital pregnancy
- Living together
- Poor communication skills
- Poor conflict-resolution skills and style

have married. Couples should walk away understanding that they will inevitably have to confront several universal issues: money, sex, parenting, in-laws, friends, household chores, and leisure time. They should also emerge knowing that marriage has predictable rough spots: The first two years are especially challenging, as are welcoming the first baby, sending a first child off to school, parenting adolescents, and facing an empty nest. These are the times when a couple's skills at communication, conflict management, affection, and problem solving are put to the greatest test. They also need to be equipped with a sense of the importance of marriage and an understanding of why it is important for them and their children to be committed to making their union a success.

Armed with skills and information, you're both better equipped to handle the challenges ahead—from choosing paint colors for your first home to deciding whose turn it is to change the baby's diaper, from dealing with moments of rebellion and inevitable emotional dry spells to weathering major crises such as job loss and illness. This pays daily dividends. Research from the University of Minnesota and Brigham Young University has found that couples who took premarriage classes reported improved communication, better conflict-management skills, higher dedication to each other, and a more upbeat view of their relationships than those who didn't.

Start early, and you may also get a reprieve from secret wedding-day distress. Experts say that many couples who ultimately divorced had a sinking feeling on the Big Day that something wasn't quite right. Taking a class early on in your engagement—or better yet, even before you decide to become engaged—can help you assess whether you're a good match and ready to tie the knot. If the answer is "maybe not" or "not yet," you can postpone or cancel your plans if necessary. "Our research has found that 15 percent of couples who start a marriage-preparation program a year before their wedding date decide not to marry," Dr. Olson says. "That number drops to 5 percent for couples who take a course just a few months before the wedding. They've already sent out the invitations and picked out their clothes and reception and honeymoon. At that point, it seems easier to go through with the wedding, even though they have doubts. We want to help people avoid that pain."

Five Reasons to Sign Up

The benefits begin almost as soon as you begin your first session and may last as long as your marriage. Among them:

- **A smoother, more joyful engagement.** Couples who've taken premarital classes often feel skeptical, reluctant, or downright scared beforehand—yet say that the experience clarifies important unresolved issues such as finances; when or if to start a family; how to raise children; and expectations about working, caring for elderly parents, and even retirement. You get a firmer foundation, great communication skills you can use to make all those nuptial decisions (chocolate or vanilla wedding cake?), and freedom to really enjoy all that wedding hoopla.

- **A happier marriage.** When University of Denver researchers conducted a telephone survey of 3,344 women and men from Arkansas, Kansas, Oklahoma, and Texas, they found out what a difference a little education can make. While just 7 percent of couples married in the 1930s and 1940s got any premarital prep, 44 percent of those married since 1990 said they had—and they reportedly were far happier. Premarital education "is associated with higher levels of marital satisfaction, lower levels of destructive conflicts, and higher levels of interpersonal commitment to spouses," according to the study. Couples went to classes for as little as 2 hours and for as many as 20 hours; in general, their odds for divorce were 31 percent lower than those who skipped this important set of lessons.

- **A clearer view of the road ahead.** Many premarriage programs include a look into the future—at the natural ups and downs of married life and the many explosions that can rock your relationship at any time. You'll learn about the inevitable, early decline in passion; about rude, everyday awakenings such as discovering your spouse sleeps with her face slathered in skin cream or never uses his laundry hamper; and at the big crises that can change anything in the blink of an eye, such as illness, accidents, and job loss.

- **Tools for weathering the storm.** Good premarriage programs teach you skills for speaking assertively about your feelings, thoughts, wants, and needs. You'll also learn how to listen empathetically so that you really hear what your spouse is saying. And the two of you will get to practice problem-solving and conflict-resolution skills. These will give you confidence that you can face life's big challenges together. One study showed that when couples completed premarital inventory questionnaires and counseling, there was a 52 percent increase in the number of couples who said they were "most satisfied" with their relationships.

- **An insurance policy against divorce.** Taking a class can cut your risk for divorce by 30 to 50 percent, various studies suggest. A comprehensive program—one that starts with an extensive inventory of your strengths and growth areas, provides classes plus mentoring by other couples, and requires you to practice new skills—could cut your odds for a breakup even further. In five Midwestern and Southern churches that instituted a premarriage program called Marriage Savers, there was a total of seven divorces among couples who wed during a recent five-year period, a small fraction of the total marriages that occurred. "One element is common to each of these remarkable churches," noted Marriage Savers founder Michael

McManus. "Each had trained a group of Mentor Couples who are willing to reach other couples at every stage of the marital life cycle: Preparation, Enrichment, Restoration, Reconciliation, and Stepfamilies. These couples have created a safety net under every marriage in their churches."

Choosing a Premarriage Class

Despite all that success, few engaged couples take advantage of marriage school. Studies show that just 30 percent of couples get even one to two hours of marriage preparation and that even among religious couples, just 36 percent had premarriage counseling. And while 90 percent of young adults agreed in one national survey that marriage education was important, just one in three intended to take a class.

The reasons? You may feel pressed for time, feel too in love to need help, or simply have no idea how to find a local program. Unless you're a member of a religious organization or other group that promotes marriage education, you may not even know that it's an option.

If that's you, we suggest you turn to the Marriage Resource Guide, at the end of this book, where you'll find a list of national premarital education programs. These groups can direct you to local classes. But whether you're looking for a class on your own or are required to take one before being married in your church or synagogue, these criteria can help you judge in advance whether it will be a thorough and useful program:

Does it use an inventory? These research-tested questionnaires dive deep into the attitudes, personality traits, relationship skills, expectations, and personal history that help determine your success as a couple. These tools are used by many popular classes. But remember: It's the skills that the class teaches you that matter most, not the self-assessment tests themselves.

Is the class led by a trained leader—or better yet, a trained "mentor couple"? The organizations that developed the three major inventories used in the United States also train group leaders. Sometimes long-married couples whose own relationships are time-tested and solid are trained together and can be inspirational role models as well as counselors.

Does it cover the big 7? Programs should at a minimum cover these seven areas shown by research to contribute to the success of a marriage.

- Compatibility
- Expectations
- Personalities and families of origin
- Communication
- Problem-solving and conflict resolution
- Intimacy and sexuality
- Long-term goals—including children and finances

How many couples will attend the class or workshop? A small group may provide more individual attention than a big group.

Is the program specifically for engaged couples? Some marriage-skills programs mix troubled couples from later stages of marriage in the same class. You'll learn most from a premarital class focused on your specific needs.

Is the program based on research? Some are, some aren't. While many solid programs are based on the clinical experiences of the psychologists and marriage therapists who developed them, you may be on the most solid ground with a program developed through years of marriage research.

Does the program look to the future? When looking into a program, ask if the class will help you and your partner agree on goals and strategies for managing and continuing to work on your most important unresolved issues.

remarriage

how the 7 stages apply
the second time around

Depending on your point of view, Lee Potts's and Rebecca Wiederkehr's marriage is either the second or third time around for each of them. Lee, a retired computer programmer, was married twice before and has three grown children from those relationships. Rebecca was a Benedictine nun for 20 years and met Lee eight years after leaving her religious community.

"I've been married now for as long as I was a nun," muses Rebecca, of St. Louis, Missouri, who maintains ties to her Benedictine abbey. "It's a strange feeling. We've been through a lot together. I remember Lee saying to me one time, 'I like that you're really there for me.' That really struck me. And when we raised Lee's daughter for three years, I realized how important that was: We had to be really for each other amid the stress of taking care of a child."

"Rebecca has my best interests at heart," Lee adds. "That makes all the difference this time around."

Remarried couples have high hopes and often face bigger, more complex challenges than first-time couples do.

Like Lee Potts and Rebecca Wiederkehr, over 40 percent of married couples in American include at least one spouse who's tied the knot before. Second (and third or fourth) chances are woven firmly into the fabric of American matrimony: As many as 60 percent of divorced women and men will march down the aisle again, many within just five years of a breakup. Still more—including growing numbers of widowed and divorced older women and men—combine households and hearts without formally saying, "I do." The remarriage phenomenon has fostered the launch of an online magazine, *Bride Again*, full of special family wedding ceremonies that include the kids, and of consultants eager to guide remarrying couples through thorny second-time-around wedding etiquette.

Remarried couples have high hopes and often face bigger, more complex challenges than first-time couples do. Among them: raising stepchildren, combining finances and households, being open to love and growth despite past disappointments, striking a balance between "making" a new marriage work and letting it mature slowly, and not letting feelings and dealings with ex-spouses interfere with their current marriage. The stakes seem higher now when it comes to sharing power and control too. It's a tall order—and may explain why up to 60 percent of remarriages fail, often faster than first marriages.

You *can* beat those odds and have a long, happy remarriage. Adapting *The 7 Stages of Marriage* to meet your needs can help. All marriages follow a similar trajectory, from early passion through inevitable disappointments, from the challenges of child-rearing to the adjustments of empty-nest and retirement years. But *re*married pairs face unique challenges, especially when building a strong bond in their early years, when raising children, and when managing money.

Here's how you can overcome some of the most common remarriage complications and make the 7 Stages work for you.

Build a Better Bond

The first two years of marriage are make-it-or-break-it years for all married couples—but even more so for those who've already been divorced or widowed. Nearly every marriage—whether it's the first or the fourth—starts in breathless passion and then plunges into the cold waters of reality. During the first 24 months of your relationship, you'll go on a wild ride as the love hormones that kept you feeling enthralled with your partner begin to ebb. You'll notice that your mate's only human, after all. And you may feel bored, disappointed, confused, irritated, or even betrayed. You may question your judgment or conclude that your spouse isn't really The One.

For remarried partners, this natural ebbing of passion can be a danger zone: It's all too easy to conclude that something's gone wrong this time too, when in fact you've simply arrived at the crucial point where fantasy clashes with reality.

A second marriage often condenses the first three stages of marriage—the Passion, Realization, and Rebellion stages—into a shorter time span than a first marriage. This is the time to work hard—and smart. Research suggests that remarried couples who build strong connections during their first two years together erase their added risk for a breakup, reducing their odds for divorce to a level on par with first-married couples. To get there, focus on the core missions of the first three stages of marriage: communication, trust, emotional and sexual intimacy, problem-solving, and a sense of shared purpose and fun. You'll ace the Passion, Realization, and Rebellion stages—and fall more naturally into the other stages of marriage—with these special tips.

Learn from the past. For your new marriage to thrive, it's important to learn the lessons hidden in the anger, pain, and conflicts—as well as the hopes and dreams—of your previous marriage. What hurts from the past can you heal—through introspection and insight or with the help of a counselor? Your incentive: Easing old emotional pain will help you avoid a potential source of conflict in your new relationship.

Look at the past to learn about your communication and conflict styles. What role did you play in the ending of your last relationship? Do you see yourself falling into similar thoughts or behaviors with your new mate? The better you understand what happened, the less likely you are to repeat the same patterns without thinking about it in your new marriage. Breaking old relationship habits isn't easy, but you'll have a head start if you can quickly recognize warning signs in your thoughts and reactions.

Let go. If you find yourself comparing your new mate to your ex, and your ex is looking better, it's a sign you haven't finished saying good-bye. This is a special risk for partners who were left behind the first time around, by a spouse who walked out or passed away due to an illness or accident. He or she may have been Mr. or Mrs. Perfect, which means you've put your new mate in an un-winnable position. Don't make your current spouse compete for your affection, or force him or her to prove their superiority. It's time to stop looking backward.

Mourn your losses. You've already been through a lot, so make sure you take the time to simply grieve the loss of your previous marriage, of hopes and dreams, of your partner, perhaps even of your home and community. You're more emotionally ready for a new marriage when you face your feelings about what you've given up. You'll also feel less hostility toward your former spouse. Research has shown that most people do not have very positive feelings toward former spouses. When couples work to reduce hostilities between former spouses, it may also enhance the new quality of the marriage.

> ## OLD THINK/NEW THINK
> ### for remarried couples
>
> **Old think**: You're wiser the second time around.
>
> **New think**: You've learned that marriage isn't easy—and you may be more committed than ever to make your new relationship work. But marriage experts point out that you still haven't figured out or practiced the skills that make marriages thrive. And experience alone won't divorce-proof your union. Learning all you can from your previous marriage and working on communication skills, problem-solving, trust, and emotional and sexual intimacy can go a long way to making things good this time.
>
> **Old think**: If I "rebound" too quickly, my new marriage is doomed.
>
> **New think**: Quick remarriage after a divorce doesn't boost the risk for breakup higher than it is for any remarried couples, found a surprising University of Utah study of 1,171 women and men. All that advice to wait a while before remarrying doesn't appear to hold true. One reason: Emotional healing from a first marriage may begin well before a divorce is finalized, the researchers suspect.

Resolve to work at your marriage—and also to let it unfold in its own time. Successful remarried couples are realistic about what can be improved upon through sheer willpower and what will take time to develop. You've probably promised yourself, and even your spouse, to "get things right" this time. It's wise to tackle relationship ripples as they happen, especially by brushing up on communication and problem-solving skills. It's also wise to let your marriage slowly develop its own character and to give yourself and your partner time and opportunities to have your own thoughts and feelings about an issue before calling a marriage meeting, laying out the plan of attack, and starting an official "marriage fix-it" project. How do you know when it's better to back off a little? If you or your partner feels overwhelmed, angry, or withdrawn, it's worth taking a break.

Nurture your Passion stage bond, even if you have kids. Crazy schedules and the emotional ups and downs of raising your kids, my kids, and our kids often means newly remarried wives and husbands miss out on the delicious, private, early bonding experiences that first-time couples get to enjoy. You need this time to connect physically and emotionally and to start the process of becoming a strong unit by developing a sense of "we." The bottom line? You need a babysitter, because you need uninterrupted time alone for fun, relaxation, romance, and, yes, sex. At the very least, take advantage of free weekends and weeknights when the children are with their noncustodial parent. Forget the laundry, leave extra office work in your tote bag, and designate these occasions as official couple time. Go out for dinner, stay in and make love, talk about your hopes and dreams.

See Realization stage letdowns as opportunities, not disasters. Waning passion doesn't indicate a problem, simply a natural shift. The rose-colored glasses you both wore from your courtship days through the first months of marriage are coming off now. You see each other more objectively.

Remarried partners may be especially tempted to write off their spouse or relationship at this point—it didn't work last time, and it sure isn't working now, the reasoning goes. Resist! Now's the time to start real relationship building.

Be honest with yourself about hidden expectations. Think carefully about what you secretly hope for. It's tricky uncovering your own expectations; this baggage is so secret you may not even realize you've got it. We all have hidden hopes and dreams for our marriages, gathered in childhood, from immersion in popular culture, and from our own experiences. You may want to be just like Mom and Dad or vow to be nothing like them; you may expect to live happily ever after because Snow White and Mary Tyler Moore did; you may secretly expect your spouse to fix emotional aches and pains from your own life. Remarried women and men may have extra expectations that have grown from the loss of their first marriages. Do you think your new spouse will make up for everything that went wrong last time? That everything must be perfect this time? Sorting realistic from unrealistic expectations gives you the chance to build what you truly desire, without leaving your partner and your marriage open to being judged by unfair—sometimes impossible—standards.

Express your true self. Courting and early marriage are all about putting your best foot forward. That's great, but at some point the rest of you needs a turn in the spotlight. If you feel you've got to keep vulnerable, angry, or seemingly difficult parts of yourself under wraps in order to make your new marriage work, you'll be lonely. And you're missing a chance to form a close connection with the other real person in the relationship: your partner. Your spouse will get a chance to love the real you only if you're willing to be yourself. Reveal more about who you are—even stuff that embarrasses you a little, or that you've kept secret. Encourage your partner to do the same while you listen supportively.

Brush up on good problem-solving skills. If loud fights, cold stand-offs, and unsolved problems were troublesome in your last marriage, you don't want a repeat this time. Take out extra insurance by practicing the sterling problem-solving techniques outlined in the Rebellion stage chapter.

Stay positive—and realistic. It's easy to rush to judgment when your partner's angry or demanding or critical. For remarried partners, that judgment could be colored by past experience—and therefore, unnecessarily harsh. Instead, try these two techniques: Listen to the information your partner's giving you, but edit out any criticisms. And give your mate the benefit of the doubt. Maybe he or she is tired, hungry, or preoccupied and doesn't see the impact of his or her actions.

Raising a Stepfamily

It's the new normal: In 2007, the number of stepfamilies in the United States is expected to surpass that of traditional nuclear families. Ironing out all the emotional adjustments and day-to-day logistics of weaving together two families is a huge challenge for a newly married couple, and it can easily take priority over building your own relationship. Your mission: Attempt to do both. A happy, stable marriage will help the kids feel secure. And the reverse is also true: Helping your children through the transition will cut the wear-and-tear on your own budding relationship.

Check the Marriage Resource Guide for books, websites, and organizations that can help you with family issues. But to get started, read on for guidelines that can help you nurture your marriage at the same time.

Be patient, be realistic. Don't expect your new, blended family to function like a picture-perfect, Ozzie-and-Harriet-era unit now—or ever. Growing an intimate, supportive, loving group takes lots of time and understanding. You're combining two cultures, and everyone's feeling the differences keenly. Be flexible. Be realistic. Let your relationship with your spouse's children develop slowly. As weeks turn into months and months into years, natural bonds will grow properly.

Shacking Up in the Golden Years

The U.S. Census Bureau recently stumbled upon a surprising trend: The number of women and men ages 65 and older cohabiting outside the bonds of matrimony nearly doubled between 1990 and 2000. In all, the government found 266,600 couples in this age group living together—and experts suspect the real numbers are far higher.

Why skip the white dress and the "I do's"? Financial simplicity and security. Marriage can mean commingling assets that took a lifetime to build and that a man or woman intends to pass along to his or her own children and grandchildren. Remarriage could also cut off a deceased spouse's pension benefits, Social Security, and health insurance coverage.

There's no license, but emotionally and physically, this is real marriage (even if your kids don't see it that way!). Guard your relationship and help it grow by taking the same steps that work for other young and not-so-young newlyweds: Talk. Build trust. Nurture intimacy. And have fun together.

Create new family rules. Discipline and responsibility are tough issues for any mom and dad, but even more so for stepfamilies, where parents and kids may be used to very different sets of rules. Avoid clashes by writing up a new set of family rules. Talk with your spouse about who in the family will handle which chores and responsibilities, and about the consequences for not doing them. Then have a family discussion about your plan. Start slowly—you might agree on just one or two rules at first, adding more as issues arise and as the family adapts to a new way of life.

Rewrite family traditions. Weaving together two families goes beyond who gets which bedroom and who sets the table. You each come to the relationship with a full set of everyday and special-day rituals that need to be reconciled so that everybody feels at home. Start sorting them out by comparing notes about your usual routines and special traditions. Acknowledge that there's no right or wrong here—if your family arrives at the breakfast table washed, dressed, and combed while his stumbles down still rumple-haired and pajama-clad, well, that's just a preference. Hold family meetings to discuss how you'll all do things in your new household. Will you establish new routines? Which rituals and traditions will you combine?

Hang in there. When University of California, Los Angeles, researchers compared the well-being of 870 teens and preteens in stepfamilies to that of 1,700 kids living with single or divorced moms alone, they found that depression increased for stepkids for a few years, then eased. A stable stepfamily, they concluded, is good for kids in the long run. One key: Fight the urge to make everything perfect. Don't force older kids to spend extra time with the family or try to pass as a non-stepfamily—the pressure of trying to force your family into a traditional mold can raise your risk for divorce.

Decide who's in charge of whose kids. "When Lee's daughter came to live with us, I jumped into trying to be Supermom," Rebecca Wiederkehr says. "And I found out I really should let the biological parent make the important decisions." In many stepfamilies, the biological parent takes charge of his or her own children, but in some families, one parent stays home and takes on child-rearing responsibilities. In others, stepparents share the responsibility. Discussing this issue fully—and revisiting it often as your relationship with stepchildren slowly grows and develops—can help your household and your marriage run smoothly.

Make respect a family value. Commit to making the needs of every family member important to the group. This kind of respect builds common ground and sends the message that everyone in the family is valued and supported—even if each of the parents retains primary responsibility for major decisions involving his or her own children.

Keep your marriage a priority. Yes, you need a babysitter. You also need daily time to reconnect. Look for 15 uninterrupted minutes where you can share your feelings and experiences. In a busy household, you might also need a weekly meeting to go over schedules and to-do lists for the next seven days or so. "The stress of parenting can make your marriage relationship bumpy," Rebecca Wiederkehr notes. "I saw how important it is for us to be there for each other and stay connected, rather than feeling divided by what's happening with children."

Build Trust regarding Money

Achieving financial harmony is a special challenge for remarried women and men. You may bring old debt or a big retirement account into your marriage. You may have different spending styles, wildly divergent philosophies about credit card debt, and mismatched notions about how much to save for emergencies, college educations, and retirement. On top of that, your lifestyles may be mismatched, regardless of your incomes: You may be comfortable with Wal-Mart jeans and camping vacations, while your partner prefers designer duds and five-star hotels.

The two of you may be bringing more financial assets into your marriage now than the first time around, and there may be more strings attached. Prenuptial and postnuptial agreements may help protect savings, investments, and property that you'd like your children or other family members to eventually inherit. But asking your partner to sign one can be seen as a breach of trust or a lack of confidence in your own shared future. It can also be interpreted as a lack of concern for your new partner's future well-being, especially if you bring more wealth into the marriage. What to do? Hire an accomplished investment advisor and consider hashing out relationship issues about money with a therapist to avoid lingering resentment. This advice can help you get started.

Face the music and talk. Get all your financial cards out on the table: the debts, the savings, and the obligations left over from a previous marriage. Be brave: Own up to big debts, tax liens, and bankruptcies in your past. In addition, talk about how you spend money and how the two of you are different or the same. And don't forget to talk about your hopes and dreams for the long term and the short term as well. *Not* talking about finances creates more problems than mismatched styles or lingering debt.

Spell out who gets what. Sometimes an ex-spouse remains the beneficiary of a partner's life insurance or retirement fund, an arrangement that may have been worked out as part of a divorce settlement. And sometimes an ex is still the beneficiary simply because no one thought to formally update the paperwork. Not knowing that could cause an unpleasant shock down the road. Our advice: Review pensions, retirement accounts, investments, and insurance policies to see who is the beneficiary and why. Are both of you adequately protected?

Figure out allowances, pocket money—and college funds—for all the kids. Equalizing day-to-day spending for children's needs and wants is tricky enough. Even tougher: reviewing how much each of you has saved for kids' college bills (and for future weddings) and whether you'll combine your efforts now. There's no simple answer: This is one area that involves talks between each of you and your ex-spouses.

getting help

finding the best counselors and enrichment programs

You fight too often—or have nothing to say. Maybe you and your partner are grappling with a wrenching issue such as infertility, infidelity, illness, or substance abuse. Or you've felt angry for far too long about the housework, the credit card bills, or sex. Perhaps you can't put your finger on it, but you know that things could be better.

Your marriage needs help. But now what?

You're in luck. These days, the two best sources of professional help for solving relationship problems—therapy and marriage-education classes—can be better than ever. And for ambitious couples hoping to improve on a good thing, a third option—couple-to-couple marriage enrichment and mentoring programs—is getting rave reviews from happy partners.

The key to success: finding the type of help that best fits your marriage and needs. Hint: It's not as simple as picking a counselor out of the yellow pages anymore.

I feel as if I've had two marriages, one before marriage enrichment and one after.

New research has unveiled some surprises about what best helps—and doesn't help—both troubled marriages and those that just need a little nudge. For one thing, not all self-described marriage counselors are pro-marriage. In one national survey of over 1,000 marriage and family therapists, 60 percent said that they are "neutral" on marriage versus divorce for their clients. Just one-third said they're committed to preserving marriages whenever possible. The danger here: A "neutral" therapist may not work hard enough to help you ride out the rough times and stay together, experts say.

Another surprise: A therapist trained to help individuals overcome challenges to happiness may not have the skills to help a couple balance "me" and "we" in ways that preserve marital bliss. "Couples are playing Russian roulette with their marriages when they pick up the phone book and call a random therapist," notes William Doherty, Ph.D., director of the Marriage and Family Therapy Program at the University of Minnesota and a leader in the movement toward marriage-friendly therapy.

Yet another surprise: A growing body of research suggests that marriage-education classes—long seen primarily as tools for engaged couples or simply nice little "tune-ups" for happy couples who want to be even happier—may offer powerful help for partners in deep conflict. In fact, the courses can be even more effective than therapy. Why? Instead of rehashing problems and dissecting fault and blame, the classes focus on teaching the skills and behaviors that make marriages work. Couples usually have plenty of insight into what's wrong; they just need new ideas and behaviors for how to make things right. The courses also reveal what to expect in a normal marriage, which helps struggling couples understand that their issues are not only common but usually surmountable. Finally, a wary spouse is often more willing to show up for an education class than for therapy.

Meanwhile, a mentor-based, couple-to-couple marriage-strengthening movement has been building in communities across the country. Grounded in the view that experienced husbands and wives are the true marriage experts, mentoring programs show the way for engaged and newlywed couples, and they help long-married pairs get through the rough patches or deal with specific challenges. In these programs, successful stepfamilies can help new stepcouples, or those couples facing chronic illness, unemployment, gambling, infidelity or addictions can be helped by couples who have successfully dealt with the same issues.

There are many mentor-based programs, including Marriage Savers, The Third Option, 10 Great Dates, and organizations like the Association for Couples in Marriage Enrichment (ACME) and Marriage Enrichment Weekend Programs. In these programs the giving is a two-way street, as the mentor couples continually strengthen their own marriages as they help others.

In fact, ACME has established chapters around the country in which small groups of couples meet regularly to share and learn about marriage. "I feel as if I've had two marriages, one before marriage enrichment and one after," says one husband interviewed for this book. "It's made all the difference in our marriage—so much so that we held a marriage-enrichment weekend for our own daughters and their husbands. The guys were reluctant beforehand, but now they all want to do it again!"

Marriage-Friendly Therapy

Therapy may be the right choice if the two of you are grappling with a deeply painful or entrenched issue, such as infidelity, that needs privacy and lots of personal attention. Therapy's also a great choice if you're not sure what the real problem is between you, if one or both of you can't talk about it, or if talking about it on your own only makes things worse. But many therapists who bill themselves as marriage counselors have little specialized training in working with couples in committed relationships.

A small but vocal group of marriage experts now warn that traditional marriage counseling may be hazardous to the health of your relationship. They point to compelling statistics: While the number of marriage and family therapists in the United States has increased 50-fold since 1970, the divorce rate has dipped just a smidgen. And, they warn, many marriage counselors have neither formal training nor extensive experience in the art of working with couples.

Fortunately, there are ways to find a marriage-friendly therapist. A new resource, the National Registry of Marriage-Friendly Therapists (online at www.marriagefriendlytherapists.com), lists well-trained therapists who've signed a pledge to work with couples on preserving healthy marriages. You can also find well-trained professionals through the American Association of Marriage and Family Therapists (online at www.amft.org). These steps can also help you find a therapist who will fight for your marriage.

Don't delay. Some research suggests that many couples wait at least six years before seeking help for serious marital problems, increasing the odds that a problem will be so entrenched and both partners will be so distressed that counseling will be less effective. You wouldn't wait years to see your family doc about a serious ache or pain. Take the same "get help, pronto" approach with your relationship.

Interview at least three therapists first. You may be able to speak at length with a therapist over the phone before deciding whether or not to schedule an appointment; others may prefer that you come in for an introductory session. Try to talk with or meet several before deciding on one. To get started, ask friends or your family doctor or gynecologist for recommendations (even divorce lawyers sometimes have an inside track on which local therapists have the best marriage-saving skills).

Ask the tough questions. Don't be afraid to find out all you can about a therapist before agreeing to start counseling with him or her. Start with these questions—and take notes so you can compare answers from more than one therapist.

- What's your training and background specifically in marriage therapy?
- How much experience do you have working on the issues that we face?
- Are your clients mostly couples or mostly individuals?
- What percentage of the couples you see stay married—and see improvements in their relationships due to their therapy with you?
- Will you work with us to keep our marriage together even though we're having problems? What are your personal values about honoring a marriage commitment despite personal differences?
- Are you licensed to practice marriage and family therapy? Do you belong to the American Association of Marriage and Family Therapists?
- What are your fees? Do you accept the type of health insurance we have?
- If you have strong religious beliefs, ask the therapist: Can you incorporate my values into your counseling—or keep them out of the room if you don't share the same beliefs or the same intensity of belief?
- How long is each session? How often are sessions scheduled? How many sessions should we expect to have? What is your policy on canceled sessions?
- How can we contact you if we have an emergency?

The Marriage-Education Alternative

Marriage-education courses, meanwhile, may offer more help than you'd expect. Ranging from weekly workshops (usually in the evening) to week-long retreats, these classes are geared toward teaching couples better skills and increasing their knowledge about winning attitudes that strengthen marriage. The thinking? Sometimes better skills are really all you need to make a breakthrough and get closer and happier on a daily basis. Start with skills; rekindled love and passion will follow once you've moved past gridlock into a closer, more empathetic relationship. We take classes in everything from how to drive a car to how to birth a baby to how to bake a pie, say proponents of marriage education, so why not take a class to learn better marriage skills our parents didn't teach us?

Once, marriage education at best meant a couple of sessions at church before you tied the knot. Today, hundreds of marriage classes of all styles and philosophies are offered in community centers and on cruise ships, in church meeting rooms and at luxury spas, in hotels and even in private homes across the United States.

The premise: There's nothing wrong with most marriages that good information, a little inspiration, some warm reassurance, and great new skills can't solve. The benefits? It can be easier to find marriage-education programs than a properly trained therapist (your church, synagogue, or community center may offer classes). There may be less delving into the specifics of your personal issues (and therefore less embarrassment or sniping "he said, she said"). And it may be easier to entice a reluctant spouse to a class than into a therapist's office. Usually there's less personal probing—most programs won't put you on the spot about sharing with the group, though some include time for private, individual coaching sessions. Often you leave with a special glow—feeling good about yourself and your commitment to each other, thanks to leaders who are unfailingly upbeat and 100 percent pro-marriage, and who have taken their own or other programs and are consequently committed to dealing with their own marriages. You also get an attitude adjustment: You're not in a bad or broken marriage, just growing.

You'll find a list of major national and regional marriage-education programs in the Marriage Resource Guide. Which is best? That's up to you. Some programs are backed by impressive research; others reflect years of trial, error, common sense, and insight on the part of longtime marriage experts.

How can you choose a marriage-education class that's right for you? These steps can help.

Read up. Most marriage-education programs have extensive websites that will tell you all about the founders' philosophies and backgrounds, as well as what to expect from the workshop itself. Many are based on books. Before choosing a class, we recommend reading the book it's based on to be sure it's right for you.

Know the fees and schedule. Costs can range from nothing for some church-based programs to several thousand dollars. And health insurance usually won't cover these programs.

Make it convenient. Choose a program that meets at a time that works well for you and your spouse. And take into consideration travel time, especially for classes that meet for several weeks. A faraway class may sound great now, but when it comes time to attend, will you be happy or able to get out the door on time and drive a long distance?

Marriage Therapists at a Glance

Many types of therapists and mental-health professionals do marriage counseling. State licensing and training vary by specialty.

Credential	Therapist	Training
L.M.F.T.	Licensed marriage and family counselor	Master's degree and course work in marriage and family therapy, as well as a minimum of 1,000 hours of supervised training with clients before being licensed.
Ph.D.	Most likely a psychologist	Doctoral degree in clinical psychology from an accredited university; licensing criteria vary by state, including number of hours of course work and supervised clinical training.
L.C.S.W.	Licensed clinical social worker	Master's degree in social work from an accredited school of social work; at least two years of post-degree supervised clinical experience required for state licensing.
D.Min., M.Div., or other	Pastoral counselor	Master's or doctoral degree in the fields of social work, professional counseling, marriage and family therapy, or psychology, as well as theological training (degree not required). Many pastoral counselors are former clergy or congregation leaders.
A.P.R.N.	Advanced practice registered nurse	Master's or doctoral degree in psychiatric/mental health nursing from an accredited nursing school; state license granted post-degree.
M.D.	Most likely a psychiatrist	Four years of medical school, followed by state licensing. One year of post-graduate residency in a hospital. A psychiatrist-in-training spends at least three additional years in psychiatric residency learning diagnosis and treatment of mental illnesses, psychotherapy (including marital therapy), and drug and other treatments.

Consider your needs, goals, and personalities. The relative anonymity and safety of a class may help the two of you break the ice and move toward a closer connection. But if it brings up painful subjects that you can't resolve together, how will you handle that? We heartily endorse marriage education and believe that for issues such as infidelity, depression, substance abuse, and anything else that's deeply painful, spending some time with a marriage therapist in addition to attending a class may be your best option.

Will it stick? Will the life-changing "Aha!" moments and new skills from a weekend workshop stay with you for the rest of your marriage? Maybe yes, maybe no. Taking a class can cut your risk for divorce, research has shown over and over again. Many couples interviewed for this book say they make a point to attend one marriage-education program each year so that they're continually learning new skills and brushing up on the old ones. It's a big commitment, but after all, isn't a marriage the biggest commitment of all, worth investing in to make it as great as it can be?

the best ever

surprising words of hope from
everyday marriages

We've saved something special for the end.

Throughout this book, you've read wise expert advice on achieving a great marriage at any stage of your journey. But sometimes it takes a kind word from a stranger to really touch your heart and motivate you to be your greatest self.

The 1,001 men and women who participated in the Reader's Digest *Marriage in America Survey* didn't get paid to participate; in fact, all that sparked their participation was an e-mail. But they willingly gave their opinions and words because—we assume—the topic of marriage meant a lot to them. That became obvious the moment we started to read what they had to say.

We asked them to share the most cherished moments—and deepest regrets—from their marriages. And so they did. They talked about moments of connection at an out-of-town diner, over eggs and coffee at 3 a.m. Of a wife waking from a coma and a husband proposing marriage from a hospital bed. Of affairs they regretted and companionship beyond anything they feel they deserve. Of children and kisses, elementary school sweethearts, and second marriages that feel just right.

As you've seen through this book, their collected wisdom is poetry, filled with hard-won joy and wisdom that speaks eloquently of the true state of marriage in the United States. Not every comment is heartwarming, mind you, and not every sentiment is universal (such as the one from a guy speaking of the joys of open marriage), but all are honest and true. We hope these moments from everyday marriages touch you as much as they moved us.

On Being Soul Mates

- My husband is my best friend, my soul mate. We have both promised each other that when the other goes, the one left behind will not date or remarry, as we both believe that we were lucky to have found the perfect mate and will be married for eternity.

- I asked the universe for my perfect match, thinking that no such thing could happen, and the universe provided. I am thankful and blessed to have my husband.

- After being married two other times, I finally got it right. I have a wonderful husband who I can talk with all the time.

- We have had an open relationship and open marriage since 1995. We both date other people, and everything is out in the open. I have two girlfriends and my wife has one boyfriend.

- Wouldn't give a nickel to do it again, but wouldn't take a million to lose her.

- I love my wife with all my heart and forever will. She is my guiding star. My everything.

- Can't live with her, can't live without her.

- Being married to my spouse has provided me with an insight to myself that I would never have achieved otherwise.

- She can't see well; I can't hear well.

- We liked each other in the fourth grade, again in the eighth grade, and still again as seniors in high school. After we both graduated from college, we got married and have been happily married for 43 years.

What I Love …

- When I wake up to my husband gently kissing my arm.

- Whenever he says or does something to show love without being prompted.

- Whenever there are deer, bunnies, or snow in our yard, and my husband sees them before I do, he always comes and gets me to see them too.

- Watching our marriage increase in quality over the last 20 years. We have learned that it's necessary to have good communication.

- Every night after work, getting a simple hug and a kiss and saying "I love you" to each other.

The Wedding

- Seeing him as my father walked me to him; his face was perfect.

- Having our children from our previous marriages in the wedding. We became a family together.

- That he flew 2,000 miles to marry me.

- The look he gave me when he saw me in my wedding dress. His face and his eyes were so full of love, as if I were the most beautiful person in the entire world.

- The day my husband asked my son (from my previous marriage) if he could have permission to marry me. Also the day my son walked me down the aisle.

- When my husband gave me the engagement and wedding rings I currently wear—both handcrafted for me—one from his family's birthplace in Ireland and one made by a designer. The love in his eyes and heart when he gave them to me were more than words could ever describe.

- Everything was so beautiful, especially my wife and two daughters who were our flower girls. Even now, two years later, I ask my wife on our anniversary if she'll marry me again!

- The day of our marriage, we went to the movies, to a Brad Paisley concert, and then we went back to our hotel. The best thing about it was that it was just like any other day, not anything fancy, just another day of Kelli and I being together.

- The moment she said, "I do." From that time on, my world's never been the same. I have her and she has me—we're the most inseparable couple.

- How absolutely beautiful she looked on our wedding day.

- Traveling 7,000 miles to Japan to marry my wife.

Children

- Finding out we were pregnant with our daughter. We found out on Christmas Eve. We'd been praying for a child for almost six years.

- My husband being with me the whole time I was giving birth to our son. He held my hand and described what he was seeing.

- The day our daughters were born. He had tears in his eyes—it showed me how much love he had for our daughters. He might look like a strong, hard man on the outside, but inside he's a very sweet, loving man.

- When my husband told me he wanted to adopt my children.

- Bringing our baby son to our company's Christmas/family day. That's when I really felt like everything had come together for us.

- The doctor letting me deliver our son.

- The day we brought our daughter home from the adoption agency.
- The birth of our first child. She was to be induced labor in the late afternoon, so I went to work and was planning to get off early, but then they had to induce her much earlier. I was across town making a delivery and had five minutes to get to the hospital. I didn't make it, but we kinda laugh about it. When our second child was born, I took the whole week off, just to make sure I wouldn't miss it!
- Watching our children become successful in their careers.

Biggest Regrets

- Time spent fighting about things that were really not important.
- Years of harsh words that cannot be erased and all the mistakes that were made that hardened our hearts and brought us to the level that we are at right now.
- That I allowed my husband early in our relationship to yell and verbally abuse me for a number of years before insisting that he go to anger management.
- My own job that took so many years away from "our" lives—it was a total worthless drain. Little money and no recognition for 18-hour days.
- Old age. There is not much golden about it. Illness and surgeries have interfered with growing old and enjoying our golden years.
- Writing a very pointed and mean e-mail to my wife during the second year of our marriage. We were on the verge of divorce.
- I most deeply regret the resentment that has built up through the years and our lack of passion.
- That my wife and my first daughter (from my previous marriage) don't get along all that well.
- Not taking my wife to a professional after she had a tubal pregnancy at the age of 35 and was never pregnant again. Had the doctor known what to do, we could have saved our only child.
- Not starting to save for retirement and children right away.
- Not getting married in my wife's country with her family around us.
- I regret my total lack of understanding of a bride's expectations for the first night of marriage.

Advice

- I love being married, but it can be challenging. If you try to maintain an attitude of fairness and an ability to admit when you're wrong, you can get through most things.

- We decided before marriage that divorce was NOT an option. Our problems would be worked out no matter what. Of course, it helped that we were at least 10 hours from the nearest in-law, so running home to Mama wasn't an option.

- Divorce is too easy these days. In a marriage, you have to keep working at it and not just focus on the bad qualities. You've got to remember the good qualities of your partner, why you loved them when you first married them.

- Keep an open mind, openly communicate, and don't let things get out of hand. Handle small slights and problems immediately. It's been positive in our marriage and has helped us to survive.

- My wife and I don't make very many decisions by ourselves, especially when it concerns family needs. We are very good about bouncing ideas off each other. We don't argue. We just state our opinion to each other and go on loving.

- We both willingly give up our wants and our needs for the other's benefit. We have always bolstered each other and tried to keep our criticisms gentle, never bringing each other down intentionally. We are always willing to forgive and forget quickly, and go forward.

- Communication is the most important thing—without it on both sides, there is no marriage. The point is not trying to change the other to fit our desires; it's taking them as they are.

Most Meaningful Moment

- The day that we walked through our brand-new home and took a second to relish the feeling that it was truly about to become ours.

- Watching the sun come up on the top of the Haleakala volcano in Hawaii.

- Recently, after an argument, instead of verbally apologizing, I came home to find that he had cooked dinner for me.

- When I came home from a business trip and the house was completely cleaned, and all over were little notes that said "I love you." I found those notes for weeks.

- How gentle, kind, and helpful my husband was when my father was dying of cancer.

- The day I banged into the garage door, and his response was, "Guess it's my turn to do something dumb now."

- My husband's "best man" speech at his friend's wedding. He told the couple that he wished them the happiness in their marriage that he has in his.

- We had been married about six months, and I had a major toothache so bad I could not stand it. He was so concerned. He called all the dentists in the area, begging each one until he found a dentist that would see me that morning. He took the entire day off work and spent the whole day taking care of me and only me.

- Reading the Hans Christian Andersen story "Great Claus and Little Claus" at a picnic for two by a river, and laughing and laughing.

- My wife surprised me with a chance to DJ at our favorite club for my birthday. She'd done all the legwork as far as setting it up and only told me when I had to start picking out music to take.

- The day he told me I was his best friend.

- Waking up on a weekend morning with a whole day of lazing around together ahead of us (important contextual note: pre-children!).

- One rainy afternoon, sitting on the couch—him on one end, me on the other with our feet in the middle—each reading a book.

- Realizing that she deserves better than me and could have found a better life, but instead she picked and stayed with me.

marriage
resource guide

There is no shortage of advice—free or for sale—when it comes to love and marriage. But only a fraction of that advice is of a caliber high enough for you to consider seriously. We've read and used much of what's out there. The following books, websites, organizations, and tools strike us as the best that are available today and are worthy of your consideration. To discover *The 7 Stages of Marriage*'s own online resources, counseling opportunities, and community, go to rd.com.

Books

Dating and Engagement

Before You Say "I Do": A Marriage Preparation Manual for Couples, revised edition. H. Norman Wright, Wes Roberts; Harvest House Publishers, 1997.

Getting Ready for Marriage Workbook: How to Really Get to Know the Person You're Going to Marry. Jerry D. Hardin, Dianne C. Sloan; Nelson Impact, 1992.

Saving Your Marriage Before It Starts: Seven Questions to Ask Before (and After) You Marry. Dr. Les Parrott III, Dr. Leslie Parrott; Zondervan, 1995.

Making Marriage Last

The Couple's Journey. Susan Campbell; Impact, 1980.

Divorce Busting: A Step-by-Step Approach to Making Your Marriage Loving Again. Michele Weiner-Davis; Simon & Schuster, 1993.

10 Great Dates to Energize Your Marriage. Claudia and David Arp; Zondervan, 1997.

The Truth About Love: The Highs, the Lows, and How You Can Make It Last Forever. Patricia Love; Fireside, 2001.

Marital Sex and Intimacy

Getting It Right the First Time—Creating a Healthy Marriage. Barry W. McCarthy, Emily J. McCarthy; Brunner-Routledge, 2004.

Hot Monogamy. Patricia Love; Plume, 1995.

Rekindling Desire: A Step-by-Step Program to Help Low-Sex and No-Sex Marriages. Barry W. McCarthy, Emily J. McCarthy; Routledge, 2003.

The Sex-Starved Marriage: Boosting Your Marriage Libido—A Couple's Guide. Michele Weiner-Davis; Simon & Schuster, 2003.

Communication

Fighting for Your Marriage: Positive Steps for Preventing Divorce and Preserving a Lasting Love. Howard J. Markman, Scott M. Stanley, Susan L. Blumberg; Jossey-Bass, 2001.

The Five Love Languages. Gary Chapman; Northfield Publishing, 2004.

Getting Real: 10 Truth Skills You Need to Live an Authentic Life. Susan Campbell; H. J. Kramer, 2001.

Getting the Love You Want: A Guide for Couples. Harville Hendrix; Owl Books, 2001.

The Power of Two: Secrets of a Strong and Loving Marriage. Susan Heitler, Ph.D., Paula Singer; New Harbinger Publications, 1997.

Saying What's Real: 7 Keys to Authentic Communication and Relationship Success. Susan Campbell; New World Library, 2005.

The Seven Principles for Making Marriage Work: A Practical Guide from the Country's Foremost Relationship Expert. John M. Gottman, Nan Silver; Three Rivers Press, 2000.

12 Hours to a Great Marriage: A Step-by-Step Guide for Making Love Last. Howard J. Markman, Scott M. Stanley, Natalie H. Jenkins, Susan L. Blumberg, Carol Whiteley; Jossey-Bass, 2003.

Commitment

The Essential Humility of Marriage: Honoring the Third Identity in Couple Therapy. Terry D. Hargrave; Zeig, Tucker & Theisen, 2000.

Mapping the Terrain of the Heart: Passion, Tenderness and the Capacity to Love. Stephen Goldbart; Jason Aronson, 1996.

The Power of Commitment: A Guide to Active, Lifelong Love. Scott M. Stanley, Gary Smalley; Jossey-Bass, 2005.

Why Marriages Succeed or Fail…And How You Can Make Yours Last. John Gottman; Simon & Schuster, 1995.

Benefits of Marriage

The Case for Marriage: Why Married People Are Happier, Healthier, and Better Off Financially. Linda Waite, Maggie Gallagher; Broadway, 2001.

Parenthood

Becoming Parents: How to Strengthen Your Marriage as Your Family Grows. Pamela L. Jordan, Scott M. Stanley, Howard J. Markman; Jossey-Bass, 2001.

1-2-3 Magic: Effective Discipline for Children 2-12. Thomas W. Phelan; Parentmagic Inc., 2003.

When Partners Become Parents: The Big Life Change for Couples. Carolyn Pape Cowan and Philip A. Cowan; Lawrence Erlbaum Associates, 1999.

Empty Nests

The Second Half of Marriage: Facing the Eight Challenges of the Empty-Nest Years. Claudia and David Arp; Zondervan, 1998.

10 Great Dates for Empty Nesters. Claudia and David Arp; Zondervan, 2004.

Retirement and Beyond

Aging Well: Surprising Guideposts to a Happier Life from the Landmark Harvard Study of Adult Development. George Vaillant; Little, Brown, 2003.

Remarriage

Getting It Right This Time: How to Create a Loving and Lasting Marriage. Barry McCarthy, Emily J. McCarthy; Brunner-Routledge: 2005.

Remarried with Children: Ten Secrets for Successfully Blending and Extending Your Family. Barbara Lebey; Bantam, 2005.

Saving Your Second Marriage Before It Starts. Dr. Les Parrott III, Dr. Leslie Parrott; Zondervan, 2001.

Infidelity

After the Affair: Healing the Pain and Rebuilding Trust When a Partner Has Been Unfaithful. Janis A. Spring; Harper Paperbacks, 1997.

My Husband's Affair (Became the Best Thing That Ever Happened to Me). Anne and Brian Bercht; Trafford Publishing, 2006.

NOT "Just Friends": Rebuilding Trust and Recovering Your Sanity After Infidelity. Shirley Glass, Jean Coppock Staeheli; Free Press, 2004.

Torn Asunder Workbook: Recovering from Extramarital Affairs. David Carder; Moody Publishers, 2001.

Depression

Depression Fallout: The Impact of Depression on Couples and What You Can Do to Preserve the Bond. Anne Sheffield; HarperCollins/Quill, 2003.

Hand-Me-Down Blues: How to Stop Depression from Spreading in Families. Michael Yapko; St. Martins, 1999.

When Someone You Love Is Depressed. Laura Rosen, Xavier Amador; Free Press, 1997.

Illness

Surviving Your Spouse's Chronic Illness: A Compassionate Guide. Chris McGonigle, Ph.D.; Henry Holt & Co., 1999.

Thriving with Heart Disease. Wayne M. Sotile; Free Press, 2003.

Caregiving

Helping Yourself Help Others: A Book for Caregivers. Rosalynn Carter, Susan K. Golant; Three Rivers Press, 1995.

Loving Your Parents When They Can No Longer Love You. Terry Hargrave; Zondervan, 2005.

Marriage-Education Programs

By the very nature of the rapidly expanding marriage-education field, this list is incomplete—new programs are constantly being added and adapted. The list below is presented to give you an idea of the great variety of courses available. For even more options, go to www.smartmarriage.com and look at its directory of programs.

Inventories

Inventories are extensive questionnaires that can help a couple assess both their strengths and the areas where they need to grow. The three most widely used and extensively researched inventories are listed here. One—RELATE—is a do-it-yourself questionnaire you take online, then see an individualized report. Two others—FOCCUS and PREPARE—must be administered by a trained counselor or facilitator. (In both cases, it's wise to attend classes or meet with a counselor to discuss your results and find ways to learn the skills you need.) While these are not programs, you can find counselors and premarriage-education programs through locater services that are maintained by the organizations that have developed these inventories.

FOCCUS

www.foccusinc.com
877-883-5422

Short for Facilitating Open Couple Communication, Understanding and Study, FOCCUS was developed by marriage and family therapists affiliated with Creighton University. Often the inventory of choice in Roman Catholic premarriage classes, it is also widely used in Protestant congregations, at synagogues, and by secular programs. A Muslim edition is also in development. FOCCUS contains 156 basic questions plus additional questions and is for remarried, interfaith and/or cohabiting couples available in English as well as Chinese, French, Italian, Korean, Polish, Portuguese, Spanish, and Vietnamese.

PREPARE

www.lifeinnovations.com
800-331-1661

Short for Premarital Personal and Relationship Evaluation, PREPARE was developed by marriage researchers from the University of Minnesota and elsewhere. It includes 165 questions that cover 14 key relationship areas including assertiveness, active listening, conflict resolution, sex, children, spirituality, and financial planning. Signing up to take the PREPARE inventory usually involves 4-6 follow-up sessions in which a trained counselor helps you talk about inventory results and then chart a course for the future. PREPARE is widely used by clergy and secular counselors alike.

RELATE

www.relate-institute.org
801-422-4359

RELATE was developed by the Marriage Study Consortium at Brigham Young University. The inventory includes 267 questions covering important relationship skills and attitudes. You can take RELATE with your partner or by yourself. The company also has a version called READY for singles who want to check whether they've got the skills they'll need when the right relationship comes along. Less expensive than FOCCUS and PREPARE, RELATE is an online inventory that you take by yourself (no counselor needed). Plan, however, to meet with a counselor to discuss the results to get the most out of the experience.

Marriage Retreats, Cruises, and Getaways

Laugh Your Way to a Better Marriage Cruise

www.laughyourway.com
866-525-2844

Created by Mark Gungor, developer of the Laugh Your Way to a Better Marriage seminar, this weeklong Caribbean cruise combines sun, fun, and a humorous approach to marriage improvement.

ANASAZI: "The Making of a Marriage"

www.anasazi.org
800-678-3445

A four-day wilderness-based marriage enrichment experience in Arizona for premarital or married couples seeking a more resilient, loving, and sustainable relationship.

Being Together: Couples Retreats

www.beingtogether.com
617-661-7890

Past retreats—to enhance intimacy and create a balance between partners—have included weekends on the Maine Coast and a weeklong retreat in Costa Rica.

Intimacy Retreats: Richard and Diana Daffner, C.S., M.A.

www.intimacyretreats.com
941-349-6804 or 877-282-4244

Vacation/workshops in romantic U.S. and international locations, including the Florida Keys, focus on renewing and enhancing intimacy.

Love Your Relationship Couples Retreats

www.loveyourrelationship.com
866-601-5683

Run by the co-developer of the well-researched PREP marriage-education program, these weekend retreats take place at a luxury spa/hotel in Boulder, Colorado.

Classes and Workshops

ACME: Building Better Marriages

www.bettermarriages.org
800-634-8325 or 336-724-1526

Teaches effective communication and problem solving, helps couples increase awareness of self and partner in addition to identifying areas for relationship growth. Presented in various formats, including one-day and multi-day sessions and self-guided activities.

Active Relationships

www.activerelationships.com
214-369-5717

The Active Relationship Center is a proactive counseling center that teaches emotional and relationship literacy, high-level thinking, and practical skills that are necessary for increasing partnership, pleasure, and teamwork within the relationship. The Active Relationship class can be taught in both private and group sessions.

African American Marriage Enrichment Program

www.aafle.org
317-274-6713

Helps African American couples establish intimate and satisfying marriages by enhancing their knowledge and skills.

www.blackmarriage.org
301-613-1316

DVD-based workshop curriculum created by Dr. Rozario Slack and Nisa Muhammad, founder of Black Marriage.

Bringing Baby Home Workshops

www.bringingbabyhomeonline.org
206-832-0355

Developed by relationship experts John and Julie Gottman, with research conducted at the University of Washington, Seattle, this workshop prepares couples for the tough job of sustaining a marriage while raising a child. This website lists local classes nationwide.

Caring Couples Network

www.gbod.org
877-899-2780

Developed by the United Methodist Church, the network sets up teams of married couples, pastors, and therapists in church congregations to help couples and families going through tough times and to prepare engaged couples for marriage.

Center for Relationship Development

www.realrelationships.com
206-281-2178

Based in Seattle, Washington, the center, run by relationship experts Dr. Les Parrott III and Dr. Leslie Parrott, offers nationwide workshops entitled Transforming Relationships to Transform Lives.

Couple Communication I and II

www.couplecommunication.com
800-328-5099

Utilizing award-winning couple communication techniques, these workshops are offered throughout the United States.

Divorce Busting

www.divorcebusting.com
815-337-8000

Marriage enrichment/divorce prevention coaches help guide couples and individuals based on the work of relationship expert Michele Weiner-Davis, author of *The Divorce Remedy* and other books.

Family Dynamics Institute

www.familydynamics.net
800-650-9995

This group runs seminars and also trains church leaders, counselors, and lay couples to lead marriage-enrichment classes.

The Gottman Institute: The Art and Science of Love Couples Workshops

www.gottman.com
888-523-9042

Based on the work of marriage researcher John Gottman, Ph.D. Focus includes building fondness and admiration, supporting each other's dreams, and turning conflict into discussions.

Imago

www.imagorelationships.org
800-729-1121

Workshops for couples and individuals; based on the idea that we unconsciously choose our partner to restore our original state of security, sense of aliveness, and freedom of expression.

Marriage Alive

www.marriagealive.com
888-690-6667

Seminars developed by marriage experts Claudia and David Arp, authors of *10 Great Dates to Energize Your Marriage* and many other relationship books.

Mars and Venus

www.marsvenus.com

877-564-6472 or 415-381-8025

Developed by John Gray, Ph.D., the originator of the book *Men Are From Mars, Women Are From Venus*, these workshops specialize in issues such as communication, dealing with differences, parenting, dating, and starting over after divorce. The program also hosts relationship workshops at a luxury organic "oxygen spa" in Mendocino, California.

National Institute of Relationship Enhancement (NIRE)

www.nire.org

800-432-6454

Weekend classes and private coaching sessions for married and engaged couples, using 10 key relationship-enhancement skills.

PAIRS

www.pairs.com

888-724-7748

Short for Practical Application of Intimate Relationship Skills, PAIRS teaches practical skills for building and rebuilding relationships. Programs range from one day to a four-month Relationship Mastery Program.

"Power of Two" Marriage Skills Couples Weekend Workshops

www.poweroftwo.org

303-388-1793

Learn proven communication skills developed by Colorado marriage therapist Susan Heitler, Ph.D.

PREP

www.prepinc.com

800-366-0166

Short for Prevention and Relationship Enhancement Program, PREP was developed in the 1980s by psychologists from the Center for Marital and Family Studies at the University of Denver. Focus is on communication skills.

Retrouvaille

www.retrouvaille.org

800-470-2230

For couples with problems like infidelity, alcoholism, gambling, and even violence; weekend workshops are taught by volunteer couples who have been through similar experiences.

Worldwide Marriage Encounter

www.wwme.org

909-863-9963

Assists couples to begin a process of self-discovery and mutual communication and acceptance, with an emphasis on religion as a focus for marital success. Facilitated by volunteer couples in coordination with clergy.

Classes by Phone or Online

The Couple's Workstation

www.relationship-help.com

626-577-2628

The Workstation is a web-based membership-only relationship-building program; includes weekly e-mail reminders about skills to practice.

Premarital Online

www.premaritalonline.com

509-532-1600

Offers programs online and over the phone for couples planning to marry.

Organizations

The following groups offer information and support.

Beyond Affairs Network

www.beyondaffairs.com

The Beyond Affairs network is a worldwide group of local support groups for people whose spouses have been unfaithful.

The National Healthy Marriage Resource Center

www.healthymarriageinfo.org

A collaboration between the U.S. Department of Health and Human Services and marriage researchers from Brigham Young University, Child Trends, Norfolk State University, Syracuse University, Texas Tech University, and the University of Minnesota, this clearinghouse provides information on marriage-education programs, research, and many other resources for couples who want to maintain and improve their marriages.

The Coalition for Marriage, Family and Couples Education

www.smartmarriages.com

202-362-3332

A nondenominational, nonpartisan, and nonsectarian organization that serves as one of the nation's best clearinghouses of information on marriage. Hosts an annual conference. Website includes extensive lists of marriage-education classes, articles, and more.

National Healthy Marriage Institute

www.healthymarriage.org

866-818-5530

Offers classes, including an online weight-loss program for couples, as well as resources for finding marriage-education programs in your community.

Finding a Marriage Therapist

The following groups can help you locate a marriage therapist or counselor.

American Association of Marriage and Family Therapists

www.aamft.org

703-838-9808

The AAMFT represents 23,000 marriage and family therapists throughout the United States, Canada, and abroad.

The National Registry of Marriage-Friendly Therapists

www.marriagefriendlytherapists.com

This locater service can help you find well-trained relationship therapists who say they're committed to keeping healthy marriages together.

American Association of Pastoral Counselors

www.aapc.org

703-385-6967

Pastoral counselors are certified mental-health professionals who have had in-depth religious and/or theological training. This organization can help you locate counselors and counseling centers that use this approach.

Index

A

acceptance, 59, 115

acts of love, 57

adult children living at home, house rules
    for, 217-18

advice, bad, 8-9

aging parents, caring for, 256-60

anger, 109, 138

apologizing, 63, 162

appreciation, expressing, 60, 78, 269-70
  in journals, 271

arguments, 9, 61-63, 109-10, 143, 211.
      See also conflict resolution
  defusing, 144
  power struggles, 139-41
  stress and, 221

assertive speaking, 107-10

B

benefits of marriage, 5, 7-9, 12-13
  books about, 328

betrayal. *See* infidelity

betrayed spouse, nine steps for, 155-60

blaming, 56, 60, 61

blended families, 307-9

body image, 253

bonding
  friendship, 158
  remarriage and, 303-7

books
  caregiving, 329
  communication, 327
  dating, 327
  depression, 328-29
  empty nest, 328
  infidelity, 328
  intimacy, 327
  marriage, 327, 328
  parenthood, 328
  remarriage, 328
  retirement, 328
  sex, 327

boomerang children, welcoming,
    212-18

boundaries, healthy, 78

brain chemicals
  passion stage of marriage, 70, 90
  realization stage of marriage, 98, 136
  rebellion stage of marriage, 136

bullying, 56, 60

burnout when caring for aging parents,
    259, 260

C

caregiving. *See also* parenthood
    aging parents, 256-60
    books about, 329
    sick spouse, 228-36
celebrations, 58
challenges to marriage, 28-30. *See also* explosion stage of marriage; realization stage of marriage; infidelity
changing oneself, 58-61, 137
children. *See also* parenthood
    adult, living at home, 212-18
    disciplining, 179, 308, 309
    relationship with, after they leave home, 203-4
    remarriage and, 307-9
chronic illness, dealing with, 228-36
church affiliation, 150-51
cohabitation, 308
commitment to marriage, 59
    books about, 328
communication, 7. *See also* conversation starters
    aging parents, caring for, and, 259
    assertive speaking, 107-10
    books about, 327
    completion stage of marriage, 270
    empty nest and, 203
    expressing love, 27-28, 55-57, 71, 80, 83-86
    finances and, 125-32, 246-47
    illness, dealing with, and, 230-32
    improving, 106-10
    infidelity and, 156-59
    intimacy cues, 102
    job loss and, 247-50
    listening, 63, 101, 110-11, 209, 232

    nonverbal, 108
    parenthood and, 173-74
    passion stage of marriage, 76
    praise, 80
    realization stage of marriage, 101, 102
    retirement and, 269
    reunion stage of marriage, 204, 207-8
    sex and, 193
    skills, practicing, 111
    spouse's weight and, 255
community service, 281. *See also* volunteer work
compatibility, 62
completion stage of marriage, 11-12, 262-87
    exercises, 268, 275, 280
    missions, 266-84
    quizzes, 51-52, 286-87
conflict resolution, 61-63, 137, 141-45, 209
    parenthood and, 170, 177-78, 179-82
confrontation, 62
conversation starters
    completion stage of marriage, 265
    dreams and goals for marriage, 114
    finances, managing, 125-26
    handling issues as a couple, 81
    for parents, 172
    for reunion stage parents, 202
    sharing religion, 153
cooperation stage of marriage, 10, 166-93
    quiz for, 42-44
cortisol, 164
couple rituals, 71, 76, 182
crisis, 28-30
    explosion stage of marriage, 11, 224-60
    needs during, 227
    response to, 28-30

criticism, 56, 60
  of parenting styles, 176-77
cruises, marriage education and, 332
cues for intimacy, 102

D

dates
  for completion stage of marriage, 285
  for cooperation stage of marriage, 183-86
  for passion stage of marriage, 77
  for realization stage of marriage, 123
  for rebellion stage of marriage, 163
  for reunion stage of marriage, 219
dating, books about, 327
debt, 123-24
decision-making
  joint, 75
  marriage and, 76
  unilateral, 56
dedication, 227
depression
  books about, 328-29
  marriage and, 236-44
  signs of, 238-39
destructive actions, 56
diet
  health and, 221
  for weight loss, 254-56
differences, irreconcilable, 9, 147
disagreements, 9, 211. *See also* arguments;
    conflict resolution; fighting
  reunion stage of marriage, 206
disciplining children, 179
  in blended families, 308, 309
distractions, throwing up, 56

division of labor in household, 102,
    116-21, 210, 282-84
  blended families and, 308
  job loss and, 249
  parenthood and, 178
divorce
  irreconcilable differences and, 147
  rebellion stage of marriage and, 134
  reduced odds for, 8, 297-98
  as the right choice, 12
  statistics, 8
domineering behavior, 60

E

education
  health, 221, 230-31
  marriage, 292-300, 315-18, 329-32
  premarital online, 299
emotional infidelity, 161
emotional intimacy, 94, 181
  building, 71, 87-89, 306-7
  in completion stage, 269-70
  empty nester and, 203
emotional skills, 28
emotions, expressing, 109. *See also* love,
    expressing
  about empty nest, 203
empathetic listening, 110-11
empathy, 101, 115, 227
empty nest. *See also* reunion stage of
    marriage
  books about, 328
  feelings about, 203
encouragement from partner, 78
engaged couples, 292-300
  books for, 327
exercise

health and, 220-21
to restore libido, 189-90
exercises
  completion stage of marriage
    business card rewriting, 278
    risk and safety, 268
    Zen and the art of now, 275
  cooperation stage of marriage
    relaxation time, 176
  passion stage of marriage
    emotional intimacy, building, 89
    expressing love, 86
    listing strengths, 82
  realization stage of marriage
    expectations, 105
    listening, 112-13
    splitting chores, 120-21
  rebellion stage of marriage
    dream self, 149
    space usage, 140
  reunion stage of marriage
    house rules for boomerang kids,
      216
    letting go of the past, 212
    uniting as a couple, 205
expectations, 102-6
  marriage and, 101
  remarriage and, 306
  sex and, 91
explosion stage of marriage, 11, 224-60
  aging parents, caring for, 256-60
  chronic illness, 228-36
  depression, 236-44
  health crisis, 228-36
  job loss, 245-51
  quiz for, 48-50
  weight gain, 251-56

expressing love, 55-57, 71, 80, 83-86
  men and, 27-28

F

family. *See also* children; parenthood
  aging parents, caring for, 254-60
  blended, 307-9
  interference from, 75, 78, 81
  relationship with
    in completion stage of marriage, 279
    in passion stage of marriage, 75, 78,
      81
  stepfamilies, 307-9
fatherhood, 178. *See also* parenthood
  empty nest and, 203
female bonding, 158
fidelity, 8. *See also* infidelity
fighting, 9, 61-63, 109-10, 143, 211. *See*
    also conflict resolution
  defusing arguments, 144
  power struggles, 139-41
  steps to avoid, 143
finances, managing. *See also* money
  debt, 123-34
  after job loss, 246-47
  in realization stage of marriage, 122-32
  remarriage and, 309-10
financial infidelity, 161
financial obligations of adult children, 217
financial planners, 132
forgiveness, 137, 160-64, 211
friends, 279
  in passion stage of marriage, 181
  same sex, 158
  supportive, 158
    for parents, 174-75
    for weight loss, 255-56

when caring for aging parents, 258
when dealing with illness, 231
when spouse is depressed, 241
friendship in marriage, 26, 101, 111-15,
179-82
fun sharing, 26, 209, 276
explosion stage of marriage, 232-33, 234

G

gender gap
dealing with illness and, 235
marriage survey results, 25, 29
sex
drives, 90-91
satisfaction of husbands vs. wives, 25
genuineness, 101, 115
grooming, importance of, 60-61, 189

H

happiness, 12
marriage and, statistics regarding, 8
personal goal setting and, 145-48
health, 13, 60, 260
crisis, 228-36
depression and, 239
education, 221, 230-31
lifestyle for, 220-22
weight gain and, 255
weight loss and, 254
high-conflict marriages, 12
holiday observance, 152
honeymoon. *See* passion stage of marriage;
second honeymoon
hormones
cortisol, 164
oxytocin, 98, 158

passion stage of marriage, 70
realization stage of marriage, 98
rebellion stage of marriage, 135, 136,
164
reunion stage of marriage, 208
swings of, 191
testosterone, 70, 208
household chores
for adult children, 217
for aging parents, 259
in completion stage, 282-84
division of labor in household, 102, 116-
21, 210, 282-84
after job loss, 249
blended families and, 308
sex and, 193
switching, 210
humor, 27-28, 181, 227 (*see also* laughter)

I

illness, dealing with, 228-36
books about, 329
imperfection, embracing, 59, 60
infidelity, 137
books about, 328
new types of, 161
recovering from, 153-60
insulting, 60
interfaith marriage, 149-50, 151
intimacy, 227
after retirement, 263-67
books about, 327
cues for, 102
emotional, 94, 181
building, 71, 87-89, 306-7
in completion stage of marriage,
269-70
empty nester and, 203

parenthood and, 181

physical, 71 (*see also* sex)

    completion stage of marriage, 272-73

    illness, dealing with, and, 234-36

    touching, 57, 71, 91-95, 193

J

job loss, dealing with, 245-51

joy, importance of, 54-58

L

laughter, importance of, 23-26, 270. *See also* humor

libido, 94

    exercises to restore, 189-90

    male-female differences in, 90-91, 94

lifespan, marriage and, 8, 13

listening, 63, 101, 209

    dealing with illness and, 232

    empathetic, 110-11

living together, 308

logic, 56

love, expressing, 55-57, 71, 80, 83-86

    men and, 27-28

M

male bonding, 158

male-female differences

    dealing with illness and, 235

    marriage survey results, 25, 29

    sex

        drives, 90-91

        satisfaction of husbands vs. wives, 25

marriage

    benefits of, 5, 7-9, 12-13

    books, 328

    challenges to, 28-30 (*see also* infidelity)

    commitment to, 59

    in completion stage, 267-72

    destructive actions in, 56

    education, 292-300, 329-32

    factors influencing success of, 294

    focusing on, 200-6

    high-conflict, 12

    institution of, 5

    interfaith, 149-51

    meaning in, 279

    motto for, 168

    organizations, 333

    protecting when spouse is depressed, 240-44

    redefining after parenthood, 174

    rules for successful, 54-63

    stages of, 9-12 (*see also specific stages*)

    statistics, 8, 19, 22, 24, 29, 30

    survey results, 16-30

    therapists, 334

    timeline, 6-9

    vision statement, 168

meaning in life, shared, 278-82

medical attention

    for depression, 239

    for sexual problems, 191, 236

medications affecting sexuality, 191, 236

men. *See also* male-female differences

    expressing love, 27-28

    friends, 158

    marriage survey results, 29

mentor-based marriage-strengthening programs, 313

missions

    completion stage of marriage, 266-84

    cooperation stage of marriage, 169-94

    explosion stage of marriage

aging parents, caring for, 258-60
depression, dealing with, 237-44
illness, dealing with, 230-36
job loss, dealing with, 246-51
weight gain, dealing with, 253-56
passion stage of marriage, 71-96
realization stage of marriage, 100-132
rebellion stage of marriage, 137-64
reunion stage of marriage, 200-222
money, 8
constraints, 167-69
debt, 123-24
job loss and, 246-47
management, 102, 122-32
realization stage of marriage and, 122-23
remarriage and, 309-10
style, 124-25
trust and, 309-10
motherhood. *See* parenthood
motto for marriage, 168
myths
cooperation stage of marriage, 187
empty nest, 203
engaged couples, 297
passion stage of marriage, 75
realization stage of marriage, 119
remarried couples, 305

N

nagging, 56, 118
name-calling, 56
needs during crisis, 227
neurotransmitters
passion stage of marriage, 70, 90
realization stage of marriage, 98
rebellion stage of marriage, 136

nonverbal communication, 108

O

online premarital education, 299
open-mindedness, 28
optimism
after job loss, 250
health and, 231
organizations, 333
oxytocin, 98, 158

P

parenthood
books about, 328
marriage and, 169-70, 171-79
stepchildren and, 307-9
parents, aging, caring for, 256-60
passion, savoring, 72-74
passion stage of marriage, 9, 68-96
mission, 71-96
myths of, 75
quiz for, 33-35
remarriage and, 305-6
past
learning from, 304
letting go of, 211, 275-76, 304
savoring, 270-72
patience, 227
peacekeeping, 56
personal goal setting, 137, 145-48, 210, 276-77
weight loss and, 254
physical intimacy, 71. *See also* sex
completion stage of marriage, 272-73
illness, dealing with, and, 233-36
touching, 57, 71, 91-95, 193

placating, 56

play, importance of, 54-58, 273-78

pleasure, importance of, 54-58, 259-60

positive attitude toward marriage, 18-21, 55, 307

   after job loss, 250-51

power struggles, 137, 139-41

praise, 80

premarital education online, 299

premarriage, 292-300

prioritizing marriage relationship, 74-80, 200-206

   in cooperation stage, 169-70

   remarriage and, 309

privacy, 57-58, 260

   for parents, 190

problem-solving, 137, 141-45, 182, 307. *See also* conflict resolution

pronouncements, avoiding, 62

purpose in life, shared, 278-82

Q

quality time, 8. *See also* together time

quizzes

   completion stage of marriage, 51-52, 286-87

   cooperation stage of marriage, 42-44

   explosion stage of marriage, 48-50

   future readiness, 286-87

   money personality, 126-27

   passion stage of marriage, 33-35

   passion style compatibility, 95-96

   realization stage of marriage, 36-37

   rebellion stage of marriage, 38-41

   reunion stage of marriage, 45-47

   stages of marriage, 32-52

transitioning into reunion stage, 214-15

when spouse is depressed, 242-43

R

rage, 138. *See also* anger

realization stage of marriage, 9-10, 98-132

   exercises, 105

   missions, 100-132

   remarriage and, 306

rebellion stage of marriage, 10, 134-64

   exercises, 140, 149

   missions, 137-64

   quiz for, 38-41

relaxation time, 275

religion, 148-53

   interfaith marriage and, 149-51

remarriage, 302-10

   books about, 328

resources, 327-34

   for caring for aging parents, 258-59

   premarital education online, 299

respect, 71, 88, 309

retirement, 262-67

   books about, 328

   planning for, 211-13

retreats, marriage, 330

reunion stage of marriage, 11, 196-222

   exercises, 205, 212, 214-15, 216

   missions, 200-222

   quiz for, 36-37, 45-47

rituals

   blended families and, 308

   couples and, 71, 76, 182

romance restoration, 170, 183-86

rudeness, 56

rules for successful marriage, 54-63

   play, pleasure, and joy, 54-58

S

second honeymoon, 203
secrecy, affairs and, 155
selfishness, 56
sense of "we," 57-58, 71, 74-80, 205
sex, 7, 12, 26
    adapting to weight gain, 253-54
    books about, 327
    completion stage of marriage, 272-73
    cooperation stage of marriage, 170,
       188-93
       planning for, 190
    drive, 94
       exercise to restore, 189-90
       male-female differences in, 90-91, 94
    illness, dealing with, and, 234-36
    infidelity and, 153-60
    passion stage of marriage, 71
       expanding vocabulary of, 90-96
    problems requiring medical attention,
       191
    reunion stage of marriage, 208
    satisfaction of husbands vs. wives, 25
    stress and, 192
    withholding, 118
socializing as a couple, 206, 260
speaking assertively, 107-10
spirituality, 137, 148-52, 282
stages of marriage, 9-12. *See also specific*
    stages
stepfamilies, 307-9
stonewalling, 56
strengths, listing of, 82
stress
    cooperation stage of marriage, 170
    friends and, 158
    health and, 164
    reducing, 221, 260
    response to, 28-30
    sex and, 192
stubbornness, 138
suicide, 239
support from friends, 158
    for parents, 174-75
    for weight loss, 255-56
    when caring for aging parents, 258
    when dealing with illness, 231
    when spouse is depressed, 241
survey of marriage, 16-30
    excerpts, 93, 128, 157, 320-25
    positive feelings in marriage, 19
    respondents, 17
    response to challenges, 30
    sexual satisfaction, 25
    time spent, 24
    traits important to marriage, 22, 24, 29

T

team approach
    to caring for aging parents, 258-60
    to parenting, 177
testosterone, 70, 208
therapists
    marriage, 313-15, 334
    types of, 317
therapy, 8-9
    for depression, 240
    marriage-friendly, 313-15
    for sexual problems, 191
timeline of marriage, 6
time scheduling
    completion stage of marriage and,
      274-75, 282-84
    cooperation stage of marriage and,
      167-69

for sex, 190

passion stage of marriage and, 78-79

reunion stage of marriage and, 203-4

survey of marriage results, 24

togetherness, 57-58, 71

passion stage of marriage,
74-80

together time, 8, 57-58

completion stage of marriage and,
274-75

reunion stage of marriage and,
204-6

touching, 57, 71, 91-95, 193. *See also*
physical intimacy

illness, dealing with, and, 233-36

traits predicting marital success, 294

trust in marriage, 21-23

breaches in, 22-23

building, 71

emotional intimacy and, 87-88

finances and, 309-10

U

unfaithful spouse, six steps for, 155-57

V

vacations, 221

marriage education and, 332

vision statement, 168

volunteer work, 277, 281-82

W

"we," sense of, 57-58, 71, 74-80, 205

wealth, 8, 13

weddings

average cost, 8

remembering, 73

weight gain, dealing with, 251-56

weight loss, dealing with, 254-56

women. *See also* male-female differences

friends, 158

marriage survey results, 29

work

community service, 281

establishing boundaries for, 79-80

infidelity, 161

job loss, dealing with, 245-51

part time, 278

volunteer, 277, 281-82

About the Authors

Sarí Harrar has been a newspaper, magazine, and book writer for more than 20 years, with a strong specialty in health and women's issues. Most recently, she was health news editor for *Prevention* magazine, where she won several awards for her feature articles. Harrar's extensive book credits include *Extraordinary Togetherness: A Woman's Guide to Love, Sex, and Intimacy; The Sugar Solution;* and *Food and You.* She is currently working as a freelance medical and science writer; her articles have appeared in *Better Homes & Gardens, Fitness,* and *American Baby,* among other publications. She won a CASE/Harvard Medical School Fellowship in 2003.

Rita DeMaria, Ph.D., has been a marriage and family therapist since 1974. In addition to maintaining a private practice, Dr. DeMaria is a staff therapist at the Philadelphia-based Council for Relationships, the nation's oldest marriage-therapy and therapist-training center in the United States, and is director of its PAIRS (Practical Application of Intimate Relationship Skills) program. She also runs Marriage Doctor, a website and counseling program aimed at teaching couples real-world skills to improve their marriages. She is the author and coauthor of several professional books on marriage therapy; is a member of the American Association for Marriage and Family Therapy, the American Academy of Family Therapy, and other industry organizations; and has been quoted frequently on relationship topics in publications such as *Redbook,* the *Chicago Tribune,* and the *Philadelphia Inquirer.*